TRIUM
FOX

Triumphant Fox

Erwin Rommel and the Rise of the *Afrika Korps*

Samuel W. Mitcham, Jr.

Cooper Square Press

Selected quotations from *The Trail of the Fox: The Search for the True Field Marshal Rommel* by David Irving, copyright 1977 by David Irving, are reprinted by permission of the publisher, E. P. Dutton.

Selections from *The Foxes of the Desert* by Paul Carell, translated by Mervyn Savitt, copyright 1960 in the British translation by E. P. Dutton and Co., Inc. in the United States and by Macdonald and Co. in the United Kingdom, is reprinted by permission of the publisher in the United States, E. P. Dutton.

Excerpts of approximately 1,000 words from *Rommel: The Desert Fox* by Desmond Young, copyright 1950 by Desmond Young, are reprinted by permission of Harper and Row, Publishers, Inc.

Excerpts of approximately 869 words from *With Rommel in the Desert* by H. W. Schmidt, copyright 1951, are reprinted by permission of G. Harrap, Ltd.

First Cooper Square Press edition 2000

This Cooper Square Press paperback edition of *Triumphant Fox* is an unabridged republication of the edition first published in Briar Cliff, New York in 1984.

Copyright © 1984 by Samuel W. Mitcham, Jr.

Designed by Louis A. Ditizio; Maps by Dr. Manik Hwang

All rights reserved.
No part of this book may be reproduced in any form or by any electronic or mechanical means, including information storage and retrieval systems, without written permission from the publisher, except by a reviewer who may quote passages in a review.
Manufactured in the United States of America

Published by Cooper Square Press
An Imprint of the Rowman & Littlefield Publishing Group
150 Fifth Avenue, Suite 911
New York, New York 10011

Distributed by National Book Network

Library of Congress Cataloging-in-Publication Data
Mitcham, Samuel W.
   Triumphant fox : Erwin Rommel and the rise of the Afrika Korps / Samuel W. Mitcham, Jr.
     p. cm.
   Originally published: New York : Stein and Day, c1984.
   Includes bibliographical references and index.
   ISBN 0-8154-1055-7 (pbk. : alk. paper)
   1. World War, 1939–1945—Regimental histories—Germany. 2. Rommel, Erwin, 1891–1944. 3. Germany. Heer. Panzerarmeekorps Afrika—History. 4. World War, 1939–1945—Campaigns—Africa, North. I. Title.

D766.82 .M52 2000
940.54'1343—dc21

00-035893

The paper used in this publication meets the minimum requirements of American National Standard for Information Sciences—Permanence of Paper for Printed Library Materials, ANSI/NISO Z39.48–1992.
Manufactured in the United States of America.

TO MY BROTHERS,
STEVE AND MARK MITCHAM

ACKNOWLEDGMENTS

I would like to thank Robert Wyatt, Linda Bonner, and Bob Bass for comments and proofreading during this effort. Also, thanks go to some very special people—John C. Lewis, Lorraine Heartfield, Charles S. Aiken, Wayne D. Shows, Addye Mae Mitcham, Wayne Mitcham, Lee Greer, Susan Stoya, Ellen Blue, and Roz McKeoun—for all of their help and encouragement along the way.

Special thanks goes to my editors, Benton Arnovitz and Daphne Hougham, for all of their hard work.

Contents

Tables

Maps

Photographs

Introduction

Field Marshal Erwin Rommel, the "Desert Fox," was perhaps the greatest military leader of our time. In recent years it has become popular to praise the antihero and to cast stones at the individual who stands head and shoulders above the crowd, and Erwin Rommel has had his share of these literary and verbal missiles aimed at his reputation. He was no god and certainly had his share of faults; nevertheless, it has been my privilege to have spent the past eight years studying him and I have drawn one inescapable conclusion: He *was* a hero. Although politically naïve and slow to recognize Hitler for the villain he was, Erwin Rommel had a high moral standard and would not tolerate those who did not live up to it—even if these people included his commander-in-chief and the rulers of Nazi Germany, whom Rommel was theoretically (but not morally) bound to obey.

This, my third volume on the man and his campaigns, deals with his life and battles up to December 31, 1941. In many ways it is the most significant volume of the three. Everything that happened after 1941 was predictable in light of what went before. It is a tale that sets the stage for tragedy, but it is nevertheless one of courage, hope, and strength of character, and of the will of a human spirit capable of rallying thousands to his side against desperate odds. It is a tale worth being told.

TRIUMPHANT FOX

1

The Rout of the Romans

Where do legends begin? It depends on the legend. The legend of Hannibal began when he crossed the Alps with his elephants; Caesar's began on the battlefields of Gaul. The birth of other military legends is harder to pinpoint. Often those who initiate and spread the legend were not present at the events that gave it birth and remain ignorant of all the facts. Such is the case of the legend of the men of the Afrika Korps, who were sent down the path to military immortality by a squat, ulcerative, middle-aged Italian vegetarian who fancied himself the last of the Caesars. His purpose, incidentally, was anything but the advancement of the reputation of the panzer troops of the German Army; nevertheless, he triggered a series of events that drew Erwin Rommel and his men into the bloody struggle for North Africa against British, Australians, South Africans, Rhodesians, Indians, New Zealanders, Palestinian Jews, Poles, Greeks, Free French, Americans, and assorted other groups. When that struggle was over, more than 100,000 men would lie dead, and the squat, ulcerative Italian would be less than two years away from his own reckoning with a Partisan death squad.

Benito Mussolini could foresee none of this on May 26, 1940, but then Mussolini is not remembered for his great foresight. He was questioning it himself that fateful summer. The previous September he had backed out of an agreement with Adolf Hitler to enter the war on the side of Germany. The Nazi dictator let him renege with a minimum loss of face, commenting caustically—though privately—to his staff that Germany would do perfectly well without the dubious help of this Latin ally.

During the next nine months, Mussolini watched with mounting dismay while Hitler's war machine won a spectacular series of victories. Poland was smashed in a month; Denmark lasted only a few hours; Norway was overrun, as was Luxembourg; the Netherlands was conquered in less than a week; Belgium held out slightly longer; the British Expeditionary Force was ejected from the mainland with heavy losses while the vaunted French Army—decimated in two weeks—had collapsed and was clearly on the verge of final defeat. The panzers seemed invincible. The Fascist dictator decided it was time to end Italy's neutrality and join the winning side. On May 26, 1940, he cornered two of his chief subordinates, Army Chief of Staff Marshal Pietro Badoglio and Air Marshal Italo Balbo, in the hall of the Palazzo Venezia in Rome. "If Italy wants to sit at the Peace Conference table when the world is to be apportioned, she must enter the war and enter it fast," he told them.

Balbo, one of the founders of the Fascist Party and now Governor of Libya and Commander-in-Chief, North Africa, exchanged negative glances with Badoglio, the conqueror of Ethiopia. Mussolini noticed this exchange and pompously declared that Italy would invade France on June 5.

Badoglio tactfully asked Mussolini if he realized what he was demanding. "Are you aware, Duce, that Italy is completely unprepared from a military point of view? You have read the routine reports. Only 20 percent of our divisions are at war strength. Over 70 percent of our armored divisions have not a single tank. We haven't even enough shirts for our soldiers. How are we expected to wage war? In our colonies there is no military preparedness. Our merchant fleet is scattered over the high seas—" The marshal tried to continue, but Mussolini cut him short. "History cannot be reckoned by the number of shirts," he snapped.[1]

Italy declared war on June 10. A few days later, France capitulated. This surrender greatly improved Mussolini's position in North Africa, as he no longer had to be concerned about an invasion of his Libyan colony from French Algeria. With his western flank thus secured, he turned to the east, where Egypt, the Suez Canal, and possibly even the Middle Eastern oilfields seemed to be within his grasp.

The worried Marshal Balbo realized that Mussolini was dreaming and that the Italians in North Africa were no match for the British, but Italo Balbo did not have long to live. On July 28, 1940, the world-famous aviator was accidently shot down near Tobruk by his own trigger-happy anti-aircraft gunners. He was replaced by the 58-year-old Marshal Rudolfo Graziani, a veteran of the East African campaigns. Graziani was known as "the Breaker of the Natives" because, while he was in charge of the pacification program in Libya, he tied native chiefs hand and foot and dropped them on native camps from several thousand feet.[2] Like Balbo, he had serious reservations about the Duce's proposed invasion of Egypt. Mussolini, however, pointed to his almost 10 to 1 numerical superiority in the desert and insisted that Graziani "cross the wire" into Egypt.*

The fall of France temporarily upset the balance of power not only in Libya but also throughout Africa. Italy had a quarter of a million men in Libya, and the Duke of Aosta commanded another 300,000 in East Africa and Ethiopia, but most of these were natives. They would be useless in a confrontation with the British, but no one yet realized that.

While Mussolini put up an appearance of great strength, the British in Egypt seemed to be very weak. Most of the British Army prepared for a Nazi invasion of the home islands, and few men could be spared for the defense of Egypt. The Western Desert Force (later redesignated the XIII Corps) under Lieutenant General Sir Richard O'Connor was composed of only two partially equipped and understrength divisions: Major General Sir Michael O'Moore Creagh's 7th Armoured and Major General Sir Noel Beresford-Pierse's 4th Indian.[3] Together they numbered about 30,000 combat effectives.

In war, numbers are frequently misleading. Nowhere is the truth of this statement better illustrated than by the example of the North African Front in 1940. The Italian Army was one of the worst in Europe. Its weapons dated from the First World War. It had little artillery and few antitank guns, and those it did possess were obsolete. Its tanks were referred to as "self-propelled coffins" by the rank and file. The soldiers' morale was understandably bad, and their fighting spirit and self-confidence was pitiful. They were smart enough to realize that they would be fighting a European war, but their leaders had armed and equipped them for a colonial conflict. Their greatest weakness lay in the infantry, which was nonmotorized, or "straight-leg." In the desert, where mobility is essential not only for victory but also for mere survival, the Italian soldier walked everywhere he went. Laboring under such a handicap, he could easily be cut off or bypassed by the fast, mobile British.

Marshal Graziani suffered from none of the delusions of grandeur that afflicted Mussolini. Graziani showed no desire to advance on Cairo and crossed the border only after the Duce informed him that if he didn't advance within two days he would be relieved of his command. On

---

*"The wire" referred to a 12-foot-high barbed-wire fence the Italians built along the Libyan-Egyptian frontier to keep the nomads from wandering across the border whenever they pleased.

September 13 Graziani's strike force, the Italian Tenth Army under General Mario Berti, advanced into Egypt. On September 16 the Italian spearhead, the 1st Blackshirt Division, reached the village of Sidi Barrani, 65 miles inside the border. Here, to the surprise of the Allies and the Germans, the Italians halted, rested, and began building up supplies. Despite their overwhelming numerical strength, they didn't move forward again. By remaining inactive for three months, they completely surrendered the initiative to a more mobile enemy.

While the British built up the armored strength of the Western Desert Force and the Italians did nothing, Hitler made his first overtures to Mussolini concerning the possibility of sending panzer troops to North Africa. The Italian leader turned down the offer, telling Badoglio: "If they get a footing in this country we shall never get rid of them."[4] Nevertheless, Hitler sent one of his most promising officers to conduct a feasibility study. Major General Ritter von Thoma had commanded the German panzer forces in the Spanish Civil War and was regarded as an expert on tank warfare. He reported to Graziani in October and set about analyzing all aspects of the situation. Thoma said later: "It (his report) emphasized that the supply problem was the decisive factor—not only because of the difficulties of the desert, but because of the British Navy's command of the Mediterranean. I said it would not be possible to maintain a large German Army there as well as a large Italian Army."

"My conclusion," Thoma continued, "was that, if a force was sent by us, it should be an armored force. Nothing less than four armored divisions would suffice . . . and this, I calculated, was also the maximum that could be effectively maintained with supplies in an advance across the desert to the Nile Valley. At the same time, I said it could only be done by replacing the Italian troops with German. Large numbers could not be supplied, and the vital thing was that every man in the invading force should be of the best possible quality."[5]

Naturally Mussolini, Badoglio, and Graziani all opposed Thoma's ideas, although Mussolini did not object to *some* German reinforcements. Hitler also objected to the report, stating that he could spare no more than one panzer division for Africa. Thoma replied that he'd better forget the whole thing, then—a remark that aggravated the Fuehrer. Hitler commented that he thought the Italians were capable of holding their own in Africa, but the soldier, who had fought side by side with them in Spain, again disagreed. He told Hitler: "One British soldier is better than twelve Italians. The Italians are good workers, but they are not fighters. They don't like noise."[6]

One cannot help but be impressed by the accuracy and the foresight of the von Thoma report. When he predicted that the supply problem would be the decisive factor in the Desert War, he was speaking with the voice of Cassandra. Like that Trojan prophetess, everyone on his own side ignored him. The British, however, were quicker to see that to win in Africa they must control the vital Mediterranean sea lanes. With the help of their secret service and a number of Italian turncoats, they set about this task.

A great many Italian officers—perhaps the majority—were pro-Royalist or at least anti-Fascist. This was particularly true in the Navy, and the incredibly efficient British secret service was never short of informants. The Italian Navy planned to send out its fleet from the southern naval base at Taranto, on the heel of the Italian peninsula, at dawn on November 11, 1940. The fleet made its final preparations to sail on the night of November 10–11, but its security was not what it should have been. Unknown to them, the British already knew their plans and were ready to launch a spoiling attack. One hour after the Italian antisubmarine nets were raised the British struck with a squadron of Swordfish torpedo planes launched from the aircraft carrier H.M.S. *Illustrious*. Three of the Italian Fleet's six battleships were struck in their hulls and knocked out for some time. The British Official History recorded: "Half of the Italian Battlefleet had been put out of action . . . by the expenditure of 11 torpedoes and the loss of two aircraft. . . ."[7]

Perhaps more important than these losses was the permanent effect this raid had on the morale of the Italian Navy. They never did attempt to face the Royal Navy in a major battle on the high seas, even when British fortunes reached low ebb. Only the Italian submariners performed credibly, leading to a worldwide joke started by the British Broadcasting Corporation: "While the U.S. Navy drinks whisky and the British Navy prefers rum, the Italian Navy sticks to port."[8] Mussolini's sailors were convinced of their inferiority to the British and never recovered their morale throughout the war.

Meanwhile, during these several weeks O'Connor and his superior, General Sir Archibald Wavell, had prepared to deal the Italian Army's morale a similar blow. They had massed a fully motorized strike force in Egypt, including modern tanks, rifles, machine guns, long-range artillery, and vastly superior air and naval detachments. General Wavell liked to do the unexpected. "Never let yourself be trammelled by the bonds of orthodoxy," he said once. "Always think for yourself . . . and remember that the herd is usually wrong."[9]

Wavell ordered General O'Connor to launch a surprise attack on the Sidi Barrani concentration on December 9. Wavell's plan called for a five-day raid that would reduce the odds in the next major campaign. Little did he know that he was starting that campaign. Sir Richard's first target was Camp Nibeiwa, south of the town of Sidi Barrani. The Italians were surprised over their breakfasts, which were never eaten. The artillery opened up at 7:00 A.M. and was immediately followed by the armor and the infantry, which rode into battle on Bren carriers. Mussolini's troops futilely attempted to mass but did not even have time to warm up the engines of their tanks. By 8:00 A.M., the battle was over. General Pietro Maletti, the garrison commander, met the British with a machine gun but was shot through the lung. He continued firing until he died, but it did no good. His 4,000 men surrendered a few minutes later. Twenty-three tanks and several artillery pieces were also taken.[10]

Wavell next turned on Sidi Barrani itself. With 31,000 men and 275 tanks he faced 81,000 Italians with 120 inferior tanks. The Royal Air Force, which had caught the Italian airmen on the ground, dominated the skies. Even so, Wavell and O'Connor must have expected a better fight than they got. Sidi Barrani fell within a few hours. Three Italian divisions—the 1st and 4th Blackshirts and the 2nd Libyan—dropped their weapons and marched off to prisoner-of-war camps.[11] Most of the 64th Catanzaro Division and part of the 1st Libyan Division were also destroyed, although the 63rd Cirene Division made good its escape.[12] By December 12 O'Connor's men had already captured 39,000 prisoners— or about 9,000 more than the total strength of the Western Desert Force. One battalion commander reported capturing an estimated "five acres of officers, 200 acres of other ranks."[13] Astonished by his success but not frightened by it, Wavell expanded his scope of operations. Instead of a five-day raid, he converted the offensive into an invasion of Libya. On December 16, he clashed with the Italians at Fort Capuzzo. The British took 38,000 prisoners, 400 guns, and 50 tanks at a cost of only 500 killed or wounded to themselves.[14]

The Italian Tenth Army deteriorated into a disorganized rabble. Men threw away their weapons and streamed to the rear, hoping to find safety in the coastal strongholds of Bardia and Tobruk. Graziani ordered his surviving units to hold these positions at all costs. At this point O'Connor had to order a temporary halt to the advance, because the Indian 4th Division had been sent to the Sudan by Churchill. O'Connor besieged Bardia but waited until the arrival of the 6th Australian Division from Palestine before assaulting it.

Both the Italian military and the Italian people put a great deal of hope in the defense of Bardia. Generally believed to be the most strongly fortified town in Libya, it was commanded by a popular hero, Lieutenant General Annibale Bergonzoli, whom everyone expected would stem the British tide. Bergonzoli was nicknamed "Electric Whiskers" because of his great energy, bad temper, and excited gesticulations, which caused "his bristling black beard to wag up and down as if it were receiving a series of magnetic shocks," to quote one American correspondent. He was no lover of luxury. In Ethiopia he would frequently go out on one-man raids, often bringing back two or three prisoners. He had also distinguished himself in Spain before being wounded in the Aragon campaign. "I am sure that 'Electric Whiskers' and his brave soldiers will stand at whatever costs," Mussolini said.[15]

On January 3, 1941, the Australian infantrymen were in position, and the storming of the Italian lines began. Two days later 45,000 more Italians capitulated. The British also inherited 462 guns, 127 tanks, and 700 trucks.[16]

At the last minute "Electric Whiskers" escaped the fall of the fortress. He walked from Bardia to Tobruk in five nights, hiding during the day. It became a point of honor for the British to capture him, but he eluded them again and again. They finally took him prisoner south of Benghazi but immediately had to rush him to Cairo: He was having an acute appendicitis attack.[17]

After the collapse of Bardia, the Italians were staggered. If the Allies could not be stopped at Bardia, then where could they be stopped? Resistance suddenly collapsed almost everywhere as panic set in throughout Libya. Defeat followed defeat for the descendants of the Romans. Tobruk, an excellent fortress, resisted only two days and yielded another 25,000 prisoners. Sollum and Derna collapsed. Benghazi was taken. At Beda Fomm 3,000 British and Australians, with only 32 tanks, captured 20,000 Italians, who had 216 field guns and approximately 100 tanks. "The police in Tel Aviv gave us a better fight than this," one Australian noted sourly.[18] Finally, the Allies reigned up at El Agheila, within striking distance of Tripoli, the last major seat of resistance in Italian North Africa. The only reason they came to a stop without completely obliterating Mussolini's North African empire was because Adolf Hitler had become aggressive again.[19] He had massed well over 600,000 men in the Balkans and was obviously preparing to invade Greece, which was already fighting the Italians in Albania. Churchill acidly rejected Wavell's advice to continue the drive to Tripoli and

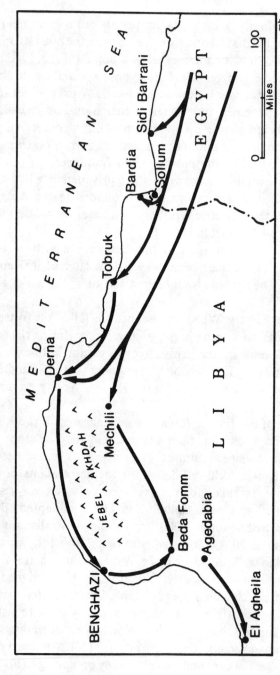

Map 1: Wavell's Cyrenaican Campaign, December 9, 1940, to February 8, 1941. In two months, Wavell's 31,000 man Western Desert Force virtually annihilated Mussolini's Libyan Army, which lost 130,000 men, 1,300 guns, 400 tanks, and 150 aircraft to a force less than a third its size. This crushing Axis defeat paved the way for German intervention in North Africa.

instead withdrew most of the experienced soldiers of the Western Desert Force and transferred them to the mountains of Greece. In doing so, he violated one of the cardinal maxims of Frederick the Great: "He who defends everything defends nothing." The British had spread themselves too thin. In Greece they suffered a disastrous defeat, at the cost of total victory in Africa.

On February 8, little of the Duce's forces remained to oppose the British. Graziani's legions were scattered and smashed. The Tenth Italian Army no longer existed. The 1st, 2nd, and 4th Blackshirt Infantry divisions had all been destroyed. Also captured were the 1st and 2nd Libyan divisions, as well as the 61st Sirte, 62nd Marmarica, 63rd Cirene, and 64th Catanzaro Infantry divisions and the Maletti Armored Group.[20] In less than two months the Italians had lost 130,000 men, 1,300 guns, 400 tanks, and 150 aircraft. Meanwhile, they had inflicted only 2,000 casualties on the attackers. All that remained to defend Tripoli was a reinforced artillery regiment at Sirte, a makeshift garrison of two infantry divisions, and parts of three other divisions, which held a 12-mile semicircular line around the city.[21] Clearly they could have been gobbled up as well if the Allies had not dissipated their strength in a futile military adventure on the mainland of Europe.[22]

Rommel summarized the effect of the campaign against Hitler's major ally in this way: "The Italian troops had, with good reason, lost all confidence in their arms and acquired a very serious inferiority complex, which was to remain with them throughout the whole war. . . ."[23]

The Fuehrer also had some observations to make. On February 3 he told Army staff officers, "The loss of North Africa could be withstood in a military sense but have a strong psychological effect on Italy. Britain could hold a pistol at Italy's head. . . . The British forces in the Mediterranean would not be tied down. The British would have the free use of a dozen divisions and could employ them most dangerously. . . . We must make every effort to prevent this. . . ."[24] He decided to send military aid to his fellow dictator. To command this "Afrika Korps" of one panzer and one light division, Hitler called on a man who had recently distinguished himself commanding the 7th Panzer Division in the French campaign: Lieutenant General Erwin Rommel.

2

Erwin Rommel and the Making of a General

Erwin Rommel was not yet 50 years old when he answered the summons to Staaken in early February 1941. He was reputed among senior German officers to be close to the Fuehrer and to owe his advancement to his political loyalty to Hitler. It was true that Rommel had seized his opportunities as they came, but his loyalty lay with the Fatherland, not with any one man or clique. Anyone who investigates his early life and career cannot help but draw the conclusion that Erwin Rommel formed his own opinions and acted on them, no matter what anyone else thought; indeed, if he had one major fault, it was that his self-reliance often bordered on pigheadedness.

The future Desert Fox was born at Heidenheim in Swabia, a district of Wuerttemberg in southern Germany, on November 15, 1891. There was little in young Rommel's background to indicate the profession he would make his life's work. His father, also called Erwin, was a schoolmaster, like his father before him.[1] He was a strict parent with a walrus moustache and slicked-down hair parted in the middle. The thing young Erwin remembered best about him was that he was always asking educational questions, which bothered and annoyed his less-than-interested son.[2]

Erwin, Senior, married Helena von Luz, the oldest daughter of the president of the government of Wuerttemberg. Herr Rommel, however, did not want a political career, as such a match might imply. He settled down with his bride and began to establish a family. Their first child, Manfred, died young. The second child, Helena, followed in her father's footsteps and became a teacher. She never married. Erwin Johannes Eugen Rommel, the future field marshal, was a middle child. He had two younger brothers. Karl, the fourth child, became an airplane pilot in the

First World War and flew reconnaissance missions in Egypt and Palestine before he was crippled by malaria. The youngest brother, Gerhardt, acquired the reputation of being the black sheep of the family. He aspired to become an opera singer but never achieved much success on the stage, or anywhere else, apparently.[3] He did, however, outlive them all. He was still alive in 1977.[4]

As a child, Erwin was weak and sickly. He didn't like to play the games the other children played; instead, he spent most of his time daydreaming. Young Rommel took no interest in hobbies, athletics, or girls. Then, as a teen-ager, he suddenly shook off his lethargy. He started a program of exercise and systematically developed his body, much as the young Theodore Roosevelt and Count von Stauffenberg did. Rommel played tennis, bicycled, skied, and learned how to skate. He acquired many of the characteristics common among Wuerttembergers—toughness, self-reliance, stubbornness, pragmatism, and thrift.[5] He was an unsophisticated person and remained so until the day he died. He took a great interest in building practical things and probably would have made a fabulous engineer, under different circumstances. At the age of 14 he and a friend built a full-scale glider in a field near Aalen. It actually flew—but not very far.[6] Nevertheless, this was an amazing accomplishment for a teenager, considering that it was 1906: only three years after the Wright brothers' famous flight.

At an early age and strictly on his own, Rommel decided to become a soldier. Except for his father, who served briefly as an artillery lieutenant, there were no military men in his family, and certainly no military tradition motivated young Rommel. His father opposed this career choice, and with good reasons. The Prussian aristocrats dominated Germany's armed forces and always had. The best Rommel could hope for was retirement at the relatively low rank of captain or major, with a modest pension.[7] Once his father was convinced that Erwin's mind was made up, however, he decided to support him. He recommended young Erwin to the Army as "thrifty, reliable, and a good gymnast." The first application went to the engineer branch, which had its quota of new recruits, so Rommel's application was rejected. An attempt to join the artillery met the same fate. Finally, he was accepted by the infantry, the toughest and least romantic of all service branches.[8] His father agreed to provide for his son's initial upkeep, pay for a minor operation, and buy him the uniform of an officer-cadet in the 124th (6th Wuerttemberg) Infantry Regiment, which young Erwin joined on July 19, 1910.[9] Three months later he was promoted to corporal, and three months after that he became a sergeant. Finally, in March 1911, he achieved one of the major ambitions of his life: He was sent to the War Academy at Danzig to undergo officer training.[10]

At the German equivalent of officers' candidate school, Rommel underwent training and testing designed to determine if he was second lieutenant material. He did quite well in rifle and drill work but only adequately in gymnastics, fencing, and riding. His commandant evaluated him as being ". . . of medium height, thin and physically rather awkward and delicate . . . [but] firm in character, with immense willpower and a keen enthusiasm. . . . Orderly, punctual, conscientious and comradely. Mentally well endowed, a strict sense of duty." In summary, he found Rommel to be "a useful soldier."[11]

At Danzig, the city that provided a pretext for the beginning of World War II, Erwin Rommel started his first and only romance. Lucie Maria Mollin was a slender, very attractive young lady with dark hair and an olive complexion. She had a nice figure, was an excellent dancer, and had won a number of dance contests. Her father, now dead, had been a West Prussian landowner and headmaster of a secondary school. Lucie was in Danzig to study languages. She and Cadet Rommel fell in love almost immediately and soon considered themselves engaged.[12] Rommel had met the only woman in his life. Only once do we have any record of his considering the possibility of being unfaithful to her, and that was in jest. The incident occurred in Normandy in 1944. He and his entourage had been out inspecting the front. They stopped at a hotel for lunch or tea and were besieged by a number of German nurses and Air Force girls, all begging for autographs and eager to meet the great Desert Fox. Later, as he got into his car, Rommel grinned at his chief engineer, Lieutenant General Wilhelm Meise, and said: "You know, Meise, some of those girls are so darned attractive I could almost be a rat!"[13] He couldn't, though, and he knew it. Fidelity was a characteristic inbred in him, strengthened by years of practice. Rommel knew in his heart that he could never be unfaithful to his wife. Loyalty was always a strong point with him, which explains in part why it took him so long to decide to act against Adolf Hitler in the climactic days of World War II, three decades later.

He and Lucie were separated for the next several years. He received his commission in January 1912 and returned to his regiment and routine of garrison life. Rommel and his fiancée wrote to each other every other day. Erwin's father died suddenly in 1913, but this had little effect on the junior second lieutenant. He had always been closer to his mother, who did not pass away until 1940, when her oldest surviving son was a major general and a rising star in the armies of the Third Reich.

Rommel spent most of the two years between getting his commission and the outbreak of World War I drilling and training the new recruits of the 7th Company, 124th Infantry Regiment. In 1914 he was attached to the 19th Field Artillery Regiment at Ulm, so he would become familiar with that branch of the service. While there he commanded a platoon of horse-drawn artillery, and he was engaged in this duty when World War I broke out.[14] Rommel immediately rejoined his parent regiment. Throughout Germany—indeed, throughout Europe—there was much joy and singing. The Continent entered the war with a light heart, for both sides were confident that they would win a quick and decisive victory.

The 124th Infantry was ordered to the Western Front. "At Kornwestheim," Rommel wrote, "I see my mother and two brothers and sister for a few moments, then the locomotive whistles that it is time for farewells. One last look, a clasp of the hands! We cross the Rhine at night, searchlights finger the skies for enemy fliers and airships. The singing dies away. The riflemen fall asleep on seats and floors. I myself am standing on the loco's footplate, staring into the open firebox or out into the rustling and whispering of the oppressive summer night. Will I ever see my mother and family again?"[15]

Up to this point, Rommel's career was perfectly average and absolutely undistinguished. His life centered around the dull routine of drill fields and training exercises designed to mold a nonelite, unpublicized infantry unit in an out-of-the-way part of Germany. His private life must have seemed equally boring to his peers, for he neither smoked, drank, nor took part in the after-dark activities of some of the other young bachelor officers. For their part, his comrades regarded Rommel as friendly but altogether too serious. On the job he was very businesslike and impersonal. His already strong will grew even stronger. He had a hard streak in him, and it frequently showed itself, for he exhibited no tolerance for those he branded as inefficient or lazy.[16]

The battlefield transformed this serious young man into a warrior of the first class. Desmond Young wrote: "From the moment that he first came under fire he stood out as the perfect fighting animal: cold, cunning, ruthless, untiring, quick of decision, [and] incredibly brave."[17] "He was the body and soul of war," one of his fellow officers commented later.[18]

He fought his first skirmish in the village of Bleid, Belgium, while the German armies drove on Paris for the first time in the twentieth century. He had been on patrol for 24 hours with little or no sleep. He was exhausted, dirty, and suffering from food poisoning. A reinforced squad of Frenchmen, perhaps 20 strong, occupied the town. With only one NCO and two privates, Platoon Leader Rommel dashed forward and starting shooting. Several Frenchmen fell, but the surprised survivors took cover. The rest of Rommel's platoon came up and a small but sharp house-to-house fight developed. Finally the Germans took the village and captured more than 50 prisoners in and around the burning hamlet. Erwin Rommel had won his first victory.[19] Although insignificant in itself, except to a few French widows and orphans, the skirmish at Bleid set the pattern of boldness that would be seen in subsequent events of a much greater magnitude.

After Bleid, the sick second lieutenant forced himself onward, toward Paris. He fainted several times, but he refused to report his illness and go to the rear. He fought in the Battle of Verdun and the retreat through the Argonne before a bullet, not a disease, finally put him into a hospital bed. Near the old Roman Road west of the town of Varennes a German attack stalled. Rommel grabbed a rifle from a wounded man and charged forward through the bushes. Coming upon five Frenchmen at a distance of 20 paces, he shot down two of them before his rifle misfired. Examining it, he discovered that he was out of ammunition! It was too late to reload now. Rommel remembered:

> There was no use thinking of escape. The bayonet was my only hope. I had been an enthusiastic bayonet fighter in time of peace and had acquired considerable proficiency. Even with odds of three to one against me, I had complete confidence in the weapon and in my ability. As I rushed forward, the enemy fired. Struck, I went head over heels and wound up a few paces in front of the enemy. A bullet, entering sideways, had shattered my upper left leg; and blood spurted from a wound as large as my fist. . . .[20]

Fortunately for Rommel, his men broke through and rescued him, but he spent the next three months in the hospital.[21]

World War I settled down to grim trench warfare in 1915. On January 29, the First Battle of Argonne raged in full force. Erwin Rommel was back in action that day, crawling on his belly through a belt of barbed wire 100 yards deep. Behind him, also on their stomachs, came the 200 men of his new command, the 9th Company, 124th Infantry Regiment. With the advantage of surprise the gray-uniformed Germans suddenly appeared in the French main positions and, with rifles and bayonets, killed those Frenchmen who failed either to flee or to surrender. Four tactically important blockhouses fell into Rommel's hands, but his position could hardly be described as enviable. The barbed wire still lay at his back, and no support arrived for his small, isolated unit. To make matters worse, the French were counterattacking. They realized that they could not allow the Boche to remain here for long. One of the blockhouses changed hands but was taken back in a sharp fight. Lieutenant Rommel, however, recognized that there could be only one end for his unit if this unequal contest continued. Taking advantage of the lull, he abandoned his foothold and escaped with the survivors of his command before the next French attack could be launched. For this exploit he was awarded the Iron Cross, First Class, a very high decoration for one so young.[22]

After a successful tour of duty as commander of the 4th Company, Rommel was promoted to first lieutenant in late September 1915 and was transferred.[23] He had hoped they would send him to the Turkish theater of operations, where his brother was an airplane pilot,[24] but instead he was posted to Muensingen, Germany, where the elite Wuerttembergische Gebirgsbatallion (Wuerttemberg Mountain Battalion) was being formed. Rommel was given command of the 2nd Company.[25]

One of Rommel's platoon leaders in this unit was Lieutenant Theodor Werner. He wrote of Rommel at this time: "When I first saw him he was slightly built, almost schoolboyish, inspired by a holy zeal, always eager and anxious to act. In some curious way his spirit permeated the entire regiment right from the start, at first barely perceptibly to most but then increasingly dramatically until everybody was inspired by his initiative, his courage, his dazzling acts of gallantry." Later Werner wrote: "Anybody who once came under the spell of his personality turned into a real soldier. However tough the strain he seemed inexhaustible. He seemed to know just what the enemy were like and how they would probably react. His plans were often startling, instinctive, obscure. He had an exceptional imagination, and it enabled him to hit on the most unexpected solutions to tough situations. When there was danger, he was always out in front, calling on us to follow. He seemed to know no fear whatever. His men idolized him and had boundless faith in him."[26]

World War I degenerated into a meat grinder as hundreds of thousands perished from machine-gun fire, heavy artillery barrages, and poison gas that made men literally cough up their lungs. For all the heroism and useless sacrifice, the trench lines remained more or less static. Rommel, meanwhile, trained, mainly in the Austrian Alps, with his new command. The object of the mountain battalion was not to fight as a unit but to commit its companies individually to more or less independent operations. They were essentially mountain shock troops, a role that suited Rommel admirably. However, an entirely different sort of role was also on his mind. In 1916 the Imperial Command granted him leave and permission to marry Lucie Mollin. The ceremony took place in Danzig on November 27, and that was that. They stayed together, a very domestic family, until his death nearly 28 years later.

Rommel's comrades reported no change in the serious young officer after he returned from his honeymoon in the winter of 1916–17. For the Fatherland, the war was going badly. Rumania imagined that Germany was beaten and joined the Allies. The men in field gray turned to meet the new antagonist. In the van of those facing this new, fresh enemy was the newlywed lieutenant.

Rommel's first independent actions on the Western Front had been on a very small scale. Now in the East, in January 1917, the scale had increased. More men followed him now, and more lives depended on his decisions. The increased responsibility bothered this serious Swabian not at all. He demonstrated this outside the Rumanian village of Gagesti, miles behind enemy lines. The fact that he was there at all showed both daring and ability. He had infiltrated enemy lines earlier in the night and, despite the bitter cold, waited for the defenders to go to sleep. Then he launched a well-coordinated attack. Although heavily outnumbering the Germans, the rudely awakened adversaries quickly surrendered. Four hundred Rumanians assembled, shocked and in many cases only partially dressed, for the long march into captivity.[27]

Gagesti represented a major victory for the young company commander. Four hundred prisoners in one evening is a big haul for any lieutenant in any army in any war. As encouraging as it must have been for Lieutenant Rommel, it was neither as impressive nor as important as his next major operation, which took place against the Italians.

Upstart Rumania's ultimate collapse seemed (and was) near at hand in the latter part of 1917, when the Wuerttemberger Mountain Battalion received its orders for the Italian Front. Here Germany's ally Austria-Hungary had suffered a series of defeats and appealed to the Kaiser for help. Wilhelm dispatched the Fourteenth Army with seven divisions and augmented by the mountaineers. The forces of Imperial Germany deployed for battle in late October. The Alps gave the Italian defenders the advantage of terrain, so the German general pitted the Wuerttem-bergers against the enemy's center. The stage was set for the battle that climaxed Rommel's World War I career.

His original orders were to secure the right flank of the Bavarian Life Guards, but the future Desert Fox soon expanded it to an independent operation. In a maneuver that was approaching standard procedure, Rommel led his enlarged command through the Italian frontlines with-out being detected. At dawn, he overran an artillery battery in a surprise bayonet charge. Meanwhile, one of the companies of Rommel's battal-ion enlarged the gap in the Italian front. The sound of the firefight alarmed the Allied commander, who ordered his reserve battalion to restore his broken front by counterattacking. Since a bayonet charge is relatively noiseless, the Italians did not yet know that Rommel was behind their lines, awaiting just such a reaction. As soon as the reserve battalion became decisively engaged, Rommel struck it in the rear with his main force. The Italians found themselves in a deadly crossfire. Soon white flags emerged. Rommel took more than 1,000 prisoners that morning, but the day had just begun.

Reinforced to six companies, Lieutenant Rommel continued to raise havoc in the enemy's rear. He occupied a camouflaged place on the main road to the pivotal fortified position of Monte Matajur. The Germans waited in silence to see what target would present itself. The one that did would no doubt have shaken a man of less daring; it was the 4th Bersaglieri Brigade marching down the road from Monte Matajur. Rommel attacked it immediately. Soon more white flags appeared, and another 50 officers and 2,000 men surrendered. Rommel could see that the war-weary Italians were unable to offer prolonged resistance to a first-class military force. Another idea dawned on him. He reformed his units and pushed the nearly exhausted infantrymen onward, right up the mountain, toward Monte Matajur. All night they struggled upward as they painfully and silently worked their way behind the fortified posi-tions. At dawn Rommel confronted the Salerno Brigade near the sum-mit. With the curtness of a German officer, he demanded their imme-diate capitulation. Remarkably, they threw up their hands as ordered. Another 43 officers and 1,500 men surrendered to the force of will of a 26-year-old lieutenant.[28]

After 50 hours of continuous movement, Rommel had captured two entire brigades and assorted other units totaling 150 officers, 9,000 men, and 81 pieces of artillery. The 7,000-foot Monte Matajur also fell into the hands of the Central Powers.[29] Rommel's total strength probably never exceeded 600 men.

For this brilliant string of successes, Rommel was promoted to captain and decorated with the Pour le Mérite, a medal roughly equivalent to the American Congressional Medal of Honor when awarded to someone of such relatively low rank. He wore this medal with the greatest pride until the day he died. This author has seen only one or two photographs of Rommel in uniform (after 1917) without his "Blue Max" dangling under his throat.

Shortly after the Battle of Monte Matajur, Rommel was reassigned to staff duty in Germany and, much to his distaste, remained in staff positions until the collapse of the Second Reich in late 1918.

For some people, the end of the war was the end of their world. Rommel, however, remained mentally unscarred by it. He simply returned home to his wife and rejoined the remnants of his parent regiment, the 124th Infantry. He settled down to garrison routine and soldiered peacefully on for the next 21 years.

At home, the daring warrior enjoyed the quiet life. Here, Lucie was the center of his world. He had no bad habits, was not interested in going out much, and preferred to stay around the house with her and the family dog. He must have been an easy husband to live with. When he went home, he left his job outside: The strife and tension of the barracks, parade ground, or battlefield rarely entered there. He was a good-tempered person at home, unconcerned with food, and an excellent fix-it man. Once he disassembled and reassembled a motorcycle in the living room, just to see what made it run. He liked stamp collecting, but he enjoyed outings to the country even more. He and Lucie frequently went skiing together, or canoeing, or horseback riding. He enjoyed dancing with his wife and taking trips on leave. Once he even visited his old battlefields in Italy, with Lucie mounted on the back of his motorcycle. Erwin Rommel had only one major fault: He attempted to play the violin, but apparently without a great deal of success.[30] In short, their life together was rather simple and perhaps colorless, but certainly peaceful, comfortable, and happy.

The most important event in their married life occurred on Christmas

Eve 1928, when their only child, christened Manfred, was born. Rommel's family life, however, remained essentially unchanged. It stayed almost completely separated from his military career.

At Stuttgart, Rommel and two of his friends, Hartmann and Hermann Aldinger, formed the Old Comrades Association of the Wuerttemberg Battalion. This group became one of Rommel's main sparetime interests. Even in the desert in World War II, with the fate of much of the Axis empire on his shoulders, he never failed to answer a letter from an old soldier who was a former member of his World War I command. This sentimental streak seldom showed itself in other affairs, but he had a definite soft spot in his heart for the veterans who had served him so well. Frequently he replied to their correspondence in his own hand. At Stuttgart in 1935, when Rommel was a rising lieutenant colonel, General von Soden invited Rommel to sit with him in the reviewing box at the annual veterans' parade. Rommel replied that he would prefer to march with his old company.[31] This incident was typical of the man.

The victorious Allies unwisely imposed the harsh Treaty of Versailles on Germany in 1919, thus setting into motion a complicated series of events that would culminate in the rise of Adolf Hitler. The German Army was limited to a strength of 100,000 men, of which only 4,000 could be officers. Among those selected to remain was Captain Rommel.

In March 1919, he received his first command in the "new" army, now called the Reichswehr. For Germany it was a time of civil unrest, rebellion, and, in places, anarchy. Rommel was sent to Friedrichshafen on Lake Constance in southwestern Germany, where he took over the 32nd Internal Security Company. This group of Red sailors at first jeered at Rommel's medals (which were no longer socially acceptable) and refused to drill. Certainly Rommel did not care whether they liked his medals or not, and he soon had them licked into shape. After the first few days he had no trouble, except on the day they were assigned to guard an illegal schnapps factory. Eventually, the 32nd Internal Security Company was considered reliable enough to use in operations against Communists, rebels, and anarchists in Muensterland and Westphalia in 1920. In one incident during this period Rommel prevented revolutionaries from storming the town hall at Gmuend; by employing fire hoses like machine guns, he dispersed the crowd. This tactic spared Rommel the agony of ordering his men to fire on Germans.[32]

Perhaps as a reward for his success with the internal security company, Rommel's next command was an infantry company in the 13th Regiment at Stuttgart. His own regiment, the 124th, had been dissolved in the reorganization. Rommel stayed in Stuttgart, very happily, until 1929. Due to the slow promotions, typical of a very small peacetime army, he did not reach the rank of major until after 1930.[33]

In September 1929, Rommel's battalion submitted one of those periodic efficiency reports that seem to be the hallmark of every modern army. His battalion commander described Rommel's abilities as "very great," particularly in the area of terrain analysis. "He has already demonstrated in war that he is an exemplary combat commander," the report continued. "He has shown very good results training and drilling his company. . . . There is more to this officer than meets the eye." The commander concluded the report by suggesting that Rommel might make a good military instructor.[34] This recommendation was acted upon, and on October 1, 1929, Rommel was transferred to the Infantry School at Dresden, as an instructor.

Rommel soon became one of the most popular teachers at the school. He was constantly challenging the cadets' minds and expanding their abilities to think for themselves. In a 1931 report, the school commandant wrote: "His tactical battle lectures, in which he describes his own war experiences, offer the cadets not only tactical but also a lot of ideological food for thought . . . [they] are always a delight to hear." A year later the senior instructor described him as "a towering personality even in a milieu of hand-picked officers. . . . A genuine leader, inspiring and arousing cheerful confidence in others. A first-rate infantry and combat instructor, constantly making suggestions and above all building up cadets' characters . . . Respected by his colleagues, worshipped by his cadets."[35]

While at the Infantry School Rommel renewed his friendship with Captain Ferdinand Schoerner, with whom he had served in Italy when they were both lieutenants. Schoerner liked to play practical jokes, and he occasionally picked Rommel as his victim. Once Schoerner hid some silverware in Rommel's pocket at a former banquet. Soon it fell out, to Rommel's great embarrassment, for it appeared that he had been trying to steal it. Schoerner enjoyed the joke, but the puritanical Rommel was less than amused. Normally, however, their rivalry was friendly. Later, Schoerner acquired the reputation of being one of Hitler's most vicious generals. Schoerner frequently had other officers shot for failing to hold their positions, despite overwhelming odds. Rommel took him aside one day during World War II and told him he should not use such methods,[36] but this plea was lost on Schoerner. The two were no longer close friends. Schoerner eventually reached the rank of field marshal and, after the war, worked for the Russians.

Teaching was not Rommel's only concern during his stay at Dresden. Here he wrote his famous book *Infantry in the Attack*. It soon became a textbook for the Swiss Army and, more important for Rommel, reached the desk of Chancellor Hitler a few years later. The former corporal read it and was impressed. The seeds that would lead to Rommel's meteoric rise, and eventually to his death, were planted.

Rommel had no way of knowing this in 1933, when he was again transferred. This time he went to Goslar, where he assumed command of the 3rd Battalion of the 17th Infantry, a mountain regiment. He amazed the younger men with his great physical endurance. On his first day in command the junior officers tried to put him in his place by inviting him to climb a nearby mountain and ski down with them. He did—three times. When Rommel challenged them to a fourth trip, the exhausted lieutenants and captains admitted defeat and declined. He was in total control of the battalion from then on. While in this command, he had his first contact with Dr. Joseph Goebbels, Heinrich Himmler, and Adolf Hitler.

The Nazi Fuehrer was to attend a parade at Goslar. The 17th Infantry was to pass in review, but when a young SS representative told Rommel that a single file of SS men would stand between his men and Hitler to provide security, Rommel flatly refused to march. He considered such an arrangement an affront to the unit's honor. The day when Adolf Hitler would need security against Rommel and kindred souls had not yet come. The young SS man, perhaps realizing that he had gone too far, asked Rommel to consult with the SS chief, Himmler, and Propaganda Minister Goebbels at the local hotel. Rommel tensely explained the situation to the important Nazis. To his surprise, they apologized. The major was perfectly correct in refusing to parade under such circumstances, they said; he should please consider the whole incident the mistake of an overly zealous subordinate. The tension subsided. Goebbels asked if the major would care to stay for lunch, and Rommel accepted the invitation.

During the meal, the club-footed Dr. Goebbels was charming, as he could very well be when he wished. Goebbels apparently realized that Rommel would not always be an insignificant major in a small garrison town. For the rest of Rommel's life, the diminutive minister would go out of his way to be nice to him, and even once suggested to Hitler that he be made commander-in-chief of the Army after Germany won World War II. For his part, the middle-aged major was quite taken with the propaganda minister but totally unimpressed with Himmler. Rommel would never have cause to alter either opinion.[37]

The parade itself took place without incident. Rommel's first meeting with Hitler was purely formal. Rommel saluted the new head of state, was introduced, and was complimented on the showing of his battalion.[38]

Considerable controversy has arisen in recent years over Rommel's political convictions. This is understandable, for Rommel's opinion of the Nazis was both politically naive and somewhat ambivalent. Certainly he never joined the party, but he did support Hitler, at least to a degree. He first viewed the Bavarian politician as an idealist with some sound ideas for putting Germany back on its feet; Hitler's association with some of the cruder Nazis he considered unfortunate. Rommel was largely taken in by the great orator, just as were millions of other Germans who fell under his spell.

On June 30, 1934, in the infamous "Night of the Long Knives," Hitler purged the Brown Shirts (SA) and took the opportunity to rid himself of several hundred real or potential political opponents at the same time. Among the pile of corpses lay two generals: Kurt von Schleicher and Kurt von Bredow. Sources differ on Rommel's opinion of the events of that evening. Brigadier Desmond Young, generally recognized as Rommel's foremost biographer, stated that Rommel believed Hitler's story that Brown Shirt leader Ernst Roehm, a notorious homosexual, was planning to overthrow the government and replace the Army with the SA. According to Young, Rommel believed the Fuehrer's actions were justified.[39] Lieutenant General Hans Speidel, Rommel's chief of staff in 1944, holds a different view. According to him, Rommel said to his friend Oskar Farny in 1934: "Now would have been a good time to throw out Hitler and his whole gang."[40] It seems impossible to say now what was the actual view of the never politically adroit future field marshal.

To complicate the hazy picture further, Rommel was personally fond of Adolf Hitler and Dr. Goebbels, at least until 1942. Rommel found much to praise about the Fuehrer, particularly after the renunciation of the Treaty of Versailles in March 1935. Now the German Armed Forces were again free to expand, and German industry could build tanks, military aircraft, heavy guns, and submarines. Many of the unemployed found jobs in either the Army or the civilian work force due to these measures. Rommel expressed confidence in Hitler, calling him the "unifier of the nation" and the "eliminator of unemployment." By 1936, he believed in the "peaceful aims and ideals" of the Fuehrer.[41]

Rommel's confidence in Hitler did not extend to the leader's subordinates, however. In 1935, the now Lieutenant Colonel Rommel clashed with a party bigwig in his first serious disagreement with the Nazis. At the time, Rommel was stationed at the War Academy at Potsdam. Late in the year he ended up on detached duty with the Hitler Youth in Berlin. The head of the Hitler Youth, Baldur von Schirach, resented Rommel's presence and attitude. The fact that the Army officer was not even a party member also disturbed von Schirach.

They did not get along well socially, either. "Rommel stayed for supper," von Schirach later recalled. "My wife drew his attention to the beautiful view onto the Bavarian Mountains from our window. This cut no ice with him. 'Thank you, but I'm very familiar with *mountains*,' he said, without so much as glancing out the window. Henriette had unintentionally given our guest his cue, because Rommel had received the Pour le Mérite in 1917 for storming some mountain or other in the Julian Alps. He now held forth on this for two hours. I found his story quite interesting, but to Henriette all such military matters were anathema and she nearly fell asleep."[42]

Colonel Rommel lost no time in vocalizing his objections to von Schirach's efforts to militarize the Hitler Youth. Rommel informed his host that he was paying too much attention to sports and military training and not enough to character development and education. The young people already seemed contemptuous of school and education, he said.

Von Schirach naturally grew defensive under Rommel's verbal attack, and an argument developed. After debating for several minutes Rommel, with a characteristic lack of tact, told von Schirach that if he were determined to train boys to be soldiers, he should first learn to be a soldier himself! Von Schirach, of course, arranged for Rommel's immediate return to the War Academy at Potsdam.[43]

Rommel thoroughly enjoyed his job as senior instructor at the War Academy. He always liked teaching the young officer-cadets. Perhaps this was inbred, because both his father and grandfather had been teachers. He encouraged the young men to think for themselves. When a cadet would try to answer one of Rommel's questions with a quote from Clausewitz, Rommel would invariably interrupt and bark: "Never mind what Clausewitz thought, what do *you* think?" Rommel never did admire Clausewitz very much; his idol was Napoleon, the man of action.[44]

Meanwhile, to his astonishment, Rommel became moderately wealthy. *Infantry in the Attack* was selling more rapidly than Rommel could have imagined. It went from one edition to another. He confided to one of his fellow instructors, Kurt Hesse: "It's astounding the money there is to be made from such books. I just don't know what to do with all the cash that's flooding in. I can't possibly use it all, I'm happy enough with what I've got already. And I don't like the idea of making money out of writing up how other good men lost their lives."[45]

During Rommel's three-year tour of duty as an instructor at Potsdam, he never associated with the members of the Nazi Party or of the High Command, despite the nearness of Potsdam to Berlin. His family life changed little. Manfred continued to grow, and he became his own man. Later he remarked: "My father had three ambitions for me: he wanted me to become a fine sportsman, a great hero, and a good mathematician. He failed on all three counts."[46]

Rommel received his promotions strictly on his own merits. In 1936, however, his career got a tremendous boost from an unexpected source. Adolf Hitler read *Infantry in the Attack* and decided to meet its author.

In September of that year Rommel was attached to Hitler's escort for the Nazi Party rally at Nuremberg. He was occupied mainly with security duties. When the rally was ending and it came time for Hitler to leave, he told Rommel to allow no more than half a dozen cars to follow him. This order meant having to stop an entire convoy of generals, cabinet ministers, and high-ranking party officials. Rommel did exactly as he had been instructed and even blocked the road with two tanks, despite the curses of some of the most powerful men in Nazi Germany. "This is monstrous, Colonel!" one of them roared. "I intend to report this to the Fuehrer!" Apparently he did, for Hitler called Rommel that night and thanked him for executing the order so well.[47]

In 1937 Rommel received a choice assignment. He assumed command of the Infantry School at Wiener Neustadt, in what is now Austria. Later he wrote that this was the happiest period of his military career. The countryside was beautiful and the duty both challenging and rewarding. Under other circumstances, Rommel might have retired here. However, a summons came from Berlin, and the 47-year-old colonel reported to his chancellor. He was given command of the Fuehrergleitbataillon, Hitler's personal bodyguard, as the German Army entered the Sudetenland. This ad hoc force consisted of about two companies of infantry armed with machine guns, rifles, antitank guns, and anti-aircraft weapons. It looked as if they would be needed. War clouds hung low on the horizon until the Allies backed down at Munich and abandoned their Czech friends. A few months later, Hitler finished off the helpless Czechoslovakian state. As he was about to enter the capital city of Prague, Hitler turned to the commander of his bodyguard, a man he had come to trust. "What would you do if you were in my place, Colonel?" he asked.

"I should get into an open car and drive through the streets to the Hradschin without an escort," Rommel replied.

Hitler followed this advice. There were no incidents.[48]

During his three periods of temporary duty as the commander of the Fuehrer Guard Battalion, Rommel's admiration for Hitler grew. Rommel witnessed none of the adverse reactions Hitler would later show to bad news. There were no temper tantrums, no unreasonable behavior, no fits. In 1939, Adolf Hitler still maintained control of all his faculties. He impressed Rommel with his actions under stress, his incredible memory, and his physical courage. The two liked and respected each other. Now Rommel was even closing his private letters with "Heil Hitler! Yours, E. Rommel."[49] Rommel came closer to being a Nazi during this period than at any other in his life. Nevertheless, he still nourished a healthy suspicion of some of Hitler's closest paladins.

Between his additional duty trips and leaves, Rommel and his family enjoyed life at Wiener Neustadt, in the mountains southwest of Vienna. The family went on many excursions and hiking trips into the Alps. They lived in a charming little house surrounded by a flower garden. Rommel often remembered this period with great pleasure. At home, he developed a new hobby: photography. In mid-1939, however, the good times ended. The international situation took a serious turn for the worse. Rommel again joined Hitler's entourage as the commander of the bodyguard. On August 23, Hitler promoted him to major general.[50] Nine days later, the panzers crossed the Polish frontier. World War II had begun.

It would be foolish to assert that Rommel did not support the invasion of Poland. Danzig was what Hitler wanted, and Danzig was a German city. Rommel and Lucie had met and fallen in love there. It had been a German town for centuries. Only since the hated Treaty of Versailles had it been a "free city." Now Germany was strong again and wanted it back, along with the surrounding land, the "Polish corridor," which divided East Prussia from the rest of the Reich. Rommel felt that Hitler was right in pressing his demands. Neither he nor his leader expected a long war.

Rommel's main problem in the Polish campaign was Hitler's constant desire to go into the combat zone personally. Of the Fuehrer at this time, Rommel later wrote: "I had great trouble with him. He always wanted to be right up with the forward troops." Hitler went so far as to expose himself to Polish sniper fire and observe the storming of a river line by the German infantry. "He seemed to enjoy being under fire," Rommel complained.[51]

The future Desert Fox made an important and dangerous enemy during this, the opening campaign of the war. Hitler wanted to drive down to the edge of the Baltic Sea at Gdynia, where Polish resistance had just ended. The road to the port was small and steep. Only Hitler's car and one other vehicle were allowed to descend. Then Rommel blocked the road. The third car belonged to the vulturelike and powerful Martin Bormann, who would soon become chief of the Nazi Party Chancellory. Bormann curtly demanded that Rommel get out of his way. Rommel replied in the same coin. "I am headquarters command-ant! This is not a kindergarten outing, and you will do as I say!" Bormann never forgot nor forgave this insult.[52]

In Poland, Rommel had a chance to observe the effects of blitzkrieg (literally, "lightning warfare") firsthand. He saw the importance of pushing forward in mechanized warfare, even if one had to bypass points of resistance and take the risk of being cut off. He learned the value of General Heinz Guderian's maxim that masses of tanks, not dribbles, should be employed against the enemy. He also recognized the impor-tance of leading tank formations from the front, and the value of close air-to-ground coordination. Although he had been in the infantry for 29 years and probably had not seen the inside of a tank before 1936, he decided his future lay in the armored branch.

On their return from Poland, Rommel approached Hitler and requested a command of his own.

Hitler took a personal interest in his new general. "What do you want?" he asked.

"Command of a panzer division," replied Rommel, without batting an eye.

Much later, Rommel commented to Major General Alfred Gause: "That was an immoderate request on my part: I did not belong to the armored branch of the service, and there were many generals who had a much stronger claim to a command of this nature."[53] Nevertheless, in February 1940 Rommel arrived at Godesberg, on the Rhine, to succeed Lieutenant General Georg Stumme as commander of the 7th Panzer Division.

The panzer division that Erwin Rommel took over in February 1940 hardly fit the standard propaganda description of an elite armored force. It was one of the four light divisions that Hitler had ordered converted into panzer units in the winter of 1939–40. It boasted only one tank regiment of three battalions, instead of the normal (1940) contingent of two regiments of two battalions each, an organizational arrangement that left Rommel with 218 tanks, or about 75 percent of the armor of a normal panzer division. To make matters worse (much worse, in fact), more than half of Rommel's tanks were captured Czechoslovakian vehicles.[54] They had simply been incorporated into the German Army in 1938. These T-38 tanks weighed only about nine tons and would be of little use against the British and the French.

Some of the German-made tanks proved to be of hardly greater value. The Panzer Mark I (PzKw I) had originally been built as a training tank and as a carrier for a 20mm anti-aircraft gun. However, nothing larger than a machine gun could be mounted on its small chassis. It was, in short, a small assault vehicle of dubious value. General Guderian, the creator of the German armored corps, explained that it was designed strictly as a training vehicle and added: "Nobody in 1932 could have guessed that one day we should have to go into action with this little tank."[55]

The Panzer Mark II (PzKw II) was somewhat of an improvement, but not much. The J Model (PzKw IIj) weighed only 10½ tons and had very thin armored protection. It could be penetrated by even the smallest enemy antitank gun.

The most important tank in Rommel's arsenal, although definitely not the most numerous, was the Panzer Mark III (PzKw III). The H Model (PzKw IIIh) weighed 23 tons and carried a five-man crew, as compared to three in the PzKw I and PzKw II. Most of Rommel's PzKw III's were an early model and weighed only 20 tons. They carried a 50mm main battle gun and two MG-34 machine guns, which made them very dangerous in both tank and combined arms battles. The maximum armored thickness of the PzKw III was 60 to 77 millimeters, depending on the model. This made them safer than the Mark I, Mark II, or the Czech tanks but hardly rendered them invulnerable to British antitank guns. Perhaps the strongest feature of the Mark III was its speed, which averaged 25 miles per hour on the road and compared favorably to the British Matilda, which had a maximum road speed of 15 miles per hour.

The fastest tank Rommel commanded in the French campaign was the Panzer Mark IV (PzKw IV), which could cover 26 miles per hour on the road. It was about the same weight as the PzKw III. Unfortunately, it was armed with a very short 75mm main battle gun, which severely restricted its range. It was best when used as an infantry support vehicle.

The men of the 7th Panzer Division were in no better shape than their panzers. The men were from the province of Thuringia, which was not noted for producing good soldiers. Rommel promptly set about bringing them up to standard. He arrived on February 10 and immediately ordered a divisional inspection, brushing aside his officers' protests that it was Sunday. After touring his new command, the Swabian sent all his regimental commanders on leave. "I won't be needing you until I've learned the ropes myself," he snapped.[56]

Rommel himself was up before 6:00 A.M. every morning. His first chore was to run a mile every morning before breakfast. He had grown overweight during his six months of relatively soft duty at Fuehrer Headquarters and found it hard "to fight back the inner Schweinehund in me that pleads, 'Stay in bed—just another fifteen minutes.'"[57]

"I don't suppose I'll find many men anxious to follow my example," he wrote Lucie. "Most of my officers are very comfortably inclined. And some are downright flabby."[58]

Erwin Rommel immediately set about correcting the situation. Training intensified almost as soon as he set up shop. Discipline quickly improved, and the division's combat efficiency increased remarkably. When the order came to attack, the 7th Panzer would be ready.

The Ghost Division's main battle force included the 25th Panzer Regiment, and the 6th and 7th Motorized Infantry regiments, also called rifle regiments. Other units included the 78th Field Artillery Regiment, and the 37th Panzer Reconnaissance, 7th Motorcycle, 58th Engineer and 42nd Antitank battalions.

The Army High Command (OKH), the Armed Forces High Command (OKW), and Hitler had a hard time agreeing on a plan for the coming invasion of France. Colonel General* (later Field Marshal)

---

*For a comparison of U.S. and German ranks, see Appendix I.

Walther von Brauchitsch, the commander-in-chief of the German Army, offered an unimaginative rehash of the Schlieffen Plan of 1914, which called for the main thrust to follow the North European Plain through the Low Countries and into France. Hitler didn't like it (it lacked the element of surprise and hadn't worked in 1914, after all), but he hesitated in putting forth a plan of his own.

Lieutenant General Erich von Manstein, the chief of staff of Army Group A, came up with the solution. He decided that the best way to destroy the French would be to launch a diversionary attack against Holland to the north and then strike through the Ardennes in Luxembourg and southern Belgium with the bulk of Germany's armor. If the Allies took the bait and rushed to meet the northern attack, as von Manstein predicted, their main forces would be cut off by the southern thrust a few days later. Colonel General Gerd von Rundstedt, the commander-in-chief of Army Group A, approved the plan, but von Brauchitsch did not, and with some valid reasons. The Ardennes, a heavily wooded area crisscrossed by streams and rivers, was dominated by steep hills and could hardly be classified as ideal terrain for armor. Von Brauchitsch initially refused even to submit the plan to Hitler; the Fuehrer only heard of it when his Army adjutant, Colonel Rudolf Schmundt, bypassed normal channels and brought it to his attention.[59] The Nazi dictator liked the idea and ordered it implemented. Von Brauchitsch was so upset by these developments that he made sure von Manstein would play no role in the execution of his plan.* The damage had been done to the field marshal's career, however; Hitler had lost confidence in him and, at the first major setback to German arms in December 1941, he sacked von Brauchitsch and himself assumed the title of supreme commander of the Army.

In May 1940, the 156 divisions of the French, Dutch, Belgian, and British armies faced 136 German divisions along a front that extended from the Swiss frontier to the North Sea. Of the German divisions, only 10 were panzer, and they were outnumbered in armored vehicles 4,200 to 2,800. In addition, the Allied tanks had an overall superiority in armament and firepower. In the three phases of warfare—land, sea, and

---

*Manstein commanded the XXXVIII Infantry Corps in France. This weak force did not take part in the drive to the Channel and was assigned only mopping-up missions later.

air—the Nazi forces held superiority only in the air. Their techniques of armored application vastly outclassed the concepts of the French and British, however, and they followed Guderian's maxim of "masses—not dribbles." The Allies scattered their tanks out over hundreds of miles. Most Allied divisions had some armored support, but no major, concentrated tank corps existed. Their opponents, on the other hand, employed huge armored formations under daring commanders who were capable of quickly swamping each unconcentrated Allied tank element they encountered before these elements could join forces and pose a serious threat to the onrushing blitzkrieg. The key to victory, therefore, lay in the superior tactics of the aggressor rather than in any mythical "wonder weapon." The alleged technical supremacy of the German war machine simply did not exist, at least in 1940.

The main German attack would be launched through the Ardennes by General Eduard von Kleist's Panzer Group.* The Group had two corps: Guderian's XIX Panzer (three panzer divisions) and Georg-Hans Reinhardt's XXXIX Panzer (two panzer divisions). Guderian concentrated on the left flank of Colonel General Sigmund Wilhelm von List's Twelfth Army, while Reinhardt assembled his men on the right flank of the same army. Rommel's division, along with the 5th Panzer Division, made up Hoth's XV Panzer Corps, which was attached to Colonel General Guenther von Kluge's Fourth Army, positioned north of the main concentration. Its one major objective was to protect Kleist's right flank against predictable Allied counterattacks from the north. Rommel's primary mission, then, was basically supportive. He soon expanded it to more than that.

The von Manstein plan worked just as its creator said it would. When German Army Group B under Colonel General Fedor von Bock attacked Holland, the bulk of the French and British forces rushed northward, on to the plains of Belgium and the Netherlands. They were not interrupted by the German Luftwaffe, which deliberately allowed them to proceed. Soon they became decisively engaged with von Bock's two armies in the northernmost part of the front. A breakthrough from the Ardennes to the sea would now cut off the main Allied armies, trap them between von Bock's men and von Rundstedt's Army Group A

---

*A Panzer group was a force of roughly army size. In late 1941 and early 1942 all Panzer groups were upgraded to Panzer army status.

(Rommel, von Kleist, von Kluge, Guderian, and company) and ensure the rapid fall of France. It could quite possibly win the war for Adolf Hitler.

The northward Allied movement hinged on the French Ninth Army, which advanced to form a line along the Meuse River from Mezieres to Namur. This hinge had to remain intact if the Nazi plan was to be thwarted; however, as it wheeled, the Ninth Army collided with Rommel, Guderian, and the bulk of the German armor.

Rommel's division crossed the Belgian frontier and penetrated to the eastern bank of the Meuse against light resistance. Most of the roadblocks it encountered were undefended, and none held out for long. Rommel did skirmish with some armored units from the 1st and 4th French Cavalry divisions, but these units were not concentrated and served only as rearguard and delaying forces. Rommel wrote later: "I have found again and again that in encounter actions, the day goes to the side that is the first to plaster its opponents with fire. . . . This applies even when the exact position of the enemy is unknown, in which case the fire must simply be sprayed over enemy-held territory. . . ."[60]

On May 12, Rommel's pursuing columns reached the Meuse bridges at Dinant and Houx. Just as they arrived, however, French engineers blew them up. Rommel had no choice but to launch a river crossing operation the next day.

Few military maneuvers, even in peacetime, are more difficult than a river crossing. The Meuse presented additional complications. In front of Rommel the banks were steep and rocky. The river itself extended to a width of 120 yards. The French defenders on the other bank were of undetermined strength, but they were no doubt strong, dug in, and ready for the German assault. The element of surprise would be totally absent. Under these handicaps, Major General Erwin Rommel planned his first major battle of the Second World War.

During the night of May 12–13, most of the Ghost Division moved into jump-off positions. Rommel's infantry concentrated near the village of Dinant. Shortly after dawn the men of the 6th Rifle Regiment crawled to the edge of the river, inflated their rubber boats, and jumped into them. Immediately, French snipers and machine gunners claimed their first victims as fire from hidden positions tore into the boats and sank them. The Germans were being slaughtered. Several wounded men, weighed down by their rifles and equipment, drowned in the current. Meanwhile, heavy French artillery plastered the eastern bank and deci-

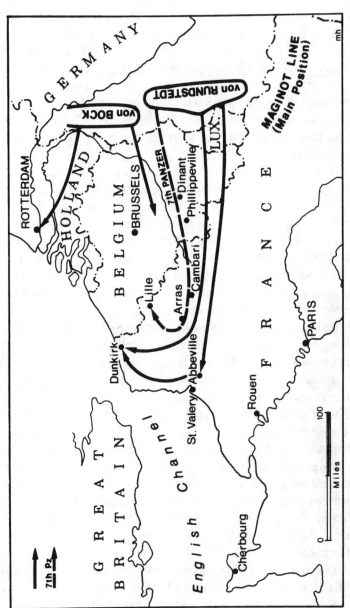

Map 2: France, 1940: Phase I. Rommel's 7th Panzer Division crossed the Meuse, routed several French divisions, breached the Maginot Line Extension, repulsed a major counterattack at Arras, helped cover the right flank of the major attack, and cut off the retreat of half of the French 1st Army at Lille. Later in the campaign it took St. Valery and Cherbourg.

mated the exposed support units. Rommel, who had no smoke companies, ordered the French houses set on fire to provide at least some concealment for his men. While watching the initial assault fall apart, Rommel saw a badly wounded man clinging to a shot-up rubber boat. The man, obviously near drowning, passed within a few yards of Rommel, who had taken a concealed position in a small woods near the riverbank. The young soldier screamed and pleaded for help. Rommel could only watch helplessly; the enemy fire was too heavy to allow him to rescue the drowning man.[61]

Meanwhile, about two miles north of Dinant, dismounted elements of the motorcycle battalion managed to secure a tenuous foothold on the west bank. With some success on his northern flank and the 6th Rifle Regiment regrouping in the center of his divisional line, Rommel turned his attention to the southern flank. Accompanied by his aide, Captain Schraepler, Rommel drove down the Meuse Road to the headquarters of the 7th Rifle Regiment, which was still desperately trying to get its men across against fierce resistance. On the way, French artillery forward observers spotted the rapidly moving German command vehicle. Their shells landed uncomfortably close. Captain Schraepler sank to the floor, gripping a mutilated arm. Other shell splinters struck the vehicle, but no direct hit was scored. Rommel reached safety, left his aide with medical personnel, and located the commander of the 7th Rifle.[62]

By the time Rommel arrived, one company of the 7th had reached the west bank, but it was immediately pinned down by the French infantry. Much of the regimental assault equipment was damaged, sunk, or burning. Rommel immediately realized that, unless speedily relieved, the 7th Rifle's bridgehead would be wiped out, and the regiment itself no longer possessed the strength to turn back a determined counterattack. Rommel ordered his artillery, heavy weapons, and panzers to fire across the river and pulverize all possible French positions with a devastating bombardment. Soon French fire lessened and Rommel decided it was now time for a second assault wave to cross the Meuse. Characteristically, he led it himself. Assuming personal command of the 2nd Battalion, 7th Rifle Regiment, he leaped into the first assault boat and was soon in the middle of the river. He would have been a sitting duck had he attempted this move two hours earlier, but the artillery had done its job, and the reinforcements suffered few casualties on their trip across the Meuse.[63]

On the west bank, Rommel had a bad moment when some French tanks appeared. Without panzers or even antitank guns, the bridgehead could easily have been eliminated. The daring Swabian decided to play a bluff: He brought the tanks under a heavy but absolutely ineffective small-arms volley. Remarkably it worked, and the French armored force retired. Encouraged by this lack of initiative on the part of the enemy, the German infantrymen advanced, captured a number of enemy positions, and steadily expanded their foothold. Satisfied with this progress, the future field marshal recrossed the river and returned to the zone of the 6th Rifle Regiment. On the return trip the French artillerymen were far too busy to bother with a single assault boat.[64]

By early afternoon, the situation was as follows: to the north, the 7th Motorcycle Battalion held the village of Grange on the west bank but could make no further progress; in the center, the 6th Rifle Regiment had suffered one repulse and was heavily engaged in a second full-scale attack; on the southern flank, the 7th Rifle Regiment held a small bridgehead, which appeared to be safe, at least for the moment.

When Rommel returned to his headquarters, both good and bad news awaited him. The 6th Rifle Regiment's attack had been successful, despite heavy casualties. Colonel von Unger, the commander of the 6th, and Colonel Michl, the antitank battalion commander, already had 20 antitank guns on the west bank, and their position looked fairly good. Engineers were racing to build a pontoon bridge across the Meuse so the panzer regiment could join the battle. The French, aware that this move could spell disaster for them, tried to prevent it by the employment of heavy artillery. The pioneers coolly ignored the storm raging about their heads. As the bridge neared the opposite bank, French countermeasures became more desperate, and they launched direct frontal assaults on Rommel's right flank and center. The Germans beat back the combined infantry-tank assault on their center and inflicted serious casualties on the Frenchmen. To the north, the counterattacks proved more successful. The light 7th Motorcycle Battalion was mauled, its commander wounded, and its adjutant killed. Rommel's right flank threatened to collapse, but the young infantrymen managed to hold out until nightfall. In the darkness, the Allied soldiers returned to their former positions.[65]

Rommel did not. The pontoon bridge was completed at dusk, but its small size made it very dangerous for tank crossings. During the night only 15 of the armored monsters reached the other side of the Meuse. At dawn, a spirited French charge could yet have smashed the German bridgehead. By 9:00 A.M., however, Rommel and Colonel Karl Rothenburg, the commander of the 25th Panzer Regiment, had gotten another 15 tanks across, bringing the total to 30.[66]

On Rommel's southern flank, Colonel von Bismarck's 7th Rifle Regiment was also making significant headway. Early in the morning Bismarck captured the village of Onhaye, four miles west of the Meuse, and signaled that he had "arrived" (*eingetroffen*) there. However, after decoding, the message read that Bismarck was "encircled" (*eigeschlossen*) in the village. The startled Rommel immediately headed for the village with all available panzers. Upon reaching Onhaye, Rommel learned of the mistake. Considerably relieved, he gave Bismarck five of his 30 tanks and led the rest into a wood area 1,000 yards north of the village. He proposed to concentrate here and plan his next move. Unfortunately for him, a French commander had had a similar idea somewhat earlier.[67]

Just as he entered the woods, Rommel's tank received hits from French artillery and antitank guns. The upper turret was damaged, and the periscope was blown away. Blood shot out of Rommel's face and onto his uniform as the tank slid down a steep slope and rolled over on its side. Bleeding profusely but not seriously wounded, the general and crew abandoned the disabled vehicle while Colonel Rothenburg covered their escape with his own tank. Other panzer commanders led their units into the woods, followed by the infantry, while Rommel learned that his signals vehicle, which always followed him, had been knocked out by a direct hit on the engine. Meanwhile, Rothenburg began systematically to clear the area of Frenchmen, a process that took until late evening. By that time, the bridgehead across the Meuse was firmly established.[68]

Rommel's method of leading from the front had earned him a blood-soaked tunic at Onhaye. Nevertheless, despite the personal danger involved, Rommel felt his style of command was not only valid and justified but also "extremely effective." He explained it this way:

> A tight combat control west of the Meuse, and flexibility to meet the changing situation, were only made possible by the fact that the divisional commander with his signal troop kept on the move and was able to give his orders direct to the regiment commanders in the forward line. Wireless alone—due to the necessity for encoding —would have taken far too long, first to get the situation reports back to Division and for Division to issue orders. . . .[69]

This method of leading from the front did have some serious drawbacks. Most obvious was the fact that the commander could easily be killed, wounded, or captured. A communications problem would be far more serious than otherwise, and command control of the battle could be lost if one well-placed enemy shell flew home. Also, an excited commander could become overly impressed with local successes and not be in a position to judge the overall situation. At various times in the years ahead, Rommel fell victim to all these circumstances. Already he had been wounded. Still, it must be concluded that he was right. The method had more credits than debits when utilized by a talented general. The leader on the spot could take decisive action at the right time with all available forces, while a commander chained to his headquarters could easily lose control of the battle. This is what happened at the Meuse, for the French missed several opportune moments for a potentially decisive counterstroke. Rommel, on the other hand, missed very little. The Meuse line was reeling.

Farther south, other important events also took place on May 14. A division from General Reinhardt's XXXIX Panzer Corps gained an insecure foothold across the river at Montherme, but the outcome of that battle remained in doubt. Guderian's XIX Panzer Corps had better luck. The Prussian pierced the Meuse line at Sedan and pushed back both the French Second and Ninth armies at their juncture. The French Ninth Army commander, General Corap, noted with increasing dismay that Rommel had forced back his center, and Guderian's attacks had seriously weakened his right flank, which seemed on the verge of collapse. During the night of May 14–15, he ordered a general withdrawal from the Meuse. This move turned out to be a fatal mistake. Guderian, Rommel, Hoth, and the other panzer leaders would allow no respite after this. The floodgates had broken. It was the beginning of the disintegration of the French Army.

Rommel could not have known all this on the morning of May 15, as he set his pursuit columns in motion after the disorganized Frenchmen. He did, however, grasp the tactical significance of the moment and determined to exploit it to the fullest. His assigned objective for the day was Cerfontaine, a town several miles west of the Meuse; he captured Cerfontaine before noon. The defenders Rommel encountered along the way had already been pounded by the Stukas, those highly effective close-support dive bombers that shot up so many unprotected Allied supply and troop columns in the early years of the war. The nervous and demoralized enemy soldiers either took to the woods or surrendered as soon as they saw the panzers approaching. In one brief engagement, the

French lost 15 tanks. Most of them were simply abandoned intact as the defenders fled. The road to Cerfontaine was littered with discarded military gear, vehicles, and panic-striken refugees.[70]

This sort of situation prevailed all along the front. To the south, Guderian and Reinhardt ripped a 60-mile hole in the Allied line and by dusk were racing through the enemy's rear toward the English Channel. On Rommel's front, General Copay desperately tried to restore his line by throwing the 1st French Armored Division and the 4th North African Division against the 7th Panzer. Events were far beyond Copay's control by now, however. Rommel destroyed both units west of Cerfontaine on the afternoon of May 15. Normally, the 1st French Armored might have performed better, but it ran out of fuel at the critical moment. Instead of continuing to resist, the entire division suddenly dissolved. Most of the French tankers took to their heels without bothering to destroy their vehicles. The 4th North African Division also collapsed and merged with the stream of humanity that clogged the roads heading west. Rommel pushed onward, and by May 16 his division was ready to attack the Maginot Line.[71]

Along the French-German border, the Maginot Line formed the most extensive system of fortifications in the history of warfare. Along the French-Belgian border, however, the line varied in depth, and in places it was even weak. It had been constructed much later and with much less lavish expenditures of money and resources, due to the shortsightedness of French politicians, who could not foresee an attack from this direction, despite the fact that the Kaiser's armies had come this way just a quarter of a century before. To be proper, this part of the line should be called the Maginot Line Extension. It was these newer, weaker fortifications that Erwin Rommel faced as dusk fell on May 15.

The enemy holding the Extension was routed, shocked, demoralized, and exhausted, both mentally and physically. Rommel's men were also tired, but they were exhilarated by their string of spectacular victories, and they expected yet another. More than that, they hoped to get past the legendary Maginot with a minimum of casualties.

Rommel, not one to be overawed by any obstacle, at least had a healthy respect for this one. He discussed his assault plans with his immediate superior, General Hermann Hoth. In this man, Rommel found a kindred soul. Like Rommel, Hoth went on to command a panzer army. As a leader on the Russian Front, Hoth would score a series of impressive victories before falling out of grace with Hitler and being removed from command in 1944.[72] Mercifully, neither Rommel nor Hoth could see into the future as they bent over their maps on the night of May 15–16.

Both generals recognized that they must keep the pressure on the French, or the resistance would stiffen, as it had in 1914; therefore, the Maginot had to be overrun at full throttle. Hoth ordered his divisional commander to break through near Sivry, 12 miles west of Cerfontaine, and continue the attack that night to the hills around Avesnes, 24 miles west of Cerfontaine.[73]

On the morning of May 16, Rommel found his way barred by a French pillbox that was protected by hedgehogs* and a steep antitank ditch. Rommel initially tried the direct approach, and he lost two tanks as a result. Quickly he changed tactics. Artillery units fired smoke rounds in and around French positions. Protected by this artificial cloud, German engineers ran pell-mell toward the pillbox and threw demolition charges into it, while Major Erdman's 37th Reconnaissance Battalion blew up the hedgehogs. French field guns and antitank weapons, positioned 1,000 yards away, tried to prevent this, but they were quickly silenced by the direct fire of Rothenburg's tanks. By nightfall the road to the west lay open.[74] The Ghost Division roared at full tilt into the darkness.

During the night of May 16–17, Rommel raced through the fortified zone. Early in the morning, the Battle of Avesnes began. Rommel left the motorcycle battalion and most of the 25th Panzer Regiment to smash this center of French resistance, and he continued on. At about 4:00 A.M. the village fell. Several more German tanks lay burning, but the Maginot Line Extension had been pierced.[75]

At dawn on May 17, Rommel was still urging his pursuit columns forward. He decided to continue on his own initiative, since radio contact with Hoth's headquarters was lost. Rommel planned to seize the Sambre River bridge at Landrecies, 11 miles west of Avesnes and 35 miles west of his original jump-off point for this surge. The bridges, as Rommel guessed, were intact and easily taken. The major general, however, remained unsatisfied. Without checking to see if the rest of his division had managed to catch up, he set off again. Finally he halted eight miles farther west, just east of the village of La Cateau, at 6:00 P.M. on May 17. Rommel had outrun his supply columns and was quite low on fuel and ammunition. He then discovered that only one panzer

---

*In this sense, hedgehogs refer to large, concrete antitank obstacles.

battalion (Sickenius') had kept up. He ordered it to hedgehog* while he doubled back to locate the rest of the scattered division.[76]

In two days, the vanguard of the 7th Panzer Division had pushed a salient 30 miles long but only two miles wide in the French front. Despite enormous risks (strong enemy forces lay on both his exposed flanks), Rommel had broken the Maginot Line Extension and secured the important Sambre River crossing. The division had lost only 35 men killed and 59 wounded and had taken over 10,000 prisoners in 48 hours. One hundred enemy tanks, 30 armored cars, and 27 field guns had been destroyed or captured by Rommel's men so far in the campaign. For this operation, Rommel received the Knights' Cross of the Iron Cross, one of Nazi Germany's most coveted decorations.[77]

During the night of May 17-18, Rommel again set out for La Cateau, this time followed by the rest of the division. He had to fight his way back, since the French had occupied Pommereville, a village halfway between Landrecies and La Cateau. After several hours of violent combat Rommel restored contact with his isolated advanced elements. Fortunately, no French counterattack had materialized against Sickenius in the meantime.[78]

Rommel never let up. Pushing his nearly exhausted veterans onward, he neared Cambrai, several miles west of La Cateau. He took Cambrai by bluff. He ordered his tanks and self-propelled guns to drive across the open fields and kick up as much dust as possible. The demoralized defenders decided the advancing enemy must have overwhelming strength and abandoned the town without firing a shot.[79]

For most of the next two days, the men of the 7th Panzer got a much-deserved rest period. Mechanics performed badly needed maintenance, and supplies caught up. Meanwhile, Rommel planned another attack for the night of May 19-20. General Hoth objected, stating that the advance must be postponed due to troop exhaustion. Rommel, however, convinced him to countermand the order on the grounds that the French must be granted no respite. The assault on the high ground southeast of the town of Arras began at 1:30 A.M. Fighting lasted until well after dawn, but Rommel carried his objectives.[80]

The next day, May 21, the 7th Panzer, with the 5th Panzer Division on its right flank and the 3rd SS Motorized Infantry Division "Totenkopf"

---

*In this sense, to hedgehog means to form a circular perimeter defense and await reinforcements.

on its left, advanced northwest in the direction of Lille. Despite the fact that his armored forces were seriously depleted due to breakdowns and combat losses, Rommel again led the pursuit. This time, though, things went differently, for the enemy finally turned on its tormentors and struck back. Three miles southwest of Arras, near the small village of Wailly, Rommel found himself faced with the most serious Allied counterattack of the French campaign.[81]

The motivation for his unusual behavior was desperation. The day before, May 20, Heinz Guderian's panzers had reached the English Channel at Abbeville, thus fulfilling the promise of the Manstein plan: The British Expeditionary Force (BEF) and most of the French armor was cut off from Paris, separated from the bulk of their supplies, fuel, and ammunition, and surrounded by the enemy on three sides, with their backs to the North Sea. They had but one chance left to save France: break through the German forces, re-establish contact to the south, and thus trap Guderian in turn. With great secrecy, to avoid detection by the Luftwaffe, they marshaled the 4th and 7th British Royal Tank regiments and the 3rd French Light Mechanized Division. Together they boasted a strength of 144 tanks of much higher quality than most of the German tanks.[82] This ad hoc force represented perhaps the last significant tactical reserve in the northern pocket. If they failed to get through the corridor and re-establish contact with the Allied armies to the south, France would be doomed to fall into Adolf Hitler's hands. All the Allies' hopes and prayers rode with them into battle. They chose as their main target a relatively weak German armored force: Erwin Rommel's 7th Panzer Division.

Rommel was standing 1,000 yards west of Wailly when he saw the first enemy tanks wipe out a small PzKw III detachment. The only other German forces in the immediate vicinity of the enemy spearhead, excluding a few infantry platoons, were an anti-aircraft battery and a howitzer battery. Rommel again assumed personal command and ordered all available forces to rally on his position. The 25th Panzer Regiment, the real muscle of the division, was too far away and too scattered to respond quickly. As the general gathered antitank and anti-aircraft guns around him, the British struck with their main force. They employed mostly Matilda infantry support tanks ("I" tanks), which carried a large (two-pounder) main gun and a machine gun. These tanks weighed 27 tons and had an armored thickness of up to 78mm. Many of the German gunners, armed with lightweight antitank rifles, could only hope to knock off a track and thus immobilize one of these terrible machines. Rommel personally gave each gun its target as bullets and shells flew all around him. A few feet away Lieutenant Most, the signals officer, fell to the ground with blood gushing from his mouth. Another officer conferred briefly with the general. While he was holding the opposite side of a map from Rommel he collapsed. Like the signals officer, he was dead.[83]

The British tanks surged recklessly on and almost succeeded in overrunning Rommel and his men. The last Matilda was knocked out within 50 yards of the main German position. Rommel had indeed been fortunate that the Allies failed to provide their tanks with sufficient infantry or artillery support, for if they had, his little combat group would have been wiped out. Their failure to destroy this island of resistance jeopardized the entire offensive. Thirty-six tanks, a full 25 percent of the total Allied armored force, were destroyed by Rommel's determined stand.[84]

Although the British continued to gain ground east and west of Rommel's position, the opportunity had been lost and the attack lost steam. The impetus was forfeited in front of Wailly. The remaining British reserves drew back to wait for the inevitable counterattack. With Rommel in command, it was not long in coming. He ordered Colonel Karl Rothenburg to charge into the enemy's flank and rear with the greater part of the 25th Panzer Regiment. He was met by the British reserves and supporting antitank weapons. A brief but bloody armored battle ensued in which Rothenburg lost six Panzer Mark III's, three PzKw IV's, and several Czech-made tanks but destroyed seven more Matildas and assorted other British equipment. Soon the Germans had crushed the British main points of resistance, and the enemy retreated. Rothenburg earned his Knights' Cross that day. Like Rommel, he held the Pour le Mérite from the First World War and therefore was one of the most decorated heroes in the Third Reich. However, his luck eventually ran out. Like so many of the other men in the Ghost Division, he was later killed on the Eastern Front.[85]

Arras was Rommel's last major engagement in the first phase of the French offensive. After Dunkirk, the 7th Panzer turned south to help finish off the rest of the French Army. On the extreme right flank of the German advance, Erwin Rommel demonstrated that he was the master of the armored pursuit. He crossed the Somme by seizing a railroad bridge intact, overran a French Colonial unit (made up of blacks), and smashed the 31st French Motorized Division at Fecamp.[86] On June 12 he captured the French port of St. Valery, taking 58 tanks, 56 guns, 17 anti-aircraft guns, 22 antitank guns, 1,133 trucks, 368 machine guns, 3,550 rifles, and 12,000 prisoners, 8,000 of whom were British.[87] A week later Rommel took Cherbourg and bagged another 30,000 prisoners, including Admiral Abrial, the commander of the French Atlantic Fleet, and four of his admirals.[88] Rommel's division pursued the enemy and at one point gained an incredible 150 miles in a single day!

Less than a week later, the French government surrendered. Rommel's division was within 200 miles of the Spanish border. During the six weeks since it crossed the Meuse, the Ghost Division had suffered 2,594 casualties, including 682 killed, 1,646 wounded, and 266 captured or missing.[89] According to one source, this figure was higher than that of any other German division in the entire French campaign.[90] One out of every five men in the division was on the list. In terms of materiel, the division lost three PzKw I's, five Mark II's, 26 Mark III's, and eight PzKw IV's, all totally destroyed.[91] Others had suffered varying degrees of damage but were repaired or repairable. The author has found no reports concerning the tanks of Czech manufacture, but a number were destroyed: This total may have run as high as 40.

During the same six-week period, the Ghost Division had done a disproportionate amount of damage to the enemy. It took 97,468 prisoners, shot down 52 aircraft, destroyed another 15 on the ground, and captured a dozen more. They captured the commander of the French Fleet (North), four other admirals, a French corps commander, the commander of the British 51st Infantry Division, 15 to 20 other generals, plus other assorted battle and supply staffs. They bagged 277 field guns, 64 antitank guns, 458 tanks and armored cars, 4,000 to 5,000 trucks, 1,500 to 2,000 cars, a like number of horse and mule wagons, 300 to 400 buses, and about the same number of military motorcycles.[92]

During the French campaign, the Nazi Army stunned the West with its blitzkrieg warfare. Despite their inferior numbers and equipment, the Germans rushed from victory to victory while two of the world's great powers struggled vainly to stop them, or even slow them down. Five major factors account for the Wehrmacht's success. They are: (1) massive concentration of armor at the correct time and place; (2) air supremacy and close air support; (3) superior individual training and morale among junior officers, NCOs, and men; (4) proper appreciation and application of the principles of mass and maneuver; and (5) bold leadership, particularly among general officers. Of these factors, no single one can be described as more important than the others, as they were inseparable in this campaign. However, Rommel's courage and leadership materially contributed to the victory over France and marked him as a rising star in the armies of the Third Reich. He had proven himself a great military commander in an army that had many excellent officers. He had made bold decisions, taken chances, accepted risks, retained the initiative, displayed great personal courage, and won battles on his own again and again. Adolf Hitler took note of the fantastic successes of his former bodyguard and decided that he was well qualified for independent command. His name was not yet a household word, but Erwin Rommel was well down the road that leads to glory and death. Both waited in the wings.

3

Birth by Attack

While Mussolini was busy losing his colonial empire, Major General Erwin Rommel was busy with occupational duties in conquered France. In his off-duty hours he frequently went hunting with the local French landowners, who tended to be sympathetic to the Germans because of their shared anti-Communist outlook. He also spent time preparing a unit history of the 7th Panzer Division. "Do you want to see how I write?" he asked his old friend from Potsdam, Colonel Kurt Hesse. He then showed Hesse a row of boxes under his bed. "Here—let's take the 23rd of May. First folder, orders received and reports sent up to my superiors. Second folder, orders to the troops and reports to me. Third folder, maps and sketches of May 23rd. Fourth folder, my photographs. Fifth folder, other items of historical interest, like letters found on the dead, captured enemy orders and home news items about my division and about myself. All this is going to occupy me on my retirement. I'm going to write a sequel to *Infantry in the Attack*."[1]

Meanwhile, Dr. Goebbels was busy making a hero out of his old friend Erwin Rommel. Goebbels seems genuinely to have liked this simple commander, and certainly he recognized Rommel's potential, even before Hitler did. When Goebbels learned of Rommel's interest in photography, Goebbels gave the major general an expensive camera. It may be seen in many of Rommel's photos of this time. Rommel took some exciting pictures with it. One was of an enemy artillery bombardment in which he was caught. Later, in Africa, he even took a picture of an Australian bayonet charge![2]

Many propagandists working for Goebbels wrote flattering stories about Rommel in France. One of them was an officer who had served with him in World War I and who rode with him again in part of the

French campaign. He wrote: "His magic word is speed, boldness is his stock in trade. He shocks the enemy, takes them unawares, outflanks them, encircles them, uses his genius and everything he's got, taking night and fog and river and obstacles in his stride. Thus his tanks carve long bloodstained trails across the map of Europe like the scalpel of a surgeon. . . . Like a film, his story goes on: isolated acts of bravery shine briefly, there are individual tragedies, crises and death. I look into his eyes. There is still the intrepid look I saw all those years ago, but something of it is overshadowed by the sheer grandiose scale of today's events."[3]

Another story read: "Yes, they know him now in France—they know this face, with its blue eyes and their hint of hidden cunning, the straight nose, the firm jaw with its lips tightly compressed when he is thinking, and the chin that says all there is to be said about these noble features— their energy, their willpower, uniformly modeled, strong and masculine to look at, but of a severity softened by the twinkling eyes and the two small wrinkles at the corners of his mouth that show he is not averse to irony and wit."[4]

Goebbels' propaganda machine even went so far as to include Rommel's division in a major film, *Victory in the West*. The Ghost Division re-enacted its crossing of the Somme. Rommel had a great time playing movie director. Many of the French black troops were hauled out of prison camps to serve as actors in the drama. Unfortunately for Rommel, they turned out to be bigger hams than he. Although they had been brave enough in the actual battle, they overacted for the cameras. They screamed, ran in terror, panicked, rolled back their eyes in fear, threw down their rifles, begged for mercy, and, in general, had a wonderful time. The scene had to be shot over and over again, with Rommel patiently trying to get them to be more subtle. He wrote Lucie: "The blacks were in it again today. The fellows had a whale of a time and thoroughly enjoyed putting up their hands all over again."[5]

Rommel's popularity in Germany spread like wildfire. His name was fast becoming a household word, thanks to the efforts of Goebbels and his propaganda ministry. Despite all this, Rommel never forgot who he was. He still wrote to Lucie regularly and took no notice of other women. In December 1940 he went on leave, but he was recalled to his unit at Bordeaux due to a threatened French revolt, which never took place; therefore, he missed Christmas with his family. He tried to go on leave again in February, but it was then that events in North Africa caught up with him. On his second evening home he was ordered to report to the Fuehrer's headquarters at Staaken immediately.

On February 6, 1941, while the British armored units closed in on Benghazi, the newly promoted Lieutenant General Rommel met with Field Marshal Walther von Brauchitsch, the commander-in-chief of the German Army. Rommel was given command of the German Afrika Korps, composed of the 5th Light and 15th Panzer divisions. The 5th Light was already en route to Tripoli and would disembark from mid-February until mid-April. The 15th Panzer would follow and be totally disembarked by the end of May. The remains of the Italian Motorized Corps in North Africa would also be placed under Rommel's supervision. The general himself was to be subordinate to Marshal Graziani. Rommel was further instructed not to assume the offensive until after the arrival of all German units. Rommel listened but apparently did not take these instructions very seriously, particularly the part about being under the command of the Italians.

Rommel's moves for the next few days are unrecorded, but he must have spent them at Fuehrer Headquarters. We do know that he met with Adolf Hitler after he talked to von Brauchitsch. The nature of Rommel's new assignment remained top secret for some time; not even his wife was informed of his whereabouts.

General Rommel reappeared in Rome on the morning of February 11. Accompanied by Hitler's adjutant, Major General Schmundt, he conferred with General Guzzoni, the chief of staff of the Commando Supremo, the Italian High Command. Rommel presented his plan for the defense of Tripolitania (northwestern Libya), and it met with complete Italian approval. This plan had the effect of shifting the main Axis concentration from Tripoli to positions 200 miles to the east, thus giving Rommel room to maneuver. After being joined by General Mario Roatta, the chief of staff of the Italian Army,[6] Rommel flew to Catania, Sicily, to coordinate air cover for his convoys with Luftwaffe Lieutenant General Hans-Ferdinand Geissler, the commander of the X Air Corps. Geissler had bad news for him. Benghazi had fallen, and the last Italian armored unit in North Africa had surrendered. Only then did Rommel truly appreciate the extent of the Italian calamity. It seemed to him that Nazi aid would arrive too late to save Tripoli unless something was done immediately. He asked Geissler to bomb the port of Benghazi the next day, but the Luftwaffe commander refused to cooperate with the Afrika

Korps commander until Schmundt put through a call to Berlin. The bombers took off the next morning.[7]

So did Rommel. He arrived in Africa on the morning of February 12 and immediately reported to General Italo Gariboldi, who had just replaced Graziani as Commander-in-Chief of the Italian Army in North Africa. Rommel presented his plan, which called for establishing a front in the Sirte sector, about 200 miles east of Tripoli. Not one step back was to be allowed. Every available soldier would be thrown into this line, including German troops, as soon as they arrived. Gariboldi was unresponsive and unenthusiastic. This attitude undoubtedly helped convince Rommel to depart from his orders (to confine himself to a reconnaissance) and assume personal command as soon as possible.[8]

A brief inspection of the Italian forces further convinced Rommel of the necessity for personal intervention. "Morale was as low as it could be," he wrote later.[9]

The only Axis forces left in Tripolitania were the X Italian Infantry Corps, consisting of the weak 27th Brescia Semimotorized* and 17th Pavia Infantry divisions, the 25th Bologna Semimotorized Division, and elements of the still-arriving 132nd Ariete Armored Division, which had only 60 tanks, all completely obsolete. The Bologna Division had already suffered heavy losses in the last days of Wavell's offensive, and Pavia's 26th Artillery Regiment, which had been sent forward, had been destroyed.[10] Nevertheless, upon Rommel's insistence, they were soon put on the march to Sirte.

The 55th Savona Infantry Division, which had also lost its artillery regiment (the 12th) to the British, as well as the remnants of the 60th Sabrata Infantry Division, remained in Tripolitania and were not placed under Rommel's control.[11] The Italian 102nd Trento Motorized Division, en route from Europe, was to be under Rommel's command, but it had not yet arrived in significant numbers.

Rommel realized that he could not count on the Italians to put up stiff resistance and that his situation was precarious, to say the least. He sent Schmundt back to Fuehrer Headquarters with a message: "If the British advance on Tripoli immediately without regard for casualties, our general situation will be very grave indeed." Schmundt wrote back to Rommel a few days later: "I reached the Berghof on Sunday and found

---

*Italian units officially designated "semimotorized" were essentially infantry rather than motorized units and will be referred to as infantry throughout the text, except in the initial reference to them.

the Fuehrer already waiting feverishly for news! I briefed him just as you said, and the Fuehrer was obviously delighted with the initiative you have shown in tackling the job, Herr General. He is deeply apprehensive about the Libyan war zone, and dreads the next two weeks."[12]

Meanwhile, on February 14, elements of the 3rd Reconnaissance Battalion under Baron Irnfried von Wechmar off-loaded at Tripoli. The first German combat unit had arrived in North Africa. The unloading went on all night, much of it by lamplight, under Rommel's personal direction. By 11:00 A.M. the next day the Reece battalion had assembled in front of Government House. They stood tall and confident, an island of military discipline and precision in a sea of rabble. This display had a visible effect on the Italians in the vicinity. Here was something they could rally on! Lieutenant Colonel Baron von Wechmar gave the order to march, and off they drove. Twenty-six hours later they reached the front.[13]

Rommel realized that one lightly armed reconnaissance battalion could do little against a British tank division. The road to Tripoli was still open for the Allies. Further to create the illusion of strength and thus encourage the British to remain inactive, Rommel established a factory in Tripoli to manufacture dummy tanks. He mounted fake turrets on Volkswagens to fool British aerial reconnaissance units into reporting that the panzers had come in large numbers. By February 21 the first 35 of these dummies had arrived at his headquarters and another 170 were under construction.[14] As of that moment, Rommel did not have a single real German tank.

The British responded to Rommel's activities with a little scouting of their own. On February 17 and 18 they appeared in strength between El Agheila and Agedabia. Rommel, fearing that Wavell might be testing the water before jumping into a new offensive, sent his German forces, reinforced by a fairly reliable Italian battalion, to make contact with the British. The Western Desert Force's reconnaissance detachments withdrew before the Germans could start a battle, however.[15]

The first skirmish between British and German forces took place on February 24. Elements of the 3rd Reconnaissance Battalion destroyed two British scout cars and brought back two prisoners. The Germans suffered no casualties in their first engagement in Africa.[16]

Meanwhile, more elements of the 5th Light Division disembarked in Tripoli. They were immediately sent to the front. The men of this division, which included the 5th Panzer Regiment (two panzer battalions), the 104th Panzer Grenadier Regiment (initially composed of the

2nd and 8th Machine Gun battalions), the 3rd Reconnaissance and 200th Engineer battalions, as well as artillery, antitank, anti-aircraft, and other units, had fought well in France. The division itself did not exist at that time, but it was formed in January 1941, when the 3rd Panzer Division (which Georg Stumme had commanded in France[17]) was divided. Nevertheless, these were veteran warriors, not green recruits.

The divisional commander was Major General Johannes Streich, an officer whom Rommel did not hold in high esteem. The two had had a bitter argument in France the year before, when Streich was commander of the 15th Panzer Regiment in Rommel's neighboring division, the 5th Panzer. They were anything but friends, and Rommel would have been better satisfied if Major General Baron Hans von Funck were still in command of the 5th Light. Streich had replaced the aristocrat only a few days before.[18]

Streich's Ia (General Staff officer, Operations; see Appendix II) was the capable Major Wolf Hausser, later chief of staff of the 14th Army in the Italian campaign in 1944. The division's Ic slot (General Staff officer, Intelligence) was held by Captain (later Colonel) von Kluge, the son of Field Marshal Guenther von Kluge, the leader of the Fourth Army in the French campaign. Soon other General Staff officers, such as Colonel Klaus von dem Borne (Rommel's first chief of staff in Africa) and Captain Baudissin, joined the staff of the Afrika Korps. Rommel was fast acquiring a group of highly qualified General Staff subordinates. This development did not entirely please him. He was suspicious of them at first, possibly thinking they would like to see him replaced by one of their own. As time passed, this attitude gave way to one of mutual trust and respect. Rommel came to realize he needed them badly, and they proved loyal to him in every respect, in some cases even unto death. This mutual admiration did not yet exist in early 1941, however.

Rommel established the headquarters of the Afrika Korps at Sirte, near the front. One visitor during this period compared the headquarters there with that of the 5th Light Division. He much preferred the relative luxury of the latter. In Streich's headquarters drinks, cigarettes, and even candy could be purchased. These things were unheard of in Rommel's Spartan setting.[19]

Rommel had observed the differences also and was not happy with them. He noticed that the General Staff officers took up residences in what were, by North African standards, luxurious quarters. As Lieutenant Heinz Schmidt recalled: "They swiftly evolved a suave and civilized routine, which required iced lemonade through the heat of the day...."[20]

One of the officers even occupied the villa of the late Marshal Balbo, who had accidently been killed over Tobruk a few months before. General Rommel resented the attitude reflected by this style of life and soon packed the whole lot off to eastern Tripolitania, where they enjoyed the same accommodations as the ordinary soldier.[21]

The commander of the Afrika Korps rapidly gained firsthand knowledge of the desert and the terrain during the buildup phase. He also experienced a *ghibli* for the first time. Of this giant sandstorm, he wrote: "Immense clouds of reddish dust obscured all visibility and forced the car's speed down to a crawl. Often the wind was so strong that it was impossible to drive along the Via Balbo [the Coastal Road, the only major paved highway in all of Libya]. Sand streamed down the windscreen like water. We gasped for breath painfully through handkerchiefs held over our faces, and sweat poured off our bodies in the unbearable heat."[22]

The men of the German Army found that the desert was much different from the common, popular misconceptions that still persist today. Swanson wrote, "of the traditional soft burning sand of the Sahara, they had found little, save in the Great Sand Desert far to the south. But there were vast stretches of hard sand and of stony ground riddled with black basaltic slabs; there were bony ridges and ribbed escarpments and deep depressions; there were flat pans which held water after the rains, where gazelles cropped the coarse grass in midsummer. There were wadi-fed flats which sprang overnight into flowery glory in spring; there were endless undulating sand and gravel dunes whose crests marched in rhythm, like waves at sea."[23] In fact, Rommel compared the desert to sea warfare on numerous occasions and found many parallels. His panzers were his battleships, and they were of primary importance. The ground was his waves, and the occupation of hundreds of square miles of it was unimportant. What did it matter who occupied a wave? Victory would be won by the combatant who destroyed the enemy's fleet while keeping his own intact. Rommel grasped this fact right away. It would take the British over a year to learn this lesson, while Hitler and the Italian High Command never learned it.

As Rommel's desert worthiness and troop strength increased, he became more and more aggressive. On his orders General Streich advanced on the Mugtaa defile, captured it, and closed it with mines. No sign of the enemy was seen.

This little operation greatly strengthened the German position, because the Sebcha el Chebira salt marsh extends from Mugtaa to a point 20 miles south of the Coastal Road. The few points on the marsh where a vehicle could cross were quickly mined.[24] Rommel's line could now be flanked only with great difficulty.

German strength in Africa grew steadily throughout February and March. By March 11, Rommel had 105 medium and 51 light German tanks in addition to the 60 Italian tanks mentioned earlier. A week later the Italian Brescia Division completed its deployment into the Mugtaa line. This freed the 5th Light from its duties of holding the front line and gave Rommel a mobile reserve for the first time since his arrival. Meanwhile, supplies poured into Tripoli. Of the 220,000 tons dispatched from Europe in February and March, only 20,000 tons were sunk, largely because the British aircraft carrier H.M.S. *Illustrious* had been neutralized. On January 10 Geissler had attacked it with about 40 Stuka dive bombers and Junker 88 medium bombers as well as a few Italian Savoia torpedo planes. The ship's flight deck was ripped apart and a fire raged out of control for several hours. The *Illustrious* just managed to reach the moorings at Malta, where it was bombed again. It would be useless for more than 11 months.[25]

On March 19, Rommel flew to Fuehrer Headquarters to receive new instructions. Hitler, as usual during this period, greeted the Swabian cordially. Hitler decorated him with the Oakleaves to the Knights' Cross of the Iron Cross for the 7th Panzer Division's exploits in the French campaign. Field Marshal von Brauchitsch extended a less friendly welcome. The High Command had no intention of launching a major offensive in North Africa, he announced. Not only that, but no further German divisions would be sent to Libya after the 15th Panzer completed disembarkation in May. Rommel was not to risk even a minor advance until all elements of the Afrika Korps had arrived. Then he might be allowed to try to take Benghazi. The Korps commander argued against such timidity. Now was the time to strike, he declared, while the British were still weak from rushing all those veterans to Greece. Germany must win a decisive victory before they could return or before new enemy formations arrived. Colonel General Franz Halder, the chief of the General Staff and a man who loathed the upstart Rommel, remembered the conversation this way: ". . . Rommel explained that he would soon conquer Egypt and the Suez Canal, and then he talked about German East Africa. I couldn't restrain a somewhat impolite smile, and asked him what he would be needing for the purpose. He thought he would need another two panzer corps. I asked him, 'Even if you had them, how are you going to supply them and feed them?' To this I received the classic reply, 'That's quite immaterial to me. That's your pigeon.'"[26]

After some mutual recriminations, Halder and von Brauchitsch rejected Rommel's advice. The stubborn Rommel decided, in turn, to ignore them. The stiff and proper High Command officers would have been shocked to learn that Rommel was contemplating a major offensive operation, the starting date of which was less than two weeks away. Furthermore, he had probably deliberately concealed this fact not only from them, but also from the supreme warlord, Adolf Hitler himself! Rommel again demonstrated his audacity, his independence of mind, and the streak of bullheadedness that were to manifest themselves in almost all his military activities. This quiet family man trusted his own genius and believed in himself and his soldiers absolutely.

British Intelligence already knew that Hitler had forbidden Rommel to undertake any large-scale offensive in the foreseeable future. They convinced Wavell that the panzers would remain idle. Wavell himself wrote that the "Italians in Tripolitania can be disregarded, and that the Germans were unlikely to accept the risk of sending large bodies of armored troops to Africa in view of the inefficiency of the Italian Navy."[27] No one in the Allied camp expected an offensive. In coming to their erroneous conclusions, the British commander-in-chief and his agents reasoned correctly. In this instance they must be excused for underestimating their opponent. No one at that time could have foreseen the effect Erwin Rommel, soon to be known universally as the Desert Fox, would have on the war in North Africa.

Rommel returned to Libya after his disappointing conferences at Fuehrer Headquarters, more determined than ever to have his own way on the question of an offensive. He decided first to test the mettle of the enemy he was facing by launching a limited-objective attack. His target was the tactically important position of El Agheila. The British had failed to defend this naturally strong position properly. The enemy force turned out to be a small vanguard, which quickly retreated 20 miles to the main Allied position at Mersa el Brega. This hasty withdrawal tipped Rommel off as to the true weakness of the enemy[28] and convinced him, if he needed any further convincing, to launch his main blow as soon as his men were ready.

The British forces that Rommel so easily brushed aside on March 24 were a far cry from the enemy that had chased the Italians across the desert in one of the greatest routs in military history. The old desert-

worthy veterans of Sidi Barrani, Bardia, and Beda Fomm had returned
to England, been sent to Greece, or were recuperating in Egypt. Britain
had virtually dissolved a victorious army in the very face of the enemy. In
mid-February 1941, as we have seen, General Wavell was ordered to
leave a bare minimum blocking force in Cyrenaica and rush all available
forces to Greece. He sent a reinforced armored brigade from the newly
arrived 2nd Armoured Division to the Balkans, along with the Australian 6th and 7th divisions, the New Zealand 2nd Division, the Polish 1st
Brigade, and a large number of nondivisional troops. The 7th Armoured
Division was withdrawn from Libya, and parts of it were sent back to the
United Kingdom. These moves left only the 9th Australian and half of
the 2nd Armoured Division to defend their desert flank. These forces
might have been sufficient for the job, even against the Germans, had
they been properly equipped and trained, but they were neither. Much of
the equipment earmarked for the two new divisions had been diverted to
the Balkans and would soon be scattered all over Greece. The 2nd
Armoured Division, which had only one brigade in Libya (the 3rd
Armoured under Brigadier R. Rimington), had one regiment of light
tanks and one equipped solely with captured Italian vehicles. The division's reconnaissance regiment, the 1st King's Dragoon's Guards, had
been converted from horses to armored cars less than two months
before. All the division's units were in a horrible mechanical state, and
their soldiers had no experience in desert warfare. The Australian 9th
Division was as bad off as the 2nd Armoured and, when inspected by
Wavell and General Sir John Dill (the chief of the Imperial General
Staff) in mid-March, was judged too immobile to remain in the forward
zone. Consequently, two of its three brigades were sent to the Jebel el
Akhar hills northeast of Benghazi, where mobile Axis columns would
lose their advantage against the Australians. The third "Aussie" brigade
remained in Tobruk due to lack of transportation.[29]

Later that month the Cyrenaican blocking force was reinforced by
another unit apparently considered unfit for service in Greece. The
Indian 3rd Motor Brigade, now attached to the 2nd Armoured Division,
consisted of three Indian cavalry regiments equipped with trucks but
without armored vehicles, artillery, or antitank guns and short of radios
and other essential equipment.[30]

If the veteran desert warriors were gone, so were the men who had led
them. The experienced General O'Connor had fallen ill and was conva-
lescing in Egypt. He was initially replaced by Lieutenant General Sir
Maitland Wilson in early February, but the talented Wilson was soon

sent to Greece. He was succeeded by Lieutenant General Sir Philip Neame, a good engineer and winner of the Victoria Cross but a man with no background in desert warfare.

The 2nd Armoured Division also had a new commander. Its former leader, Major General J. C. Tilly, had died suddenly and was succeeded by Major General Michael D. Gambier-Parry, who was also new to the Sahara.[31]

The new leaders soon upset their commander-in-chief, who inspected their units in mid-March. Later, Wavell described British dispositions at that time as "just crazy,"[32] and although changed somewhat on his orders, they were not much better by the end of March. At that time the 2nd Support Group (a mobile, heavy-weapons unit of approximately regimental size) of the 2nd Armoured Division* held the commanding heights of Mersa el Brega. The 3rd Armoured Brigade centered its line five miles to the northeast, near the Gulf of Sirte. Two brigades of the Australian division still encamped northeast of Benghazi, while the division's third brigade still lay immobilized at Tobruk, far to the rear. The 3rd Indian Motor Brigade formed the tactical reserve at El Mechili, about 100 miles east of Benghazi. Obviously it would be of no immediate help if the front were attacked. In short, the British forces were hopelessly scattered, despite the protestations of Major General Gambier-Parry, who wanted to keep his division as concentrated as possible, just in case Rommel did decide to try something after all. Neame, however, saw no danger and rejected his advice.

The British main defensive line extended from the sea through the heights of Mersa el Brega south to Bir es Suera. South of here the terrain was sandy, spotted with salt marshes, and almost impassable to vehicles. Rommel took in the situation after one or two reconnaissance flights: If he allowed the British to dig in and to establish minefields, barriers, trench systems and so forth, they would be very hard to roust out. He therefore decided to strike as soon as possible, while he would still have the element of surprise.

The great advance, since known as Rommel's First Cyrenaican Campaign, began at dawn on March 31. At 9:50 A.M. parties of the 3rd Reconnaissance Battalion clashed with the screening elements of the 2nd Support Group. Initially the British prevailed. The reconnaissance

---

*Throughout this book all Allied units are British unless otherwise indicated. The 2nd Support Group was commanded at this time by Brigadier H. B. Latham.

troops withdrew but soon returned with the 5th Panzer Regiment, and the battle began in earnest. Again the Allies won the opening round. That afternoon, however, the 8th Machine Gun Battalion, led by the incredibly brave Lieutenant Colonel Gustav Ponath, broke through the British right flank and headed north. Supported by Stuka dive bombers, the Germans advanced through hastily constructed British minefields in the 100-degree heat. The Mersa el Brega position fell at about 5:30 P.M. Rommel captured 30 trucks and 50 Bren carriers as the Allies retreated. [33]

The next day the Afrika Korps set out in pursuit. The 5th Panzer Regiment, 8th Machine Gun Battalion, 3rd Reconnaissance Battalion, and supporting units followed the Allies along the Coastal Road while the 2nd Machine Gun Battalion tried unsuccessfully to get around their desert flank and cut off their retreat. By April 2, Rommel concluded that Agedabia should be attacked, even though his orders specifically forbade him to do this. The miserable little village fell to the infantry of the 5th Light after a short skirmish. Farther to the south, the 2nd Battalion of the 5th Panzer Regiment, on the right flank of the German thrust, destroyed seven British tanks of the 5th Royal Tank Regiment (RTR) against a loss of three panzers. Again the British retreated but Rommel could not follow, because the Afrika Korps was out of gasoline! His supply experts told Rommel that it would take at least four days to bring up the fuel required for a pursuit. This report did not suit Rommel, who ordered all the light vehicles and trucks in the 5th Light to be unloaded and sent back for fuel and ammunition. For 24 hours the panzer forces lay immobilized—a dangerous situation indeed. The risk paid off, however; the advance resumed the next day. [34]

While the blitzkrieg rolled forward, Neame and Wavell conferred. Wavell committed a major error when he assumed that Rommel, a man still inexperienced in desert warfare, would not commit his major force to a cross-country advance. Thinking the commander of the Afrika Korps would travel along the paved Coastal Road, he ordered Neame to defend the road and try to pierce Rommel's right flank as he advanced toward Benghazi. In taking this course of action they ignored the objections of Gambier-Parry, who wanted to withdraw the 2nd Support Group from the coastal area to within supporting range of the 3rd Armoured Brigade on the desert flank, even if it meant exposing Benghazi to capture. By failing to listen to Gambier-Parry's advice, Wavell and Neame hopelessly divided the 2nd Armoured Division. When Rommel struck out across the desert—the very thing the Allies least expected him to do—they did not have the strength on hand to stop him

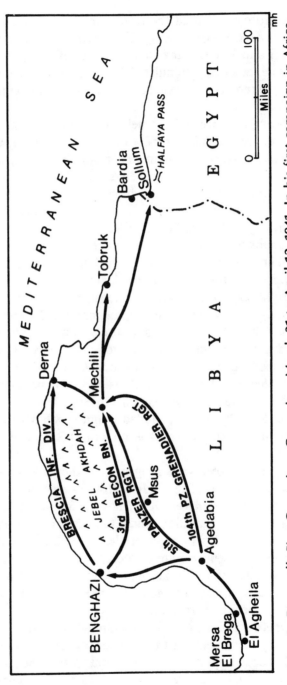

Map 3: Rommel's First Cyrenaican Campaign, March 31 to April 12, 1941. In his first campaign in Africa, Rommel surprised the Allies at Mersa El Brega, smashed the British 2nd Armored Division, routed the Western Desert Force, penetrated to the Egyptian frontier, lay siege to Tobruk and began the legend of the Afrika Korps.

and therefore committed the mechanically unreliable 3rd Armoured Brigade to a retreat across very difficult terrain at a time when it had only 22 cruiser and 25 light tanks left and was suffering breakdowns at the rate of one tank every 10 miles.[35] The only British armored division in Libya was exposed to defeat in detail—a situation Rommel was quick to exploit.

At dawn on April 3 Rommel was moving again. He divided his command into four (and later five) columns. Relatively weak forces (the 3rd Reconnaissance Battalion under von Wechmar, followed by the Brescia Infantry Division) were sent up the tarred highway, covering the left flank of the main advance, which was moving across the desert at a rapid pace. This northern force was placed under the command of German Major General Heinrich Kirchheim, who was in Africa on a visit but suddenly found himself pressed into active service. Eventually the northern prong of the attack reached the Jebel el Akhar hills, where it was divided into the so-called northern and southern Brescia columns.

The right flank of the German offensive was much stronger than the left. The right flank consisted of some motorized infantry detachments from the 5th Light, the Fabris motorcycle unit, and the Santa Maria armored unit from the Ariete Division, as well as a few miscellaneous formations. Its commander was Colonel Count Gerhard von Schwerin, who later led the 116th Panzer Division in Russia and France. Group von Schwerin was followed by Group Streich (under Major General Johannes Streich), which included Ponath's 8th Machine Gun Battalion, a squadron of tanks from the 5th Panzer Regiment, and an antitank company.

The German center was stronger than either of its flanks. Forces here included a battalion of the Italian Ariete Armored Division (40 poor tanks), the 5th Panzer Regiment (minus a few small detachments), the 2nd Machine Gun Battalion, and a few artillery and support units, all under the supervision of Colonel Herbert Olbrich, commander of the 5th Panzer Regiment. Rommel ordered him to attack Msus via Solluch. This meant that the Swabian had weighed his advance well into the desert—exactly where the enemy least expected him—a move that set the pattern for future operations.

Rommel's basic plan was exceedingly bold. It called for a triple converging movement on the huge enemy supply dump at Mechili. Rommel hoped to pin down, attack, and destroy the main Allied forces long before they could retire into the fortress of Tobruk. This plan clearly violated the cardinal military principle of concentration, but

Rommel threw caution to the winds in his effort to score a decisive victory.

Each column except Streich's had intermediate objectives: Benghazi for the left, Msus for the center, and the area east of Mechili for the right. Schwerin's column's mission on the right probably was the most important. If he could work his way behind the 2nd Armoured Division and 3rd Indian Motor Brigade, he could delay their escape and give Rommel time to come up with the rest of the Afrika Korps and perhaps completely destroy the Allied desert army.

The capture of Msus was also a vital military objective. It was the largest British supply dump west of Tobruk and had huge quantities of fuel stored in underground tanks. Rommel wanted both Msus and Mechili, intact if possible, but in flames if necessary. Without them, the British would have no choice but to abandon most of Cyrenaica (northeastern Libya) and retreat to the Tobruk area, within 100 miles of the Egyptain frontier. If Rommel could pull off his victory and then capture Tobruk, his next advance might well carry him to the Suez Canal.

The battle on the left flank reached its climax first. On April 3, Rommel gave Baron von Wechmar permission to take Benghazi, despite the objections of General Streich. The commander of the 5th Light thought the state of his vehicles demanded a halt. He had a point: They did need to be modified and adapted to desert conditions. The tanks, for instance, needed an overhaul ever 1,500 miles, instead of every 3,000 miles, as had been the case in Europe. One might imagine Rommel's response to such objections, however. ". . . I could not allow this to affect the issue," he tersely commented later. "One cannot permit unique opportunities to slip by for the sake of trifles."[36]

Not all the German leaders showed the same timidity as Streich. Wechmar, for example, was positively eager to capture the city, which had a great deal of political importance to the Italians. "I commission you to represent us at the Benghazi victory parade," Rommel told him.[37] This remark was all the baron needed. In the best tradition of a panzer leader, he set out in immediate pursuit of the enemy rear guard. The 2nd Support Group, too weak since their battering at Mersa el Brega to go it alone, retreated rapidly, while Neame ordered the Benghazi demolition plan executed. Among other things, 4,000 tons of captured Italian ammunition were blown up. The harbor was a total mess by April 4. Meanwhile, Neame ordered the Australians to fight a delaying action in the Jebel el Akdar hills and then retreat to Tobruk while the support group covered its rear and the British 3rd Armoured and Indian 3rd Motor brigades, as well as miscellaneous units (including an Australian antitank regiment), concentrated at Mechili.[38] The idea of concentrating was a good one; unfortunately for the British, it came too late.

Like the British, Italian Marshal Italo Gariboldi was upset, but for entirely different reasons. He was angry because his orders were being ignored. The only way he could get his commands obeyed, he decided, was to have a personal confrontation with Rommel and insist on obedience. He was also in for an education.

When Rommel returned to Afrika Korps Headquarters, now located at Agedabia, on the evening of April 4, he found Gariboldi waiting for him. "I am very displeased—" he started.

"I'm one up on you," interrupted the Desert Fox. "I'm furious."

"You have contravened Rome's directives—and mine. You should not have gone beyond the frontier of Tripolitania and you are already in Cyrenaica."

"I hope to be further on still tomorrow," Rommel retorted.

"Impossible," snapped Gariboldi. "You are to stay here and await orders from the Commando Supremo."

"You can stay here if you like. I'm going on," replied the obstinant Swabian.[39]

The argument became heated, but Rommel refused to kill such a promising start. "I was not going to stand for it . . ." he wrote later. "I stated my views plainly and without equivocation."[40] Knowing something of Rommel, one can readily grasp the implications of his remark. He certainly did not spare Gariboldi's feelings. The argument grew in volume until, at the best possible moment, a message arrived from the German High Command. It authorized Rommel to proceed—something he had already determined to do anyway. Gariboldi turned on his heel and stalked out. Later that night Colonel von Wechmar occupied Benghazi. The British had evacuated the city a few hours before.

Alarm spread throughout Allied ranks as the Nazi flood continued unabated. France came to the minds of many of the veterans on both sides. The retreat reached incredible speed and threatened to degenerate into a full-scale rout.

On April 4, panic swept through the French troops who garrisoned Msus. Rumors circulated that Hitler's soldiers were closing in, about to attack. Suddenly the French spotted the approaching tanks. Surely they were panzers! The signal was given immediately to blow up the petroleum depots. Thousands of gallons of precious fuel went up in huge balls of smoke and fire. The tank column drew nearer. They were not panzers at all, but the bulk of the British 3rd Armoured Brigade. The tanks had come to Msus to refuel; now they would have to be resupplied from some as of yet unknown source or be destroyed, for they did not have enough diesel to reach Mechili.[41]

When the 3rd Armoured left Msus for the Charruba area (halfway between Benghazi and Mechili) on the afternoon of April 4, its 5th Royal Tank Regiment had only nine cruiser and 14 light tanks left. The 6th RTR, which was made up solely of captured Italian tanks, was also in bad shape. Throughout the night they retreated across the desert, refueling their better tanks from the fuel compartments of the worst, until there was no gasoline left. By nightfall on April 5, the 6th RTR had only two tanks remaining, while the 5th was reduced to about eight. "[The] 3rd Armoured Brigade was no longer of any use as a fighting formation . . ." the British *Official History* recorded.[42]

With Benghazi captured and Msus in flames, Rommel turned his attention toward Mechili on April 4. He did not change his original plan in any of its essentials. The British base camp would face a three-pronged converging attack. The 3rd Reconnaissance would form the northern pincer by moving across the desert south of the Jebel el Akhar hills, due east of Mechili. The Ariete, now nearing Msus, would attack through the village and continue the march northeast to Mechili. The 5th Panzer Regiment was ordered to sweep through the desert village of Ben Gania and the Bir Tengeder,* thus getting into the British rear. They were then to pivot northwest and attack the Allied stronghold from the southeast, along with von Schwerin's combat group. These moves would effectively cut off the British retreat. The Brescia Division would continue to advance along the Coastal Road in the far northern sector and clear the hilly Jebel el Akhar region of any rear guards the Australians might have left behind.[43]

By the end of the day the 5th Panzer Regiment had occupied the village of Ben Gania. In the northern area of operations the 3rd Recon took El Regima, 15 miles due east of Benghazi, after a brief skirmish with the Australian rear guard.[44] To the north, the bulk of the Brescia

---

*A *bir* (theoretically, at least) is a water hole.

Division continued its march along the Via Balbia, with most of its men on foot. The Italian infantrymen suffered greatly in the oppressive heat.

Rommel's policy of unrelenting pursuit and leading from the front was paying handsome dividends, just as it had in France. Throughout this campaign, General Neame issued his orders from his headquarters at Barce, 50 miles northeast of Benghazi. He never once visited the front and most of his commands were based on information that was out of date well before he received it. He never seemed to understand just how bad off mechanically the 2nd Armoured Division was, for example. His fast-moving opponent never allowed him to regain his balance or exercise the slightest degree of control over the battle. British troops were soon to refer to this battle and their hasty withdrawal as "the Tobruk Derby," or "the Benghazi Handicap."[45]

So far everything had gone more or less according to plan; on April 5, however, confusion began to set in. The Ariete lagged behind, and Olbricht was unable to occupy Msus on schedule as a result. Due to fuel shortages and maintenance problems, the 5th Panzer also dropped behind schedule and was strung out over 20 to 30 miles of desert. Rommel pushed his men forward as rapidly as he could, for he still hoped to fight a decisive battle at Mechili before the bulk of the Western Desert Force (now called the Cyrenaican Command) escaped. With this in mind his Intelligence officer, Captain Baudissin of the General Staff, flew a reconnaissance mission near Mechili. The British shot down his airplane. Baudissin survived the crash but was soon captured.[46] Rommel had lost a valuable officer, the first of many.

"A hard time was in store for the Germans, for their General drove them ruthlessly," Major General Playfair noted in the British *Official History*. A good example of Rommel's attitude is his reply to General Streich when he asked for time to pull maintenance on his tank engines. "Out of the question. I don't let my men rest and I'm not going to spare the machines. We'll see about all that later." When the commander of the 5th Light complained his division was running short of fuel, Rommel responded: "Sort it out for yourself. I want to be able to leave tomorrow morning."

"Impossible, General," responded Streich. "I need four days."

"I couldn't care less," snapped Rommel. "We are not going to let the chance of a victory slip on the ridiculous pretext that you have no more fuel. Take it from the non-essential vehicles. They will catch up later."[47]

Toward nightfall on April 5 the Desert Fox joined the 8th Machine

Gun Battalion (at the head of Group Streich) and personally led it throughout the night toward Mechili.[48] At 6:30 A.M. the next day, Erwin Rommel was only 15 miles south of the town. Unfortunately, he had only a single combat battalion with him. Shortly afterward the advanced elements of Group von Schwerin arrived, but Streich and the rest of his division were nowhere to be seen. At last Rommel's aides located him, far from where he was supposed to be. This discovery led to another of their periodic arguments. Rommel ordered him to attack Mechili at 3:00 P.M. Streich refused to do so. His division, he said, was scattered across 100 miles of desert, and many of his vehicles had overheated engines or no gasoline. Rommel lost his temper and called Streich a coward. The commander of the 5th Light was furious. He unhooked his Knights' Cross from his neck and roared: "Withdraw that remark, or I'll throw this at your feet!" Rommel, of course, had gone too far, because, whatever else he was, Johannes Streich was no coward. The Desert Fox muttered a halfhearted apology but chalked up another black mark against the slow leader.[49]

It was the afternoon of that day before elements of the 5th Light Division finally captured the burned-out remains of Msus. Rommel had wanted to begin the Battle of Mechili that day. Now he was 85 miles short of his objective.[50]

April 7 went no better than April 6 had for the Afrika Korps. The Italians, already behind schedule, ran out of fuel and lagged far, far behind. Olbricht got lost and Rommel, in his Storch airplane, went out to find him. He spotted a column and ordered his pilot to fly down beside it, only to discover that it was British. The pilot immediately applied power and banked away sharply. The enemy opened fire and struck the aircraft but did no significant damage. The occupants of the Storch remained untouched.[51]

It was the night of April 7–8 before a furious General Rommel could get an assault force into position near Mechili. By then several of the disorganized Allied units had slipped through his grasp, and Colonel Olbricht, with the most powerful battle group in the army, was still many miles away. The survivors of the 2nd Armoured Division passed up their opportunity to escape and were soon loosely surrounded in the supply base. That night they tried to break out but were stopped by Colonel von Holtzendorff's 104th Panzer Grenadier Regiment and von Schwerin's panzer squadron.[52] Rommel would have the chance to smash the British after all, but it was more due to the errors of his enemies than to the speed of his subordinates.[53]

The Afrika Korps was finally in position at dawn on April 8. The attack started at 6:00 A.M. Rommel left Major General Streich to direct the detailed ground battle while he gave overall instructions from the air. Soon after takeoff he flew over an Italian engineer battalion at an altitude of 150 feet. Apparently they had never seen a Storch before and mistook it for an Allied airplane. They started firing wildly in all directions. Rommel should have been killed, or shot down at the very least. Not a single bullet touched the aircraft, however: a pitiful display of marksmanship! Rommel's luck had held again.[54]

Later in the morning the general spotted an 88mm anti-aircraft gun position. He assumed there was a stronger force in the area and ordered his pilot to land, which proved to be a serious mistake. The terrain below was uneven, and the airplane piled up, although no one was hurt. On further examination, Rommel discovered that the 88 was not only alone, but also disabled. Worse yet, the British were taking an interest in it, no doubt provoked by the crash of the strange airplane. Rommel and the gun crew had to flee across the desert in a truck, chased by the enemy. By the time Erwin Rommel eluded his pursuers and found his way back to the main body of the Afrika Korps, Mechili had fallen, with its fuel dumps intact.[55]

Rommel's experiment in directing the battle from the air turned out to be a total failure. It was the first and only time he tried this method of command. Following Mechili, he returned to the concept of leading from the front.

When he finally arrived at the village, Rommel set about inspecting the prize that Streich had captured. He found that the 2nd Armoured Division had ceased to exist as an organized opponent. Of its major subordinate unit—the 3rd Armoured Brigade—only four tanks managed to escape to the Coastal Road, and all of these were knocked out by German pursuit forces before they could reach Tobruk.[56] Major General Gambier-Parry, the divisional commander, and Brigadier Vaughan, the commander of the Indian 3rd Motor Brigade, were among the 3,000 prisoners.[57]

During his inspection, Rommel found three huge British command vehicles, which the staff of the Afrika Korps immediately christened "Mammoths." After a short discussion with a group of captured British officers, Rommel checked out the vehicles and appropriated them for himself. Inside one of the Mammoths he found a pair of sun-and-sand glasses. He picked them up, took a liking to them, smiled, and said:

"Booty permissible, I take it, even for a General." The glasses stayed with him from then on.[58]

As great as the victory at Mechili was, the forces of the Third Reich scored another success that day that may have been even more moment-ous. British Generals Neame and O'Connor left for the rear in the same staff car. O'Connor had recently returned from Egypt and had been offered command of the battle on April 3 but turned it down, saying, "changing horses in midstream would not really help matters."[59] Later he admitted, "I cannot pretend that I was happy at the thought of taking over command in the middle of a battle which was already lost."[60] Still, at Wavell's urgent request, he agreed to serve as Neame's adviser and remained with him until they completely lost touch with the 2nd Armoured Division and Neame's headquarters was about to be overrun by the northern Brescia column. Then they drove down the Coastal Road for Tobruk in the same staff car. They never made it. The British Headquarters convoy ran into Lieutenant Colonel Ponath's 8th Ma-chine Gun Battalion near Derna; it had taken the town and cut the Via Balbia without their knowledge. Lieutenant General Neame and Sir Richard found themselves staring down the barrel of a Nazi machine gun with but two choices: surrender or die. Slowly they raised their hands.[61] Brigadier J. F. B. Combe, the desert warfare expert and former commander of the 11th Hussars, was also captured. Like O'Connor, Combe had been sent forward from Egypt to advise Neame. Of the senior officers of the Cyrenaican command, only Brigadier A. F. Hard-ing, the senior staff officer who was busy setting up a new command post at Tobruk, escaped.[62]

The capture of General O'Connor, the foremost tank commander in the British Army, must be considered as important as the destruction of the 2nd Armoured Division, for he was the only Britisher who was equal to or nearly equal to Rommel's caliber, and as such he was irreplaceable. Later Wavell wanted to offer six Italian generals in exchange for O'Con-nor, but the War Office would not allow it—it would appear to the public, they said, that they were discriminating in favor of generals! Sir Richard remained in an Italian POW camp until 1943.

The greater part of the Cyrenaican Command (née Western Desert Force) had been smashed by Rommel's sudden blitzkrieg. The brilliant Swabian, true to his maxim of never allowing a beaten enemy the chance to recover, quickly pressed his men onward again. Only the fortress of Tobruk lay between him and the Suez Canal. The town was defended by Major General Leslie J. Morshead and his tough Australian 9th Infantry Division.

4

Tobruk

While the Afrika Korps isolated and annihilated the 2nd Armoured Division, Morsehead's Australian 9th Infantry Division retreated as rapidly as its transport would allow, trying to reach Tmimi (about 50 miles west of Tobruk) before Rommel could cut off its retreat. By the night of April 7–8, two brigades of the division plus the remnants of the 2nd Support Group were concentrated behind strong rear guards near Acroma, 15 miles west of the fortress. At Tobruk, the division's third brigade, the 24th Australian, dug in for the attack that was sure to come. It was joined here by the Australian 18th Brigade of the Australian 7th Infantry Division. The 7th was en route to Greece by sea when Rommel scored his breakthrough, and the 18th had been diverted to Tobruk.[1] Meanwhile, Erwin Rommel closed in at full speed, trying to swamp the beaten foe before he could reorganize and make a determined stand within the fortress. On April 8, the same day Mechili fell, he received fresh reinforcements in the form of the 605th Antitank Battalion, the vanguard of the 15th Panzer Division. At their head rode Major General Henrich von Prittwitz, a promising and energetic divisional commander. Rommel immediately placed him in charge of a pursuit force: a combat group made up of the 3rd Reconnaissance, the 8th Machine Gun, and 605th Antitank (AT) battalions. Before the day was out they took 800 more prisoners along the Coastal Road and streamed forward again, in the direction of Tobruk, the last major seat of Allied resistance in Libya.[2]

Rommel was not the only one who realized the value of the small Arabian city. It could hardly be classified as a city at all, at least by Western standards. In 1941 it boasted a population of only 4,000 persons, who lived in a few hundred white houses among a handful of dusty palm trees. The major activities in the area were its water distillation plant (capable of providing 40,000 gallons a day)[3] and its port. Herein lay its military importance, a fact Winston Churchill quickly grasped. As he received dispatches describing the latest series of defeats for the Allied forces, he dictated the message that may have saved the British Empire. On April 7, he informed Wavell that Tobruk was to be defended "to the death, without thought of retirement."[4] Wavell appointed Major General J. D. Lavarack (the commander of the Australian 7th Division) acting garrison commander and immediately began to reinforce him by sea with everything available. By the time Rommel was ready to attack the fortress, Major General Morshead, the permanent garrison commander who arrived with his division on April 9, had the equivalent of six full infantry brigades, four regiments of artillery, two antitank regiments, 75 anti-aircraft guns, 45 tanks, and a total of 36,000 men.[5] All these units together represented a formidable force, which Rommel dared not bypass. Furthermore, it grew stronger as time elapsed, because the Royal Navy never ceased to reinforce it by sea. Churchill remarked, "Nothing but a raid dare go past Tobruk." While this statement was not strictly true, Rommel certainly could not charge full tilt into Egypt with this thorn in his side.

Tobruk, however, had more than a nuisance value for the Allied High Command. It was the best port between Tunis and Alexandria and much superior to either of Rommel's main ports of Tripoli or Benghazi. Without Tobruk, the Axis lines of communication and supply extended several hundred miles. With Tobruk, Rommel would have a fine forward base and could easily invade Egypt and perhaps capture the oilfields and the Suez Canal. Without a forward harbor, he had gone almost as far as he could go. In short, both antagonists recognized the value of this prize, and both were prepared to pay whatever price was necessary to have it.

On April 9, Rommel sent the Brescia and later the 102nd Trento Motorized Division to attack Tobruk from the west, while the 5th Light swept across the desert to strike the city from the southeast. Streich was to deliver the main blow. To Rommel's annoyance, the 5th Light did not get off the mark on time due to a *ghibli*. It then proceeded at too slow a pace, due to maintenance problems that Rommel felt should have been ignored.[6] Mentally he chalked up another black mark against General Streich and Colonel Olbrich. No attack on Tobruk was launched that day.

At dawn on April 10, the 3rd Reconnaissance Battalion was still 30 miles west of Tobruk (following the Australian rear guard) and still had not started its flanking movement to the south. Rommel sent it to El

Adem, the southern gateway to the city. The rest of the 5th Light moved out to cut off the fortress from the east. Again the slow progress did not satisfy Rommel, who demanded more immediate results. Since he could not get the 5th Light to respond properly, he decided to light a fire under Major General von Prittwitz. He burst into his tent on the morning of April 10, while it was still dark outside, and told him to get a move on. "The British are escaping," he emphasized to the commander of the 15th Panzer Division. This conversation had tragic results within a few hours. The embarrassed Prittwitz left his tent in a rush, jumped in a car borrowed from Count von Schwerin, and headed for the front. Neither he nor Rommel expected the Australian rearguards to turn and fight, but they did, 25 miles west of Tobruk. One of the antitank gunners scored a direct hit on Prittwitz's staff car which, in his haste, he had ordered too far forward. The general and his driver were both killed instantly. The Afrika Korps had lost its first general.[7]

Colonel Schwerin was furious when he heard of von Prittwitz's death. He tensely informed Rommel of the incident. "That was the first time I saw him crack," von Schwerin recalled later. "He went pale, turned on his heel and drove off again without another word."[8]

The Swabian drove south of Tobruk, followed by a number of trucks to check on the progress of the enveloping movement. Suddenly his lookout shouted. Two small vehicles were trying to catch up to them from the rear. Rommel looked through his binoculars. One of the cars was definitely British. "Get the gun ready!" he ordered. A soldier manned the 20mm anti-aircraft gun, which could easily have torn the approaching vehicles apart. They came closer—it was an angry Major General Streich, who was raving about the death of Major General von Prittwitz.

Rommel was now angry himself. Streich almost always had this effect on him, and he was certainly not in the mood to talk to him now. "How dare you drive after me in a British car!" Rommel roared before Streich could speak. "I was about to have the gun open fire on you."

Streich looked at Rommel with contempt. "In that case, you would have managed to kill both your panzer division commanders in one day, Herr General," he replied coolly.[9]

The next day, April 11, Group Streich finally completed the envelopment of Tobruk to the east, while Group von Schwerin (formerly Prittzwitz) closed in on the south, and the Brescia Infantry Division dug in to the west. The men inside could no longer be supplied by land. Also that day the Stukas raided the fortress for the first time. These low-level dive bombers proved to be as effective in the desert as they had been in Poland and France. Their arrival must have been somewhat of a relief to Rommel, who had been without air cover for two days. The reason for this was fundamental: Rommel had simply outrun his air support. Now the Luftwaffe had brought up its sophisticated equipment and established new airfields, from which German air power again asserted itself.[10]

Farther to the east the 3rd Reconnaissance under Baron von Weckmar and elements of Lieutenant Colonel Knabe's 15th Motorcycle Battalion occupied the town of Bardia, 65 miles east of Tobruk, on the Libyan-Egyptian frontier. In doing so, Rommel's men re-established the boundaries of the old Italian North Africa to what they had been before Mussolini invaded Ethiopia. More importantly, they had started the construction of an early-warning system. Soon German reconnaissance units established a screen far into the desert. Any attempt to relieve Tobruk could now be detected well in advance, and countermeasures could be taken before Rommel's rear was seriously threatened.

On the night of April 11, Lieutenant General Erwin Rommel still had no idea of the extent or depth of the fortresses' defenses. He had requested copies of the city's defense plans from Rome, but his allies were slow in producing them. Realizing that the enemy was growing stronger every day, he made a tough decision: He would attack blind the next afternoon. Predictably, Colonel Olbrich objected. "I am afraid that my tanks are not battleworthy," he said.

"You will attack nevertheless," was Rommel's retort, "and to be sure that you carry out my orders, I shall be with you."[11]

Tobruk proved to be better prepared for such a move than Rommel guessed. Its defenses included two lines of strongpoints interconnected by trenches and completely sunk into the ground. They boasted a series of heavily concreted dugouts and improved natural caves, with an average of one platoon per position. Each such unit had antitank and anti-aircraft protection, along with overlapping direct and indirect artillery support. The outer defensive belt was surrounded by a deep antitank ditch, which the Australians cleverly camouflaged by covering it with planks and putting sand on top of these. The Germans would not be able to see it until they were falling into it. The ditch itself was seven feet deep and ten feet wide, with straight sides, so the panzers could not negotiate it. The communications and support trenches were hidden in the same manner as the antitank ditch. German aerial reconnaissance was of little value against such camouflage. A barbed wire belt of up to 30 yards in width protected the outer defenses, in addition to minefields. The second belt of strongpoints lay 2,000 to 3,000 yards behind the first. These belts extended 35 miles, in a radius of 20 miles, and were defended by stubborn adversaries: a tough obstacle indeed for a korps that was yet hardly more than a division in strength.[12]

The first of four major attempts to take Tobruk came on April 12. Initially, the 5th Panzer Regiment attacked the Australian 20th Infantry Brigade in the southern sector just west of the El Adem Road. The assault, which was delivered by 20 panzers, was dispersed mainly by artillery fire, although some Axis infantrymen did reach the antitank ditch before being driven back. The ditch surprised the Germans, who could neither bridge nor outflank it. After suffering several casualties, they withdrew in confusion. The fierceness of the resistance surprised Rommel, who expected to meet only disorganized units previously routed in Cyrenaica. The second part of the attack, also launched without benefit of reconnaissance, was made by the Italian Brescia Infantry Division to the west of the 5th Panzer, and it was also checked. Regretfully, Rommel had to wait until the rest of his units could catch up. He ordered Streich to prepare a major offensive for the night of April 13–14.[13]

Even if General Rommel had known the strength of the defenders, there can be little doubt that he would still have tried to storm the fortress. Rommel was obsessed with taking it, for it was the key to freedom of maneuver in North Africa. On April 13, at 6:00 P.M., he unleashed his second major assault, which started just before nightfall. Lieutenant Colonel Ponath led the way with his machine-gun battalion, supported by a battalion of anti-aircraft guns. They crawled forward, broke into the British perimeter, and demolished a section of the antitank ditch. Now the panzers could cross. With Olbrich coming up behind, Ponath's men formed a spearhead and continued to advance toward the port of Tobruk.[14]

The bulk of the 5th Panzer Regiment followed Ponath at 12:30 A.M. the next morning. They made excellent progress initially, despite the darkness, but they had penetrated on too narrow a front. The Italians assigned to cover their flanks failed to do so. Then, within a few miles of the town, Colonel Olbrich met stiff resistance from Fort Pilastrino and the 1st Royal Artillery Regiment, which fired on him through open sights. No doubt worried about being cut off, since he had no flank security whatsoever, the commander of the 5th Panzer Regiment ordered a retreat when he was attacked by British cruiser tanks. He left behind 16 out of the 38 tanks committed to the breakthrough, but his withdrawal was tantamount to abandoning Ponath and his men to their fate. When he heard the news, Erwin Rommel was furious and immediately ordered the attack to resume. The objective was no longer to take the fortress but to rescue the stranded battalion, which the Australians had surrounded. Desperately Rommel tried to rally the men of the Italian Ariete Armored Division and hurl them into the battle. It proved to be a slow process. Noon passed before he had them in line. Then a few British artillery rounds landed nearby. "The confusion was indescribable," Rommel wrote later. "The division broke up in complete disorder, turned tail and streamed back in several directions."[15] Rommel was unable to save the isolated unit, which "went to ground." Ponath had already lost a quarter of his strength when Olbrich abandoned him, and the colonel himself had been twice wounded. "We're cornered like rats," he told his men. "Well then, we've got to survive and, in order to survive, we must be more rat-like than the rats opposite. You can't dig too deep, and you've got to make yourselves look like a bit of the landscape." He held out for four days, carrying out nightly raids for food, water, and ammunition. Finally, at 11:00 P.M. on April 20, his unit was reduced to a handful of men and his command post was surrounded. Ponath charged out with a few survivors and eight rounds left in his revolver. An Australian, firing at nearly point-blank range, blew his brains out with a rifle.[16]

The 8th Machine Gun Battalion was all but wiped out. Only 116 of its 500 men escaped the repeated attempts of the garrison to destroy them; most of those who survived infiltrated enemy lines on the night of April 14–15.[17]

An embittered Erwin Rommel blamed General Streich and Colonel Olbrich for the tragedy of Colonel Ponath and his men. "Your panzers did not give their best and left the infantry in the lurch!" he snapped at Streich and Olbrich. The major general tried to defend his actions, but Rommel refused to listen to any excuses. He accused both unhappy commanders of lacking resolution. On the evening of the next assault Rommel told Streich: "I expect this attack to be made with the utmost resolution under your personal leadership."[18] This was clearly a "come back victorious or don't come back at all" type order.

The next attack came two days later, at 5:00 P.M. on April 16. Rommel wanted to threaten the city by taking Ras el Madauer (Hill 187). From here he would be in a position to dominate much of the Australian line. The Ariete Armored Division and the 62nd Infantry Regiment of the Trento Motorized Division led the way, with several German companies advancing directly behind them. The Italians also received heavy German artillery support. By utilizing this method, Rommel hoped to steady his allies and get better service out of them than he had during the Ponath disaster.

Ariete, the best of the latter-day Roman legions with Rommel at this time, was in pitiful shape. It had started the offensive with 100 tanks, but mechanical failures caused the loss of over 80 percent of its armored strength before it even skirmished with the enemy. Those tanks that remained, or that could be repaired quickly, were no match for Allied tanks or antitank guns. In fact, there was a standing joke in the Afrika Korps. The question: "Why are the Italians such brave soldiers?" The answer: "Because they are ready to go to war with the equipment they have."[19] Rommel wrote: "It made one's hair stand on end to see the sort of equipment with which the Duce had sent his troops into battle."[20]

At first all went well with the attack. A small tank battalion from Ariete (18 tanks) overran Australian positions and seized the hill. Unfortunately, they halted on the highest point, instead of on the southern slope of Ras el Madauer. Enemy forward observers quickly took note of this unusual behavior, and the spearhead was plastered by artillery fire. Suddenly one of their periodic panics gripped the Italians. They began pouring to the rear, or rushed toward the Australians to surrender in droves. They had not yet learned (but soon would learn) that the Australians were less keen on taking Italian prisoners than anyone they would encounter in the Desert War. Major Schraepler, now recovered from his wound on the Meuse Road the year before, rushed forward in a vain attempt to rally the Italians. In the end he narrowly avoided capture himself.[21]

Neither General Streich nor Colonel Olbrich were killed or wounded in this battle. Shortly afterward, both the 5th Light Division and 5th Panzer Regiment had new commanders. Indeed, there were almost wholesale firings in the higher ranks of the Afrika Korps. Rommel was, in general, not satisfied with many of the men he had inherited. He always demanded two qualities from his officers: loyalty and efficiency. All too frequently, Rommel felt, his closest subordinates lacked one or both of these qualities.

All good commanders have the ability to fire. Rommel set about cleaning house and did so with a vengeance. Major Ernst Bolbrinker replaced Colonel Olbrich and was soon replaced himself by Colonel Fritz Stephan.[22] The chief of staff of the Afrika Korps, Colonel Klaus von dem Borne, was also sent home, although why is unclear; it is possible that von dem Borne could not stand up physically to the harsh desert environment. Rommel's first aide and longtime personal friend, Captain Hermann Aldinger, returned to Europe at about this time with health problems. Major Ehlers, the Korps' operations officer, proved the worst of the lot. He wrote Berlin that Rommel's poor leadership was responsible for the German failure to take Tobruk. It is probable that he was trying to engineer Rommel's removal. The Swabian commander relieved him of his duties, sent him home, and eventually secured his dismissal from the General Staff. Streich was temporarily replaced by Major General Heinrich Kirchheim, who had returned from the hospital after being wounded. General Rommel lived to regret this appointment, however, and Kirchheim was replaced by Major General Johannes von Ravenstein.[23]

There were howls of protest in Berlin, of course, because the favorites and spies of Halder and certain other senior General Staff officers were being wiped out in a bloodless version of the Night of the Long Knives. Halder and his friends, who had been agitating for Rommel's dismissal, did not expect him to have the gall to strike down their African-based confederates. Rommel was determined to rid himself of these people nevertheless and replace them with loyal subordinates. The political infighting at this time caused Rommel a great deal of nervous strain. It would continue, to a greater or lesser extent, for the next four years and would intensify, in fact, when the Halder-type officer was gradually replaced by Hitler's lackeys.[24] Perhaps it was with some relief that Rommel turned to face the Australians and the British. He knew where he stood with them.

On April 17 the fighting around Tobruk began again. Two heavy companies of the 15th Motorized Battalion, which had arrived in Tripoli only seven days before, were thrown into the conflict. Led by Rommel's adjutant, Major Schraepher, they met fierce resistance and soon all their heavy weapons and antitank guns were knocked out by Allied artillery fire.[25] Again the Afrika Korps had failed to score a victory. Ariete supported the 15th and lost five tanks in the fighting.[26]

With the situation at Tobruk stabilizing along siege lines, Rommel decided that he must wait until more armored elements of the 15th Panzer Division could be transported from southern Europe to the front. In the meantime the High Command awarded Lieutenant Colonel Baron Irmfried von Wechmar a much-deserved Knights' Cross. Rommel decided to decorate the daring commander personally. On April 19 he set out to do so.

During April the 3rd Reconnaissance Battalion had advanced as far as Sollum, a few miles inside Egypt, and now occupied defensive positions near there. Rommel presented von Wechmar with his prize and then combined business with pleasure by thoroughly inspecting every trench, gun emplacement, and terrain feature in the area. He had Colonel Wechmar describe the capture of Capuzzo in minute detail. Like a child with a new toy, Rommel checked out everything and everybody that came into his view. He talked with privates, crawled into vehicles, and climbed into and around positions. "At the end of the day everybody was tired but Rommel," his aide remembered.[27]

On the way back Rommel's staff contingent was attacked by the Royal Air Force. Two Hurricane fighters seemed to come from nowhere and strafed the vehicles in three separate passes each. The dispatch rider sought cover too late and was shot in the head. The radio van was ripped apart and totally destroyed by enemy machine-gun fire. In the Mammoth, Rommel and his driver were initially surprised; then they grabbed for the protective armored shields in an attempt to close the steel windows. They were not quick enough. A bullet missed Rommel's head by inches. Another tore into the driver's stomach. When the Hurricanes disappeared, Rommel and the other survivors wrapped the wounded man in blankets and laid him in the back of the command vehicle. He showed no indication of the pain he was in. Rommel jumped behind the wheel of the Mammoth and drove on all night. He delivered the driver to a hospital after dawn.

Following the strafing incident, Rommel prepared for yet another assault on Tobruk. He asked the Commando Supremo to send over two more static (that is, Italian nonmotorized infantry) divisions. With these men in the siege line outside Tobruk, Rommel could pull out his motorized forces, form a tactical reserve and strike again. He set the date for the attack as April 30.

Franz Halder, the chief of the General Staff, was also making plans of his own, for his intense dislike for the aggressive desert commander was growing daily in April 1941. "Rommel has not sent in a single clear report, and I have a feeling that things are in a mess . . ." he wrote in his diary. "All day long he rushes about between his widely scattered units and stages reconnaissance raids in which he fritters away his strength. . . . His motor vehicles are in poor condition and many of the tank engines need replacing . . . cannot meet his senseless demands. . . . It is essential to have the situation cleared up without delay. . . ."[28] To "clear up the situation," Halder sent a deputy chief of the General Staff, General Friedrich Paulus, on a fact-finding mission to North Africa. Paulus, Halder noted in his diary, was "perhaps the only man with enough influence to head off this soldier gone stark mad."[29]

Paulus arrived at Rommel's Headquarters on April 27 to find him planning his April 30 attack. Paulus initially forbade it, but when Marshal Gariboldi showed up the next day and approved Rommel's plans there was little Paulus could do but relent. The operation called for another attack on Ras el Madauer (on the southwestern side of the Australian siege line) with half of the 5th Light and elements of the still-arriving 15th Panzer Division. Over 70 panzers would be employed in the operation. Because Rommel had totally lost faith in General Streich, he placed Major General Kirchheim in charge of the operation.[30]

Before Rommel could advance, the Australians carried out a series of daring night raids of their own. Each night they would go out, infiltrate Axis lines, and ambush a convoy or knock out a command post. Rommel considered these men "the best of soldiers, with their cold-blooded ability to carry out reconnaissance raids night after night."[31] The largest and possibly most daring of these forays was a night attack on Hill 201, which was held by the Italian Fabris battalion. The defenders immediately ran away, abandoning an important position and two artillery batteries in the process. Rommel dashed to the point of the breakthrough with the nearest German unit, the 605th Antitank Battalion, only to find that the enemy had returned to his own lines. Of the Italian performance, Rommel wrote: "Needless to say, I was not very pleased with this curious behavior in the face of the enemy."[32] Despite these diversions by the Australians, the attack of April 30 went off on schedule, however.

At 6:30 P.M. the Stukas flew in at low level and blasted the Australian strongpoints. Moments later these same positions were pulverized by German artillery. Before the Australians could regain their equilibrium, the panzers were on them. The Australians defended themselves desperately, but they could not prevent Rommel from surrounding Ras el Madauer. At 9:00 P.M. the hill fell to the German infantry. The attack now had a good chance of storming the fortress, but General Kirchheim allowed himself to be bogged down by fighting local actions against individual bunkers instead of bypassing them. In this type of hand-to-hand fighting the Australians had no equal. Small pockets might be wiped out, but they did not surrender. Rommel said: "The Australians fought with remarkable tenacity. Even their wounded went on defending themselves with small arms fire, and stayed in the fight to their last breath. They were immensely big and powerful men. . . ."[33]

After several bitterly contested firefights, the German advance lost its momentum because the armor of the 5th Light advanced offcourse due to early-morning fog, ran into a minefield covered by antitank fire, and was forced to withdraw. On the left flank, the 15th Panzer Division was also checked, and soon the Australians began counterattacking. "The strongpoints taken will be held at all costs," Rommel ordered.[34] Despite this command, several were retaken by the Allies. However, the fighting soon entered a temporary lull when a sandstrom reduced visibility to zero.

Just before the storm, Rommel delivered a second attack, this one in the Pilastrino sector, just to the northwest of Ras el Madauer, but it also stalled short of its objective. Fort Pilastrino occupied a commanding position behind the Allied front line. Rommel told his staff, "Whoever holds Pilastrino is in a position to read the others' cards. This is the key point of the Tobruk defenses."[35] He sent a regimental combat team under Major Schraepler to take it. They gained some ground but were halted by the fierce determination and courage of the Australians. The fighting raged unabated until the wind put an end to the killing. Both sides suffered heavy casualties, but nothing had been decided.

The *ghibli* did not end all activity, however. Under the cover of dust, Lieutenant General Rommel brought up supplies and ammunition so Schraepler could begin the assault again. He did so as soon as the wind died down, but with no more success than before. Rommel went forward himself and received a severe rebuke from a sergeant major who mistook the dirty corps commander for an impetuous private. Rommel's personal example did no good this time: Fort Pilastrino remained in enemy hands.

On May 1, the battle began to go against the Germans. Major General Baron Hans-Karl von Esebeck, the new commander of the 15th Panzer Division, reported to Rommel that day: "Our troops and particularly officers have suffered heavy casualties from infantry and antitank fire coming from numerous undetected bunkers and from saturation artillery fire. Most units have 50% casualties, some even more. Morale is still absolutely magnificent, both among our shock troops, who went in as planned to attack the objectives, and among the infantry companies, who followed them eastward in heavy close combat with the reviving bunker crews and held out despite artillery fire."[36] Still, despite the bravery of the troops, the advance was stalled. On the afternoon of May 1 Rommel tried to extend the right flank of the penetration and roll up the British line. This move forced Morshead to commit part of his armored reserve, and five precious British tanks were destroyed, but the Axis attempt was stopped.

Even though the Afrika Korps had not made its decisive breakthrough, it had scored some important tactical gains that the Australians tried to wipe out on May 2, 3, and 4. The major attack came on the night of May 3–4, when Morshead committed his reserve brigade, the Australian 18th Infantry, in a counterattack against Ras el Madauer. The fighting raged almost until dawn, but the Allies were beaten back. When the battle ended, the Axis forces had gained ground on a three-mile front, but with a maximum depth of less than two miles. All Rommel had gained was a good observation post and a staging ground for future operations. The cost had been 650 German and 500 Italian casualties. Now both sides settled down for a long siege, mercifully unaware that it would last 221 more days. Stalemate had set in on the North African Front.[37]

5

"Battleaxe"

And what was happening on the frontier while Rommel was trying to batter his way into Tobruk? First of all, Wavell was busy creating a new Western Desert Force. It should be kept in mind that, of the two divisions in Neame's old Cyrenaican command, one was trapped in Tobruk and the other had been destroyed. The commander-in-chief for the Middle East quickly established a new, temporary command called Mobile Force, placed it under Brigadier W. H. E. Gott, and then sent him every mobile unit he could lay his hands on to keep the Germans out of Egypt. By the second week in April, Gott had the 22nd Guards Brigade and the 11th Hussars Regiment, both up from Egypt, as well as what was left of the 2nd Support Group. On April 8 Wavell named Lieutenant General Sir Noel Beresford-Peirse—until then commander of the Indian 4th Division—as chief of the Western Desert Force. Beresford-Peirse's new command included his own old division, what was left of the Australian 7th (now fortifying Mersa Matruh, Egypt, in case Tobruk fell and Rommel advanced on the Nile), and the incompletely formed British 6th Infantry Division (under Major General J. F. Evetts) in Egypt,[1] as well as Gott's command. Of Beresford-Peirse's three divisions, only the Indians were equipped well enough to meet the Afrika Korps in a mobile campaign.

The new Western Desert Force did not have long to wait before meeting the Germans. On April 10 the 3rd Reconnaissance Battalion advanced on the coastal town of Bardia, while Lieutenant Colonel Knabe's 15th Motorcycle Battalion attacked Sollum. Bardia fell on April 11, and Capuzzo and Sollum were taken two days later. At about this same time, all German forces on the frontier were placed under the command of Colonel Maximilian von Herff (commander of the 115th Panzer Grenadier Regiment). For the next two weeks von Herff and

Gott skirmished almost continuously until Herff finally defeated the Mobile Force in a frontier battle on April 25–26. After that Gott retreated in Egypt and the German-Italian troops began preparing their border screen for the next Allied onslaught. It consisted mainly of motorized outposts with a few desert strongpoints lying in between. The border troops soon discarded their motorcycles, which had been so valuable in Europe but were worthless in the desert sand. Most of them were replaced by the scout car. This vehicle and the 88mm anti-aircraft gun became the backbone of the screen, which extended miles into the desert. It was anchored on the north by the Halfaya Pass, 65 miles east of Tobruk. The Halfaya and Sollum passes were of the utmost importance, because a large coastal escarpment extended from near Tobruk all the way to deep within Egypt—almost to El Alamein, in fact. Only at these two passes could the escarpment be negotiated by armored and soft-skinned vehicles. The British challenged the screen in May. They could afford to do so, because they had been greatly reinforced in one of the most daring operations of the war.

In London in April 1941, Prime Minister Winston Churchill became alarmed by the rapid German advance in Cyrenaica. On April 20, with Tobruk under siege, aides informed him that the 15th Panzer Division had definitely landed combat units in Africa. The next day Churchill ordered the implementation of Operation "Tiger." It called for a convoy of five merchant ships, loaded with 295 of the latest-model tanks and 50 fighter airplanes, to journey from England to Egypt via the Strait of Gibraltar instead of by the longer and safer route around the Cape of Good Hope in southern Africa. This bold decision exposed the convoy to attack by Italian submarines and Axis airplanes, but if successful it would mean an early offensive for the British, who hoped to relieve the Tobruk garrison before Rommel grew strong enough to overpower it.

Churchill signaled Wavell while "Tiger" was en route: "If this consignment gets through the hazards of passage . . . no German should remain in Cyrenaica by the end of the month of June."[2] Pressure on Wavell to attack increased after British Intelligence intercepted Paulus's dispatches to Hitler, describing Rommel's supply deficiencies.

On May 12, Tiger reached Alexandria. It had caught the Axis flat-footed. On the way, the Royal Air Force flew escort missions from its base on the island of Malta. Its pilots bombed Benghazi and sank an Italian cruiser, three Italian destroyers, and several smaller vessels. "Tiger" itself only lost one ship: The Empire Song struck a mine and sank with 57 tanks and 10 Hurricanes on board. The Royal Navy delivered 238 tanks and 43 Hurricanes to the Western Desert Force. Of the tanks, 35 were of the latest-model heavy infantry (or "I") tank, the Matilda II, which weighed 26½ tons. Wavell also received 82 Mark II cruiser tanks (which weighed 14 tons each) and 21 Mark IV tanks. The latter were primarily reconnaissance vehicles, for they weighed only 5½ tons but reached speeds of up to 40 miles per hour.

Meanwhile, on the other side of the hill, things were not going so well for Erwin Rommel and his Afrika Korps. He continued the Siege of Tobruk, of course, primarily because he had no choice. Although the Luftwaffe succeeded in driving the Royal Air Force from the skies (the last Hurricane left Tobruk on April 25), the Royal Navy continued to resupply the fortress at night despite the risks and the casualties involved. Rommel was faced with a two-front war: one on the Egyptian frontier, the other at Tobruk. He could not concentrate against one without exposing his rear to an attack by the other, and without concentrating his forces either attack would be doomed to failure, so the siege ground on.

In May Rommel's supply situation deteriorated drastically. That month the Afrika Korps and its allied formations needed 50,000 tons of supplies to operate properly, but they received only 29,000 tons.[3] With such a supply deficiency, only limited-scale operations were possible. Rommel engaged in as few of these as possible, in order to conserve his strength for the offensive that he knew was coming.

The failure to capture Tobruk put the initiative back in Allied hands. The General Staff officers in Berlin lost no time denouncing Rommel for failing to obey their instructions of two months before. Colonel General Halder, for example, wrote in his diary on April 23: "Reports from officers coming from this theater, as well as a personal letter, show that Rommel is in no way equal to his task."[4] Later he added: "By overstepping his orders, Rommel has brought about a position for which our present supply capabilities are insufficient."[5] The feud continued between the commander of the Afrika Korps and the chief of the General Staff and would continue until Hitler dismissed Halder in September 1942.

On May 12, Paulus submitted his report to OKH. Not surprisingly, Paulus judged the Afrika Korps' position to be tactically bad and administratively worse. It was not as critical as it might have been, however. Paulus, who would later surrender the Sixth Army to the

Russians at Stalingrad, recommended that more Luftwaffe resources be devoted to protecting the sea routes from Italy to Tripoli and Benghazi, but he did not suggest that the Afrika Korps be significantly reinforced.

The arrogant General (later Field Marshal) Erhard Milch of the Luftwaffe also graced the Afrika Korps with a visit in May 1941. Major General von Esebeck escorted him about camp one day but did not care much for this duty. The general remembered: "We all prayed the R.A.F. would favor us with a good heavy raid while he was there. Fortunately the R.A.F. obliged. General Milch was wearing a beautiful white uniform. I could not have been more delighted than when I saw him dive into a slit trench. When he came out, I was even more pleased to see that it was the trench into which the servants had thrown the refuse from the kitchen."[6]

Von Esebeck himself did not remain the commander of the 15th Panzer Division for long. He was wounded in the face by a shell splinter near Tobruk in July. They evacuated him to Europe, where he soon recovered, but the High Command refused to allow him to return to the Afrika Korps. Later he led a panzer division on the Russian Front, until he was arrested in 1944 for his part in the conspiracy to assassinate Adolf Hitler. He spent the rest of the war in a concentration camp.[7]

Rommel did not share Baron von Esebeck's low opinion of General Milch. Rommel personally liked the Luftwaffe general, and Milch returned this feeling in kind. "The time I spent with him was short but sweet," Goering's deputy wrote later. "He was very happy about the increase in fighter plane strength, as he was one of our more air-minded generals. He was quite starry-eyed about his prospects. Bending very close to his maps—he was desperately shortsighted—he exclaimed, 'Look, Milch, there's Tobruk. I'm going to take it. There's the Halfaya Pass. I'll take that too. There's Cairo. I'll take that. And there—there is the Suez Canal. I'm taking that as well!' What else could I say to that except: 'And here am I. Take me too!'" Rommel's headquarters was filled with good-natured laughter.[8]

May 11 marked the end of the first month of the Siege of Tobruk. German artillery and Stukas were reducing the city to rubble. Only one building—General Morshead's operational headquarters—remained standing. Conditions among the Australians worsened after Luftwaffe bombs damaged the port facilities. They ran out of bread but had an abundance of flies, rats, and fleas. The German Air Force further added to their misery by establishing forward air bases within 10 miles of the front lines. Sometimes the Australian infantry could hear the Stuka pilots warming up their engines for their morning air raids.

Bad as all this was, conditions were far worse for Erwin Rommel's infantrymen. Their "bunkers" were merely trenches, dynamited into the rocky soil and lined with concrete. The men were forced to lie motionless in their positions all day, in the hot desert sun, because the Australians ranked among the best snipers in the world and received an unlimited amount of ammunition. Like their food, the Germans got only a limited supply of bullets each day. Under these circumstances, the inevitable flies and the heat became almost unbearable. Fortunately, they were relieved by frequent sandstorms. In these, the Australians went underground, while the Germans and Italians began to move about and live again. When the wind stopped, the Allies came out and the Germans went back to ground. The Desert War was not without its paradoxes.

German food proved to be universally bad. The cooks usually arrived with the meal about midnight. The soup was of poor quality, but was readily eaten because it was warm, and desert nights are bitterly cold. In addition to soup, the cooks served processed cheese and sardines, with black bread. They had to eat olive oil instead of butter, which spoiled too rapidly there. Sometimes the soldiers were given *Alter Mann* (old man)—bully beef with the letters "A.M." on the tin can. The Germans called it *armer Mussolini* (poor Mussolini). The less charitable Italians referred to it as *asino morte* (dead donkey).[9]

The bad diet was already beginning to cause health problems. "Even our twenty-five year olds are already losing their teeth," one officer wrote, "and their guns just won't stop bleeding. It's not going to be an easy summer."[10]

The worst suffering during the siege occurred on the western sector, where both sides lay in rocky trenches. The hard terrain would not allow them to dig proper shelters, and they had to lie in small foxholes all day long.

In June some new members of the General Staff reported to the headquarters of the Afrika Korps. They included Major General Alfred Gause, an Eastern Prussian engineer officer who replaced Colonel von dem Borne as chief of staff. Also present was Major (later Major General) Frederick Wilhelm von Mellenthin, a former cavalryman who was now the Intelligence officer for the Korps. Rommel received the newcomers frigidly. He had not overcome his suspicion of General Staff officers. This time he had considerable justification: Gause had been ordered not to place himself under Rommel's command. The lieutenant general quickly informed all within earshot that he alone commanded every single German soldier in Africa. Gause had no choice but to subordinate himself to Rommel. Gause probably would have done so anyway; he was a loyal man with little talent for intrigue.

Of his new commander, Major von Mellenthin later wrote: "Rommel was not an easy man to serve; he spared those around him as little as he spared himself. An iron constitution and nerves of steel were needed to work with Rommel, but I must emphasize that although Rommel was sometimes embarrassingly outspoken with senior commanders, yet once he was convinced of the efficiency and loyalty of those in his immediate entourage, he never had a harsh word for them."[11]

Since the tanks that Tiger delivered were of the newer models, some crew training would be required before committing them to the major summer offensive, which the British planners christened Operation "Battleaxe." While the preparations for "Battleaxe" were in progress, Wavell decided to try to improve his position by launching Operation Brevity with the troops on hand. These troops, which were encamped in western Egypt, included the 7th Armoured, 22nd Guards, and 2nd Rifle Brigades, as well as the 4th Royal Tank Regiment, all under a veteran desert warrior, soon-to-be Major General Gott. He planned a three-pronged advance: The 2nd Rifle Brigade, supported by the 8th Royal Field Artillery Regiment, would advance on the northern (coastal) flank against the lower (north) end of the Halfaya Pass and later on to Sollum. In the center the 22nd Guards Brigade would strike along the southern side of the coastal escarpment and take the upper Halfaya Pass and Fort Capuzzo. Because the coastal escarpment was impassable to vehicles, the 2nd Rifle and 22nd Guards brigades could not physically cooperate. The 4th RTR, with 24 "I" tanks, was to support the guards. On the desert (southern) flank, the 7th Armoured Brigade was to advance on Sidi Azeiz and deal with the German reinforcements. The 7th Armoured consisted of only the 2nd Royal Tank Regiment (only 29 cruiser tanks) and the 7th Support Group,[12] with mechanized infantry battalions, antitank guns, and heavy support weapons included.

The British attacked on May 15 and immediately overran the vital Halfaya Pass, although the 4th Royal Tank Regiment lost seven tanks to unexpectedly stiff Italian resistance. Some of the defenders escaped to the difficult terrain north of the pass and continued to fight. It took the 2nd Rifle Brigade the rest of the day to roust them out. Meanwhile, the infantrymen of the 22nd Guards Brigade took Capuzzo, and the 7th

Armoured brushed aside weak resistance in the desert. "Brevity" had started off well enough, but Erwin Rommel—tipped off by his Wireless Intercept Service that something was afoot—reacted violently. The 2nd Battalion of the 5th Panzer Regiment counterattacked against the Allied center, overran the Durham Light Infantry Battalion, and inflicted heavy casualties on the unprotected foot soldiers. Despite this victory, Colonel von Herff did not have the forces to stop a division-sized mobile strike force. That night he asked Rommel's permission to retreat to positions west of Sidi Azeiz. Perhaps Herff was concerned about being cut off by the 7th Armoured Brigade, which had flanked him to the south. Rommel, however, sent him another panzer battalion and ordered him to continue fighting his delaying action the next day.[13]

May 16 was a day of indecisive fighting. Herff continued to delay the British while Rommel concentrated units from both the 5th Light and 15th Panzer divisions for his major counterattack, set for the next day. W. H. E. Gott, however, became nervous because the Afrika Korps was concentrating and his center was in joepardy. That night he retreated to the Sidi Omar-Sidi Suleiman line and went over to the defensive. "Brevity" was over, and it was a failure for the British. They had gained only the important Halfaya Pass, but at a cost of 18 tanks and about 200 men—over 160 of them in the Durham Light Infantry. The Germans had lost three panzers, 12 men killed, and 61 wounded. The Axis forces lost about 200 captured, mostly at Capuzzo and Halfaya Pass.[14]

Taking and holding the critical Halfaya Pass turned out to be two different things for the Allies. Rommel concentrated approximately 160 German tanks in the sector.[15] This force was placed under the command of Colonel von Herff and included the muscle of the Afrika Korps. Herff had both the Korps panzer regiments (the 5th and the newly arrived 8th), the 104th Artillery Regiment, and the 33rd Panzer Artillery Regiment, plus supporting panzer grenadier units. This battle turned out to be Herff's last major operation with the Afrika Korps, for soon afterward he transferred to the SS and eventually became Heinrich Himmler's chief of personnel.[16] Herff's improvised force counterattacked the British at Sollum on May 26. The battle was well fought on the German side. Initially the 5th Panzer Regiment carried out a diversion to the south. The British armor took the bait and followed it. Meanwhile, the 8th Panzer Regiment under Lieutenant Colonel Hans Kramer circled around and caught the Allies in the rear, while the 15th Motorized and 33rd Reconnaissance battalions carried out a frontal assault. The 104th Artillery and 33rd Panzer artillery regiments supported the attacks.[17]

The perfect coordination of artillery, armor, and infantry that character-
ized this operation became the trademark of the Afrika Korps. In North
Africa, as had been the case in France, the British frequently sent armor
or infantry into battle, one unsupported by the other. Rommel, on the
other hand, used a system of mutual and overlapping support that gave
all elements the maximum protection possible. Normally a line of antitank forces preceded the advance of the Korps. After they shot up the
enemy's armor, Rommel unleashed the panzers to deal with the Allied
infantry. Often the armored and antitank elements "leapfrogged": The
panzers brought the enemy under fire with their main battle guns and
thus kept his head down while the antitank gunners rushed forward and
took up advantageous positions. Then, while the panzers advanced, the
AT gunners pelted the enemy's positions with deadly antitank fire. If the
enemy stood his ground, he invited annihilation from a converging
assault. If he retreated, the Germans simply repeated the process until
the foe surrendered, dispersed, or fled. Although this method of attack
seldom varied in principle, it was never the same tactically. The attacks
were always tailored to the terrain.

The principles of command and control used by Rommel and his
senior commanders also differed greatly from those of the British. The
commander on the spot directed all German ground forces. All too often
the British defenses were commanded by individuals situated miles to the
rear who had no grasp of the true situation. The panzer leader, frequently Rommel himself, knew exactly what the situation was at any
given moment because he could see it, sense it, and influence it. Above
all, he could recognize the decisive moment and deal out crushing defeats
by launching concentrated attacks, while the British commanders let
opportune moments pass because they simply did not know what was
going on.

On May 26, Rommel's tactics enabled him to isolate the 3rd Cold-
stream Guards Battalion at Halfaya Pass and simultaneously concentrate most of Group von Herff against it. The guards' commander,
Lieutenant Colonel Moubray, had no choice but to abandon the strategic pass in the predawn hours of May 27. He extracted his command
skillfully but nevertheless suffered 173 casualties and lost four artillery
pieces, eight antitank guns, and five "I" tanks. The only British gain in
"Brevity" had been wiped out.[18]

Despite his victories, Rommel continued to be burdened by backstab-
bing from his enemies in Berlin. On May 25 Field Marshal von Brau-

chitsch sent Rommel a signal that the Swabian called "a colossal rocket." In his message, the commander-in-chief of the Army told Rommel: "You are to avoid reporting too optimistically or too pessimistically under the immediate influence of events." He implied that Rommel was too emotional to command a field army.

Rommel wrote Lucie concerning the dispatch. "I had a big rocket from the Army High Command—to my mind quite unjustified—in gratitude for all we have achieved so far. I'm not going to take it lying down, and a letter is already on its way to von B." "Bellyaching," he added in another letter, "is so easy if you're not having to sweat things out."[19]

Rommel realized what the British were up to in early June 1941. He knew that the "Tiger Cubs" would be released soon, but he did not know when or where. He greatly strengthened Halfaya Pass by sending German infantry and artillery to hold it. The garrison commander was the Reverend Captain Wilhelm "Papa" Bach, a battalion commander in the 104th Panzer Grenadier Regiment and soon-to-be hero in the Third Reich. Other than the transfer of Bach and his men to Halfaya, plus a few other, minor tactical shifts, Rommel could do little but train his men and wait. He needed 1,500 tons of supplies each day, but he received less than 1,000 tons a day. The Axis failure to capture the strategic island of Malta, located midway between Tripoli and Sicily, was costing him dearly. Forty percent of Rommel's supplies sank in May and June. Most of the cargo carriers sunk during that period were bombed or torpedoed by ships, submarines, or airplanes operating from Malta.

The men of the Afrika Korps, undersupplied and underfed, braced themselves for the attack in a desert heat of up to 107 degrees daily. Temperatures inside the panzers reached 160 degrees. Many young men ended up in the hospital because of heat exhaustion or dysentery.[20] Others, however, took their places, and morale remained incredibly high. The Afrika Korps was already an elite unit, a fact the whole world was about to learn, if it did not know it already.

On the other side of "the wire"—that huge barbed-wire fence that divided Libya and Egypt—Beresford-Peirse assembled his troops at Sidi Omar, from which he could attack either toward Halfaya and Sollum, or to Tobruk via Capuzzo. Rommel had no way of knowing in which direction the main blow would fall.

The Swabian general anticipated the Allied advance by shifting the 8th Panzer Regiment from the Tobruk area to the Sollum sector. The infantry of the 15th Panzer Division remained at Tobruk for the time being, to prevent a breakout by the garrison.

The Allies would badly outnumber Rommel when their summer offensive began. They had over 300 tanks against 80 for the 15th Panzer and probably a few less than that in the 5th Light. The Afrika Korps had approximately 95 PzKw III's and IV's in both its divisions combined. These were the only tanks of real value in Rommel's arsenal. He would not even use the Italian Ariete Armored Division in this battle because of its poor tank maintenance and the poor quality of its equipment. The British also had superior artillery forces but only local air superiority. The RAF had 116 fighters against 60 supporting Rommel, and it outnumbered the Luftwaffe in eastern Libya 128 to 79 in bombers (including dive bombers). The 70 operational fighters and 25 bombers the Italians contributed counted for little.[21] Overall, the odds against Rommel were about 2½ to 3 to 1.

Rommel was keenly aware of the international importance of the coming fight. Not only was the positional advantage of the Afrika Korps threatened, but also the political implications were immense. For the first time the German Wehrmacht would have to fight a major defensive battle. The whole world had witnessed the blitzkrieg, but was the Nazi Army effective only as an offensive tool? Could it win battles when it did not possess the initiative? Hundreds of millions of people had their eyes on Erwin Rommel and the Afrika Korps in the summer of 1941.

General Beresford-Peirse's plan called for two main attacks. The Indian 4th Division (now under Major General F. W. Messervy), with heavy armored support from the 4th Armoured Brigade, was to storm the Halfaya Pass, while the 22nd Guards Brigade and the rest of the 4th Armoured overran Point 206 and Capuzzo and then wheeled east to take Sollum from the rear. The left (desert) flank of both forces would be covered by Major General Michael O'Moore Creagh's 7th Armoured Division (now composed of the 4th and 7th Armoured brigades and the 7th Support Group), which was to take Hafid Ridge. After the fall of the major frontier strongpoints, the 7th Armoured Division would seek a decisive tank battle against the 15th Panzer Division. If it seemed that a major tank battle was imminent, the 4th Armoured Brigade was to rejoin the 7th Armoured Division. Meanwhile, Morshead's Tobruk garrison would break the siege and attack Rommel's rear. The conclusion of this action would be the elimination of all German forces in North Africa.

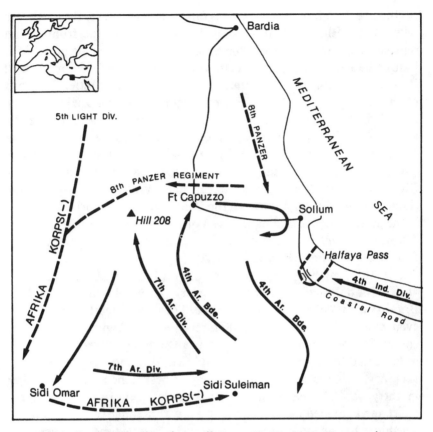

Map 4: Operation "Battleaxe," June 15-17, 1941. Despite being outnumbered more than 2 to 1, Rommel smashed the British offensive, losing 25 tanks while destroying or capturing 100 Allied tanks. This battle was doubly important as it was the first time Hitler's armies had to fight a defensive battle. It also allowed Rommel to maintain the Siege of Tobruk.

On June 8 Rommel completed his final preparations for the battle. He relieved the 5th Light (and Colonel von Herff) on the frontier and replaced them with the 15th Panzer Division. All elements of the 15th Panzer had now completed their trip to Africa, and Major General Walter Neumann-Silkow assumed command on the frontier. His units on the border included the 8th Panzer Regiment (two panzer battalions), the 33rd Reconnaissance Battalion, a battery of the 33rd Panzer Artillery Regiment, the 1st Battalion of the 104th Panzer Grenadier Regiment, Bach's battalion at Halfaya Pass, the 33rd Antitank Battalion (with a dozen 50mm antitank guns and 21 37mm antitank guns), the 15th Motorcycle Battalion, an anti-aircraft battery of 13 88mm guns, and three battalions of infantry from the Italian Trento Motorized Division in the Sollum–Capuzzo area. The rest of Trento was stationed at Bardia. The 15th Panzer had four major strongpoints to defend: the Halfaya Pass, Qalala, Point 206, and Point 208 (the Hafid Ridge).[22]

The Allied offensive began at 4:00 A.M. on June 15. Messervy's Indian 4th Division slashed at Halfaya with a large group of Mark II's, perhaps Britain's most deadly tank at this time. They were met, however, by an even more dangerous foe: the 88mm anti-aircraft gun. This weapon could effectively engage a target at a range of 11,000 yards—over six miles. In addition, a good crew could fire 20 rounds in a minute with accuracy. Rommel's crews were among the best in the Reich. The Indian infantry were decimated, and their attack stalled. Tanks were ripped apart and exploded long before they got within range to fire effectively. The bitter but unequal struggle continued for some time, but eventually the Allies withdrew with heavy losses. Eleven of the 12 British tanks engaged above the pass (that is, south of it) were destroyed. North of the escarpment, four of the six committed British tanks ended up in a minefield. From this moment on, soldiers on both sides referred to Halfaya as "Hellfire Pass."[23]

Later in the day the Allies made another attempt and this time made some progress. They captured the village of Halfaya, which the 88's proceeded to reduce to rubble. The garrison continued to hold the pass against all comers.[24]

Although bogged down on the coastal plain, Beresford-Peirse scored some local successes on the inland plateau. Late on the afternoon of June 15, Capuzzo fell to a force of 90 Matilda tanks from the 4th Armoured Brigade. Point 206 was also captured, but the overall issue was still in doubt as night fell.

Rommel's strategy was not yet apparent as dawn broke on June 16, but essentially it was this: Hold the panzers in reserve while the Allies exhausted themselves against his strongpoints; then, at just the right moment, counterattack and rout them. For this type of plan to succeed, the defending commander must have nerves of steel. Here, in "Battleaxe," Rommel proved himself a master of the art of defense for the first time. At Arras in the French campaign he had defended only until he could bring up his panzers and attack. Here, on the Libyan frontier, the panzers were near enough for immediate use, but Rommel deliberately withheld them so that the enemy could bleed himself white against fixed defenses. Rommel's unwillingness to make a major commitment of his armor on June 15 demonstrated his strength of character as well as his military versatility. He proved that he could fight defensive as well as offensive battles and win them.

On June 16, the British again did pretty much as Rommel wanted them to. They railed against Halfaya, depleting an entire division against a relatively small number of Axis soldiers.

The second day of the Battle of Halfaya Pass was fought in 130-degree temperature, with little water for the defenders. Rommel signaled Bach: "The Pass must be held under all circumstances." The preacher-turned-soldier complied by beating off five separate attacks. He even managed to retake the ruins of the former village of Halfaya.[25]

Finally, Beresford-Peirse realized that he would have to bypass Halfaya. He would, no doubt, have reached this conclusion earlier if he had been at the front. His headquarters, however, lay 60 miles behind the lines, too far for him to influence the battle personally. We must not criticize him too severely, though, for his actions conformed to current British command and control doctrines.

In modifying his original plan, Beresford-Peirse split his army into three main combat groups. On the right (coastal) flank, the Indian infantry continued to besiege Halfaya Pass, although they launched no more costly frontal attacks. In the center, strong armored forces advanced on Sollum (behind the pass), while the third group, including most of the 7th Armoured Division, tried to flank the Afrika Korps to the south. By late morning on the 16th, the 7th Armoured Division neared Point 208, the southern anchor of Rommel's line.

An elite German formation defended Point 208 (also known as Hafid Ridge). This unit was the 1st Oasis Company under Lieutenant Paulewicz. In addition to his own company, Paulewicz had a machine-gun section, a battery of 37mm antitank guns, and a battery of the legendary 88mm anti-aircraft guns. Initially the British 7th Armoured Brigade attacked with at least 70 tanks. The Germans held their fire until the tanks were well within range of the 88's and then blasted them with a concentrated volley. Eleven Mark II's exploded within minutes, and the rest retreated rapidly. Later in the afternoon the British attacked again, and again were repulsed. Seventeen more Mark II's were knocked out.[26]

The fame of the 88mm AA guns would grow out of this battle and that of the Halfaya Pass. In these fights small German units defeated and disabled greatly superior Allied forces, mainly because the Germans used the 88.

Late in the afternoon of June 16, the British tried for a third time to take the vital Point 208. This time they left their tanks behind and sent in nothing but infantry. The results were as bad as before. The Allied infantrymen were mowed down by machine-gun fire. Again the survivors withdrew, not to return. They had lost too much time and too many men and tanks against relatively minor positions.[27] Now, on the afternoon of June 16, Rommel decided the moment for the grand counterstroke had arrived.

Earlier in the day, on the Sollum (central) sector, the Allies finally shook themselves free of Rommel's holding forces and burst through his line. The Axis front threatened to collapse as the British 4th Armoured Brigade overran Capuzzo and drove on toward Sollum. If they took this coastal town, they would be in a position to overrun the German rear and would have cut off Bach from the rest of the Axis army. Rommel could not afford to let this happen, so he committed a part of his reserves before he really wanted to. The Swabian sent the 8th Panzer Regiment into a head-on collision with the 4th Armoured Brigade, supported by the 31st Royal Field Artillery Regiment and parts of the 22nd Guards Brigade. Initially the Germans won, but the British fell back to Capuzzo, rallied, and made a determined stand. The panzers could make no penetration, and soon the battlefield was littered with burning German armored vehicles. The 8th Panzer Regiment lost 50 of its 80 tanks in the Battle of Capuzzo.* Nevertheless, Rommel still had a division in reserve; Beresford-Peirse had practically no reserves left.

Despite the heavy tank losses, the fighting at Capuzzo stabilized the situation on the Axis front and prevented the 4th Armoured Brigade from joining the rest of the 7th Armoured Division to the south. With a

---

*The term "lost" refers both to tanks completely destroyed and those that were later recovered and repaired (i.e., those "lost" for operational purposes during a particular battle).

Erwin Rommel, commander of Panzer Group Afrika, late 1941 or early 1942
(*U.S. National Archives*)

Rommel when he was commander of the 7th Panzer Division in France, 1940 (*U.S. National Archives*)

(below) A Czechoslovakian T-38 tank of the 7th Panzer Division. These tanks had been incorporated into the German Army in 1938. *(U.S. National Archives)*

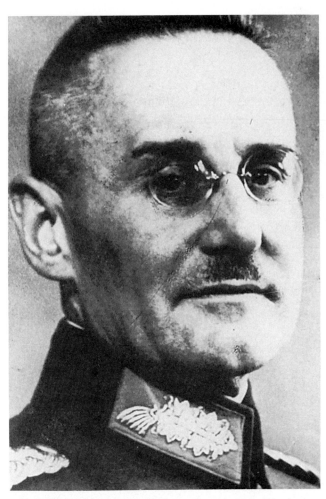

(above) One of Rommel's archrivals at Fuehrer Headquarters, Colonel General Fritz Halder, chief of the General Staff. Halder opposed the North African adventure from the beginning, constantly tried to limit German involvement there, and intensely disliked Rommel personally. *(U.S. National Archives)*

(left) An Afrika Korps soldier in the summer of 1941. Soon afterward they discarded this helmet and appeared mainly in floppy-type caps for the rest of the Desert War. *(U.S. National Archives)*

A German tank commander quenches his thirst, 1941. This young man is wearing the Iron Cross, First Class; the ribbon for the Iron Cross, Second Class; and the close combat badge for 25 or more armored engagements. Although it is difficult to tell from this photo, his tank seems to be a Panzer Mark IV with a short-barrel gun, which greatly reduced its effectiveness. *(U.S. National Archives)*

Rommel's friend Lieutenant Colonel (later Lieutenant General) Fritz Bayerlein, who went on to command a panzer division on the Western Front. *(U.S. National Archives)*

Rommel, with an angry expression, gives orders to aides, 1941. *(U.S. National Archives)*

(above) One of the British tanks destroyed by an 88mm anti-aircraft gun is being examined by German soldiers. This captured German photo is dated September 26, 1941. *(U.S. National Archives)*

(below) A Panzer Mark III rolls down a trail in the desert. Since enemy contact is not expected, all crew members except the driver ride on the outside of the tank. *(U.S. Army photo)*

(above) A panzer company, accompanied by supporting vehicles, crosses the desert in 1941. The lead tank is traveling in reverse. *(U.S. National Archives)*

(below) A British Mark III tank, captured by and incorporated into the Afrika Korps during the "Crusader" battles, late 1941. Because they were fighting a "poor man's war," Rommel's troops frequently relied on captured enemy equipment and supplies. *(U.S. National Archives)*

(above) A panzer formation throws up dust in the Western Desert, 1941. Dust, sandstorms, and haze frequently caused poor visibility and confusion on the desert battlefields throughout the war. *(U.S. National Archives)*

(below) A platoon of PzKw III's checks its bearings in the desert. Note the short-barrel main battle gun on the lead tank, which sports a command pennant. Tank tracks have been welded to the front of these panzers to give them additional armored protection. *(U.S. Army photo)*

(above) Elements of a panzer regiment under British fire, December 1941
(U.S. National Archives)

(below) An 88mm anti-aircraft gun being used in an antitank role, in action at the Battle of Sidi Rezegh, 1941. *(U.S. National Archives)*

Colonel General Erwin Rommel has just presented General Cruewell with a birthday present at the latter's headquarters, 40 kilometers southeast of Derna on March 20, 1942. Cruewell commanded the Afrika Korps during the "Crusader" battles and was promoted to deputy commander of Panzer Army Afrika shortly thereafter. Less than two months after this photo was taken, he was captured by the British. Notice the Italian cameramen in the background. *(U.S. Army photo)*

Rommel being congratulated by Adolf Hitler on his 1941 victories in the desert. The major general in the background is probably Rudolf Schmundt. Rommel's relationship with Hitler soured in 1942, and by 1944 he was actively plotting the Fuehrer's overthrow. *(U.S. National Archives)*

(above) A panzer crew in camp, 1941. The tank is a PzKw III. The pennant indicates that it is a command tank. *(U.S. National Archives)*

(below) This photo shows a camouflaged Afrika Korps truck depot near Derna. It is dated September 15, 1941. The typical desert terrain is also shown. *(U.S. National Archives)*

(above) A damaged Volkswagen is hauled by a truck during the retreat from Tobruk, late 1941 or early 1942. *(U.S. National Archives)*

(below) The Coastal Road minefield, 1941. *(U.S. National Archives)*

The German retreat from Tobruk. The crew of a heavy field gun breaks camp and prepares to continue its withdrawal from Cyrenaica. (U.S. National Archives)

(facing page) A German truck is stuck in the sand, 1941. The truck in the rear is attempting to extricate it. The symbol of the Afrika Korps is clearly visible on the door. (U.S. National Archives)

(above) A camouflaged German supply tent with sentry, 1941. *(U.S. National Archives)*

(below) The German graveyard 40 miles southwest of Derna. *(U.S. National Archives)*

bloody stalemate developing on the northern and central flanks, Rommel ordered von Ravenstein's 5th Light Division forward to the south. This was Rommel's decisive attack. Major General Ravenstein caught the 7th Armoured still shaken from its defeat at Point 208 and in an exposed position. The British armored division was decisively defeated six miles west of Sidi Omar. As night fell, the 7th Armoured Brigade had only 21 operational tanks left. Sidi Omar was the turning point in Operation "Battleaxe."[28] The main division in the Western Desert Force was, for the moment at least, a broken reed.

With the Allied southern flank wavering, Rommel came up with an exceedingly bold plan. Under the cover of darkness he denuded his center and sent the remains of the 8th Panzer Regiment to reinforce the 5th Light Division. This move was extremely dangerous. A major Allied thrust from Capuzzo to Tobruk could not help but be successful. The strong Australian garrison, the 4th Armoured and 22nd Guards brigades, and the battered but intact Indian 4th Division were all available for such an attack, and all that was left to oppose them were elements of the weak reconnaissance battalions, which had no tanks at all, and the weak Ariete Division. An attack could easily have cut off Rommel's main force and left it isolated deep in the desert. Since the Afrika Korps was already low on fuel, it is very conceivable that the Axis might have lost all of North Africa that day if the British had acted quickly. However, it was all a question of speed, and Erwin Rommel struck first, as usual. Of this moment, when he decided to take the great risk, Rommel later wrote: "This [the Battle of Sidi Omar] was the turning point. . . . I immediately ordered the 15th Panzer Division to disengage all its mobile forces as quickly as possible and, leaving only the essential minimum to hold the position north of Capuzzo, to go forward on the northern flank of the victorious 5th Light Division towards Sidi Suleiman [an important position deep in the enemy's southern flank]. The decisive moment had come. It is often possible to decide the issue of a battle merely by making an unexpected shift of one's main weight."[29]

At dawn on June 17 the 5th Light drove deep into the Allies' communication and supply zone. The tank regiment of the 15th Panzer covered the 5th Light's northern flank and then swung toward the coast. Soon Neumann-Silkow's men were in the rear of the British and Indian forces in the Capuzzo and Halfaya Pass areas. The Allies, who could have cut off Rommel only a few hours before, now found themselves nearly cut off in turn. They escaped after a struggle but lost many vehicles, some of which had to be abandoned due to lack of gasoline. During the clashes of

June 17, all of which took place in the British rear, Rommel lost 25 tanks, as opposed to 100 for the Allies. The enemy front collapsed, and they rushed pell-mell toward the Egyptian frontier. At 4:00 P.M. Rommel reached Halfaya and relieved Bach's battered command. "Battleaxe," or the Battle of Sollum, as the Germans called it, was over.

Few people were killed in this fight, because it was primarily a tank battle. Table 1 shows the exact figures. Most of the Allied casualties fell at Halfaya Pass and in the infantry attack on Point 208. Rommel's men suffered the highest casualties when the 4th Armoured Brigade unexpectedly broke into Capuzzo on June 15. The real measure of the battle is shown in Table 2. The British and their allies lost over 100 tanks but could recover none of them because the Germans possessed the battlefield. On the other hand, Rommel's mechanics immediately set about repairing damaged vehicles. Within a matter of weeks the Afrika Korps reached approximately the same armored strength level it had attained before the battle, excluding reinforcements received from Europe. As for Churchill's forces, many of the precious "Tiger Cubs" were either burned out or, worse yet, fixed and incorporated into the Nazi war machine. This was too much for the Prime Minister. He relieved General Wavell of his duties and replaced him with Sir Claude Auchinleck. General Sir Noel Beresford-Peirse's days as commander of the Western Desert Force were also numbered.

In retrospect, there were six main reasons for the Allied defeat in "Battleaxe." First, their commanders, especially Beresford-Peirse, headquartered too far to the rear. Second, Wavell succumbed to political pressure from London and launched the offensive too soon, before his tankers could get enough experience in operating their new machines. Third, their tank tactics were inferior to those of the Afrika Korps.

Table 1

Losses During "Battleaxe"

	Killed	Wounded	Missing	Total
Allies	122	588	259	969
Axis	93	350	235	678

Source: Playfair II, p. 171.

Rommel concentrated his panzers against Allied infantry and soft-skin vehicles and sent antitank gunners after the British tanks. Fourth, the Germans used superior combined arms tactics (that is, the proper mixture of infantry, armor, artillery, and antitank forces), while the Allies violated the principle of mutual support. Fifth, Hitler's war machine momentarily had a degree of technical superiority over its Western opponents. The 2-pounder gun on most of the British tanks was not equal to the 50mm gun on the Panzer Mark III, the main battle tank of the Afrika Korps (see Chapter 7). The technological superiority of the 88mm anti-aircraft gun needs no further discussion. Finally, the Germans' tank recovery methods greatly outclassed those of the British. Rommel's mechanics recovered disabled panzers even under fire, and repaired them closer to the front line than the Allies; therefore, the "turnaround time" for returning a damaged panzer to the battle was much less than that for a damaged British tank. A seventh factor must be added to the list of reasons for the Allied defeat in "Battleaxe": The Axis commander simply had no equal on the other side. In fact, the Rommel legend was already taking hold on both sides of the line.

Rommel's bravery in battle was matched only by his seeming invulnerability. Time and time again the vehicle he was riding in would be shot up. Erwin Rommel would stroll away unscathed. Men only a few feet away from him would be blown to bits. Rommel's only damage would be a dirty uniform and perhaps a slight strain of the eardrums. Most of the veterans of the North African campaign could relate stories of his brushes with death. Death itself, however, seemed carefully to be avoiding Erwin Rommel. Why should it disturb someone who served it so well? As the legend of the Desert Fox grew, stories of his courage and

Table 2

Tank Losses During "Battleaxe"

	Tanks Destroyed	Tanks Disabled
Allies	+100	?
Afrika Korps	12	50

Source: Carell, p. 44; Playfair (II, p. 171) reported that the British lost 27 cruisers and 64 "I" tanks destroyed, but does not report disabled and abandoned tank losses.

incredible escapes crossed the line and perhaps grew a little in the telling. British Intelligence officers reported as early as mid-1941 that "Rommel's very name and legend are in the process of becoming a psychological danger to the British Army."[30]

About the Rommel legend, an outstanding German writer, Paul Carell, put it best when he wrote:

> Rommel's men considered him to be invulnerable. "No bullet has ever been forged for the Old Man," they used to say in amazement, or with a shake of the head, when he had once more sensed the danger and moved off in his armored car, just before a shell had burst. They lay in the desert under a hail of enemy machinegun fire—could not even put their noses out of their slit trenches without the risk of having their heads blown off. The attack was halted, Rommel came rushing up and stood upright in the trench, shielding his eyes with his hands against the sun. "What the hell's the matter with you fellows? When things get a bit hot over there you don't have to belly-flop every time!" Hardly had he gone than there were casualties once more. It was always the same story. Many of the old desert foxes have told me similar stories—men who returned home with the Iron Cross and the Knights' Cross and who certainly were not scared of a bombardment. Yes, no bullet had ever been forged for Erwin Rommel.[31]

Soon after "Battleaxe," British Intelligence tried twice to capture or kill Lieutenant General Rommel. On the first try, commandoes attempted to raid his headquarters, then located west of Tobruk. They were captured within a few hundred yards of his truck. A short time later Rommel moved his headquarters to a position near Bardia, closer to the front. He found a beach from which he could swim (usually nude) in the Mediterranean. One day a group of British snipers fired on him and only narrowly missed their target. The Desert Fox dove behind a stone wall, and the snipers escaped into the hills. Rommel remained unperturbed by the assassination attempt. "I must be worth quite a lot to the Englishmen," he said to his aide and then laughed.[32]

In July 1941, Hitler ordered the reorganization of Axis forces in Africa. He promoted Rommel from the rank of lieutenant general to general of panzer troops. He also created the Panzer Group Afrika and placed Rommel in charge. General Ferdinand Schaal, who had commanded the 10th Panzer Division in France, was selected to replace Rommel as commander of the Afrika Korps. Unfortunately, Schaal was not physically able to remain in Africa more than a few days. His successor, General Philip Mueller-Gebhard, contracted dysentery almost as soon as he arrived in Libya.[33] A fourth commander for the Korps had to be selected, and Lieutenant General Ludwig Cruewell, the former leader of the 2nd Motorized Division in France and the 11th Panzer Division in the Balkans campaign, was named in October. His turned out to be an excellent appointment indeed. Major General Gause remained Rommel's chief of staff, while Colonel Fritz Bayerlein was named chief of staff of the Afrika Korps. The 5th Light Division was upgraded and redesignated 21st Panzer Division, but it received no new units. Major General von Ravenstein remained in charge. Each panzer division now had a panzer regiment of two battalions, a panzer grenadier regiment of two battalions, a reconnaissance battalion (which included an armored car company), an antitank battalion, an engineer battalion, a signal battalion, and an artillery regiment of three battalions, as well as miscellaneous supply and support units.

During the reorganization, Rommel received authorization to form a new division, although he got no reinforcements. Initially this formation was called the Afrika Division, but it eventually was designated the 90th Light. It soon had four battalions of infantry, but it lacked the trucks or armored cars to make them mobile. Eventually the 90th Light was fleshed out to a strength of three full motorized infantry regiments, and the 190th Panzer Battalion was created to support it. Improvised units of this type seldom become elite formations. For some unexplainable reason, this one did. The enemy came to look upon them as very capable fighters, a truly dangerous enemy for whom no challenge was too risky to be taken. Rommel trusted them as much as he did the Afrika Korps, of which they were not a part. For aspiring divisional commanders, however, the leadership of the 90th Light was frequently a ticket to the hospital, or worse. No other command in the entire German Army, as far as I can determine, used up commanders as quickly as the 90th Light did. At least two commanding generals in North Africa were killed at the head of this formation, and several others suffered painful wounds. Probably the last German general killed in action in World War II was Afrika Korps veteran Lieutenant General Ernst Baade, the leader of the rebuilt 90th Light Division (then called the 90th Panzer Grenadier). He died in Italy on the last day of the war.[34]

The order of battle of Panzer Group Afrika in July 1941 is shown in

Table 3. Table 4 gives the breakdown of the German elements of Panzer Group Afrika at the same period.

After "Battleaxe" and the formation of Panzer Group Afrika, neither side had the strength to attack the other. Except for an occasional skirmish near the besieged fortress of Tobruk, or an occasional patrol on the frontier, a long lull descended on the war in the desert. It was the longest halt in operations that ever took place in that theater. This pause in military action gives us the opportunity to examine Rommel a bit more closely, both as a military commander and as a human being.

Table 3

Order of Battle of Panzer Group Afrika,
July 1941

Panzer Group Afrika—General Erwin Rommel

    Afrika Korps—Lieutenant General Ludwig Cruewell
        21st Panzer Division
        15th Panzer Division

    90th Light Division*

    Italian XX Motorized Corps†
        Ariete Armored Division
        Trieste Motorized Division
        Trento Motorized Division*

    Italian XXI Infantry Corps‡
        Pavia Division‡
        Bologna Division‡
        Brescia Division‡
        Savona Division

*Not completely formed.
†Ordered to coordinate with Rommel; not officially attached
  to Panzer Group Afrika until November 1941.
‡Besieging Tobruk.

Table 4

Order of Battle of the German Contingent,
Panzer Group Afrika, July 1941

Afrika Korps
    21st Panzer Division
        5th Panzer Regiment
        104th Panzer Grenadier Regiment
        3rd Reconnaissance Battalion
        104th Panzer Artillery Regiment
        200th Engineer Battalion

    15th Panzer Division
        8th Panzer Regiment
        115th Panzer Grenadier Regiment
        33rd Reconnaissance Battalion
        33rd Panzer Artillery Regiment
        33rd Engineer Battalion

    90th Light Division
        361st Infantry Regiment*
        155th Infantry Regiment*
        200th Infantry Regiment*
        580th Reconnaissance Battalion*
        900th Engineer Battalion*

*Not completely formed.

6

The Lull

From Erwin Rommel's victory at the Battle of Sollum in June until the beginning of the British Winter Offensive in late November, a period of relative calm descended on the North African Front. Rommel, of course, was far from idle. His supply deficiencies, aggravated by the inefficiency of the Italian Navy, prevented him from assuming the offensive, so he busied himself with defensive matters and prepared for the next onslaught.

Almost every day the commander of Panzer Group Afrika visited the young desert warriors, keeping them on their toes and boosting their morale. The mutual trust and admiration already established grew by leaps and bounds. Major General von Esebeck remembers: "He was always gay when he was speaking to young men. He had a smile and a joke for everyone who seemed to be doing his job. There was nothing he liked better than to talk with a man from his own part of the country in the Swabian dialect. He had a very warm heart. . . ."[1]

War changed his personal habits very little. Life only became a little harder and a little more primitive, but Rommel thrived on it, at least until 1942, when the strain began to undermine his health. Those days were yet to come, however. He still did not seem to care what he ate, and frequently he forgot to eat at all. He usually carried a few sandwiches or a can of sardines and a piece of bread with him in the mornings. Quite often they returned with him at night, uneaten. For drink he carried only a small flask of cold tea, with lemon. Since Rommel realized that the more you drink in the desert the more you want, he usually brought the flask back untouched as well. One day Rommel invited an Italian general to lunch with him in the field. "It was rather awkward," Rommel said later. "I had only three slices of bread and they were all stale. Never mind, they eat too much [anyway]."[2]

Rommel's evening meal, the longest of the day, never lasted more than 20 minutes. He would have simple food, with an occasional glass of wine, but only with the meal. After dinner he would order the radio turned on, but only for the news, never for the music. After this he would write to his wife. If a major campaign was in progress, he sometimes had his batman, Corporal Herbert Gunther, write to her for him. He also continued his correspondence with his World War I comrades. Normally these letters were written in the general's own hand; very seldom were they dictated and typed, or written by an aide and simply signed by Rommel. No letter from these old veterans ever went unanswered. After replying to any letters from these old friends, Rommel filled the rest of the evening with official correspondence. He might occasionally read a newspaper, but novels and radio programs (other than the news) had no place in his schedule.[3]

His relationship with other officers was strictly professional and formal most of the time. One of his aides, Lieutenant Heinz Schmidt, wrote: "He seldom mentioned his family or his private life, and, indeed, was almost reticent about intimate affairs of any sort. It was months before he called me anything but the formal Lieutenant, and only after he decided that I was more than a necessary additional limb did he address me by name, bother to find out my age, whether I was happy, or indeed, even think of me other than as something that filled a uniform and answered a command. It was, in fact, almost strange, after a long acquaintance, to find the impersonal General actually human."[4]

Around himself Rommel gradually drew a staff of friends and professionals, who composed the nerve center of the Afrika Korps and Panzer Group Afrika. They included Gause, Colonel (later Lieutenant General) Siegfried Westphal, Colonel (later Lieutenant General) Fritz Bayerlein, Major (later Major General) Frederick Wilhelm von Mellenthin, and others. Ability was the chief criterion Rommel used in choosing his associates, although being a Swabian was also a plus.[5]

Perhaps the two most diverse of Rommel's subordinates were Major General Johannes von Ravenstein and Major von Mellenthin. Ravenstein was a civilian at heart. He had fought in World War I, and he had even won the Pour le Mérite in June 1918. At the end of hostilities, however, he did not apply to remain in the service, for he had no desire for a career on active duty. He founded a small news agency in Duisburg and married a beautiful Portuguese countess. This solid, well-to-do citizen would have been perfectly happy to have been allowed to continue his pleasant existence in his small city indefinitely, but the war intervened. Ravenstein was called up in 1939 and fought in Poland, Bulgaria, and Greece. His courage and natural abilities as a soldier enabled him to rise rapidly. In mid-1941 he succeeded the unfortunate Colonel Olbrich as commander of the 5th Panzer Regiment. Before the Halfaya Pass–Sollum battles he found himself commanding the division.[6] He demonstrated undeniable talent in his part in turning back "Battleaxe" and soon ranked second only to Rommel as the most feared German commander in Africa.

Major von Mellenthin, on the other hand, was born and bred a soldier. His father, Lieutenant Colonel of Artillery Paul Henning von Mellenthin, was killed in action in the First World War, when Frederick was thirteen. The colonel's son grew up with a strong militaristic tradition and was very proud that he was the great-great grandson of Prince August of Prussia, a nephew of Frederick the Great. Mellenthin enlisted in the 7th Cavalry Regiment at Breslau in 1924, as a private. Due to the small officer corps imposed on Germany by the Treaty of Versailles, he could not become a lieutenant until 1928. In 1935 he was selected to serve on the General Staff and worked for Field Marshal Erwin von Witzleben.[7] This leader was commander-in-chief in the West for a period but was retired by Hitler and eventually hanged for his part in the attempt on Hitler's life in 1944. Mellenthin, however, remained politically uncontaminated and continued his advancement to the rank of major. He participated in the French and Balkan campaigns before joining the Afrika Korps in 1941. This was his first really major assignment, and Mellenthin acquitted himself well. He continued to serve with Rommel until amoebic dysentery laid him low during the El Alamein fighting. After his recovery, the High Command sent him to Russia. From late 1942 until 1945 he served in a number of important positions: chief of staff of the XXXXVIII Panzer Corps, chief of the General Staff of the 4th Panzer Army, and acting commander of the 9th Panzer Division. He ended up as chief of staff of the 5th Panzer Army in the defense of the Ruhr Pocket, where he was captured. His older brother, Horst, commanded an infantry corps on the Russian Front and rose to the rank of general of infantry.[8]

Another tough, experienced officer reported to Rommel during the lull. Colonel Fritz Bayerlein was described by Desmond Young as a "stocky, tough little terrier of a man."[9] He joined the Kaiser's army when he was 16 and fought in the First World War. After the collapse of the Second Reich he could not find a job in the troubled civilian economy, so he re-enlisted in 1921. After much hard work and studying he earned a commission and finally a ticket to the General Staff College in 1932. From 1935, he soldiered strictly with the panzer branch. He was operations officer for Heinz Guderian's Second Panzer Group and was fighting on the Eastern Front when the summons to North Africa reached him. This transfer almost certainly came at Rommel's request. The two had known each other since the early 1930s.[10]

Initially Rommel's aide in North Africa was Captain Aldinger, a small, slender man who had served with then-Lieutenant Rommel in World War I. However, the years had taken their toll on Aldinger. After the Battle of Sollum his health gave way, and he returned to Europe.

Lieutenant Heinz Schmidt, who had been born in South Africa, succeeded Aldinger. Hitler's draft had converted this young university student into an infantry platoon leader in the invasion of Poland. Perhaps because of his previous experience in Africa, the High Command sent him to Italian Eritrea, where he commanded a company of German naval merchant volunteers. He barely escaped the Italian collapse in East Africa, in the rear of an obsolete aircraft with three drunk Italian pilots.[11] Rommel did not seem to like him at first but later came to appreciate him. Eventually Schmidt asked to be transferred to a combat unit. Rommel's reaction to this request is instructive. Schmidt recalled: "Rommel's eyes flickered for a moment and then he looked me hard in the eye. . . . Still eyeing me sharply, Rommel asked in a half-jocular manner: 'Are you tired of working for me, Schmidt?'"

"'No, no, Herr General,' I answered quickly, if not quite truthfully, 'but as a young officer I should like to be back with the troops.'

"'Quite right, Schmidt,' was Rommel's unexpected reply. 'As a lieutenant I should have done exactly the same. . . .' And he added with an unusual twinkle: 'A staff officer's life does not appeal to me either.'"[12]

Schmidt went on to command a company of infantry in Africa, and he escaped the final collapse in Tunisia because, at the last moment, the High Command approved his request to get married. He ended up in Army Group C in Italy.

Lieutenant Count von Schweppenburg, a one-armed veteran, replaced Schmidt but remained with Rommel only a few weeks.[13]

Captain Schraepler, Rommel's aide from the French campaign, followed him to Libya after recovering from his wounds. Little is known about his private life except that he was married. He was promoted to major in late 1940 or early 1941 and served as Rommel's adjutant while he commanded the Afrika Korps. Schraepler was undoubtedly very brave, as he demonstrated in France and in the initial attacks on Tobruk.

His end was tragic. He was accidentally run over and crushed by the Mammoth during the British Winter Offensive of 1941.

Among Rommel's other staff officers was Captain Alfred Berndt, a fanatical Nazi who formerly worked in Goebbels' Ministry of Propaganda. Berndt wrote a war book and did much to advance Rommel's popularity with the German public. Berndt frequently served as an intermediary between the Desert Fox and the Nazis, since he was politically acceptable to Hitler, had important contacts, and was liked by both Rommel and the Fuehrer. Later in the war Berndt returned to the Propaganda Ministry but fell out of favor with Goebbels and was forced to resign. He promptly joined the SS and rose to the rank of major. Unlike Schmidt and most of the others, he did not survive the war. He was killed in Hungary, fighting the Russians, in 1945.

Besides competent staff officers and commanders, Rommel also surrounded himself with a personal bodyguard, at least in theory. In reality, this unit did almost everything but guard Rommel's body. It was actually a personal battle group of approximately battalion size that Rommel could throw into battle at a moment's notice, whenever and wherever he saw fit. Even this function, however, was theoretical, for Rommel usually outran this *Kampfstaffel* (battle staff) just as he outran the rest of the Panzer Group. The *Kampfstaffel* did, however, see more than its share of emergency situations. It was finally wiped out at El Alamein in November 1942. It consisted of a tank company, a mixed antitank/anti-aircraft company, a small reconnaissance unit, and a signals detachment.

A typical day in the life of Erwin Rommel tested the strength and stamina of much younger men. Physically, Rommel was a man of stronger than average constitution, even though he was, surprisingly, somewhat overweight. In his war years, he was never able to thin his waistline, despite his Spartan environment. He was somewhat self-conscious about it, but it never slowed him down. Rommel had blue-gray eyes, with "unusual humor wrinkles slanting downward from above the corners of his eyes to the outer edges of his cheekbones."[14] He had a strong chin and mouth. All in all, he was of about average appearance. His manner was simple, and he enjoyed a good laugh. However, beneath the skin lay the iron determination that propelled him forward when much younger men could no longer find the strength. Years of skiing and mountain climbing had kept him in excellent condition for someone over 50. One young Nazi paratrooper, himself a skiing champion, said of Rommel: "He had the strength of a horse. I never saw another man like him. No need for food, no need for drink, no need for sleep. He could wear out men twenty and thirty years younger. If anything he was *too* hard, on himself and everybody else."[15]

No discomfort bothered this man, or at least nothing could make him admit that he was bothered. Like Napoleon, whom he admired, or Stonewall Jackson in the previous century, he could sleep with his head on a table for a few minutes and wake up completely alert and ready to go again for hours. During active campaigning, the general was always up and shaved by 6:00 A.M. He wore a standard German uniform: breeches, boots, and jacket. Only on the hottest days would he wear shorts. The only liberty he took with the dress code was a checkered scarf, which he wore around his neck in the winter.

Heinz Schmidt described a typical day with Rommel this way:

"Punctually at 7:00 A.M. we leave on one of our customary front-line visits. . . . On the horizon in no-man's land we often spot enemy patrol cars. They cannot guess how fat a prize is moving within eye-shot of their binoculars.

"Rommel studies our own positions from vantage points on the enemy's side. He examines then through his field-glasses with the painstaking care of a scientist using a microscope. He snorts: he has seen something that displeases him. We leap into the car after him. He stands up as we head straight for the strongpoint he has surveyed.

"The sentry on duty stares at Rommel wide-eyed. 'Why don't you salute?' the General barks. The soldier jumps to attention, petrified, speechless.

"'Where is the outpost commander?' Rommel demands angrily.

"'He is asleep, Herr . . . er . . . Major!' the sentry stutters . . .

"'Ja, Herr Soldat,' snaps Rommel. 'It seems as if everybody is asleep here. Please wake this—gentleman.'

"The sentry need not move. The flushed face of a young officer appears at the entrance of a dug-out nearby. When he sees the general, he comes smartly to attention, salutes and reports: 'Outpost Franke—nothing special to report.'

"'How do you know, Herr Lieutenant? Rommels raps out at him. 'You have been sleeping—and beautifully, too.'

"The lieutenant has nothing to say. There is a grim pause. Rommel says, 'Herr Lieutenant, your post is not being run in accordance with my instructions. Your shelter is too prominent. The post is not camouflaged.

Your men are running about—while you sleep! I shall return tomorrow and satisfy myself that my requirements are satisfied in every particular. Good morning, Herr Lieutenant.'"[16]

They drive off before the young officer can respond.

At the next outpost Rommel is pleased. His manner changes completely. He is quite friendly and complimentary to the lieutenant in command. "A well-selected position and good dispositions," he says. ". . . One good strong-point must serve as well as two indifferently planned and manned. . . . How are you off for ammunition and supplies?"

"We have plenty of ammunition, Herr General, and food for three days."

"For three days, my friend? You require provisions for three weeks. But . . . never mind, we will see to that."

Again he thanks the young man and is off once more. Schmidt remembers: "At every OP the General leaves his car. Although nearly twice my age, he shows no sign of fatique; my legs are sore and heavy as lead, for it is heavy going in the sand. . . ."[17]

Rommel believed that the fighting on the North African Front was the most sophisticated and up-to-date mode of battle experienced in the Second World War. Of course, he could not have foreseen the atomic bomb. On the subject of modern warfare, Rommel wrote: "North Africa may well have been the theatre in which the war was waged in its most modern guise. . . . It was only in the desert that the principles of armored warfare as they were taught in theory before the war could be fully applied and thoroughly developed. It was only in the desert that real tank battles were fought by large-scale formations."[18]

Rommel frequently compared desert warfare to war at sea. "No admiral ever won a naval battle from a shore base," he was fond of saying.[19] The Sahara even resembled the sea, with its huge areas of open space, its unpredictable storms, and its shifting waves. The waves were made of sand instead of water, and the tank took the place of the destroyer, but many of the other naval principles remained constant. Speed and the quick decision were trumps. Major General J. F. C. Fuller, one of the fathers of the theory of the blitzkrieg, explained the Allied defeats this way: "In rapidity of decision and velocity of movement the Germans completely outclassed their enemy and mainly because Rommel . . . normally took personal command of his armor. . . . It was not that the British generals were less able than the German. It was that their education was out of date. It was built on the trench warfare of 1914–1918 and not on the armoured warfare they were called upon to direct."[20]

Rommel himself once remarked, "Why should I bother about the superior number of British tanks when their commanders always use them in driblets? Against those driblets I am stronger with my army."

In recent years many people have incorrectly attributed Rommel's success to the superiority of his equipment. This alleged technical superiority of the German Army was a myth, at least before 1944, when the Panzer Mark V (Panther) and Panzer Mark VI (Tiger) tanks made their appearance in significant numbers. Rommel fought his North African battles with the PzKw III and IV model tanks, which were equaled in performance by a number of Allied models and were inferior to the Grants and Shermans, manufactured by the United States and exported to Great Britain. Rommel's chief of Intelligence put it this way: "Contrary to the generally accepted view, the German tanks did not have any advantage in quality over their opponents, and in numbers they were always inferior."[21] He attributed the success of the Afrika Korps to three major factors: the superior quality of German antitank guns, the high level of cooperation achieved by various branches of the German Army, and the magnificent tactical methods employed by the Afrika Korps and the 90th Light Division.[22]

Although Rommel emphasized mobility in his battles, he wasn't blind to the importance of the key position. Strongpoints were created to deny the enemy vital terrain features, such as the Sollum and Halfaya passes. To the recently promoted Major Reverend Bach and his officers, the general said, "Every defended point must be a complete defensive system in itself. Every weapon must be sited so that it is able to fire in every direction. . . . Sufficient water, ammunition, and supplies for three weeks must be available. And every man is to sleep prepared for action. . . .

"The final decision of any struggle if the enemy attacks will probably rest with the panzers and motorized units behind the line. Where the decision is reached is immaterial. A battle is won when the enemy is destroyed. Remember one thing—every individual position must hold, regardless of what the general situation appears to be. Our panzer and motorized formations will not leave you in the lurch, even if you should not see them for weeks. . . ."[23]

While the members of his staff admired Rommel and remained completely loyal to him in spite of pressure from Berlin, there were some areas of disagreement. F. W. von Mellenthin complained: "Rommel had some strange ideas on the principles of staff work. A particularly irksome characteristic was his interference in details which should have been the responsibility of the Chief of Staff. As a rule, Rommel expected his Chief of Staff to accompany him on visits to the front—which frequently meant into the very forefront of the battle. This was contrary to the accepted general staff principle, that the Chief of Staff is deputy of the Commander-in-Chief during the latter's absence. But Rommel liked to have his principal advisor always at his elbow, and if he became a casualty, well——he could always be replaced."[24]

Mellenthin had some reason to complain. A few months later he would find himself with a machine gun in his fists, fighting like a private, hand-to-hand against the Australian infantry. Gause, Westphal, and Bayerlein—all top General Staff officers—would at various times in the months ahead end up in hospitals because they got too close to the action. However, as von Mellenthin stated, they were always replaced.

Rommel himself was almost killed several times on these visits to the front. Once his own men almost did him in. Carell recorded the incident this way: "Time and time again an irresolute commander who had halted his tank would hear a loud knocking against his steel giant. When he opened the turret he would see Lieutenant Baron von Schlippenback, Rommel's aide, using an iron crowbar as a knocker. Crowbars were always carried in Rommel's car. They were the modern counterpart of the Prussian King's cane. Rommel stood up in the car, and as soon as the tank commander appeared in the turret he shouted: 'Get cracking! On your way! Attacks don't succeed by standing still.' On one occasion these exhortations to battle nearly ended in disaster. 'Once more we had approached a halted tank from behind,' Lieutenant von Schlippenbach told me. 'I had already jumped out of the car with my crowbar. At this moment the tank came under fire. The driver put it into reverse and backed into our car. Rommel only just managed to jump out in time.'"[25]

Rommel took great pride in the treatment given by his soldiers to enemy prisoners. He had very strong views on the subject of morality in war and proper military conduct. Afrika Korps troopers were not normally permitted even to deny water to their captives, much less beat or shoot them. Rommel's first friction with Hitler occurred over this point. This friction, which increased as the war went against Germany and Hitler became more and more vicious, escalated until Rommel came to despise the leader he once idolized. One prime example of Hitler's hatred and inhumanity toward enemy prisoners is the Fuehrer Order dated October 18, 1942. It read in part:

> From now on all enemies on so-called commando missions in Europe or Africa challenged by German troops, even if they are to all appearances soldiers in uniform or demolition troops, whether armed or unarmed, in battle or in flight, are to be slaughtered to the last man. . . . Even if these individuals, when found, should apparently be prepared to give themselves up, no pardon is to be granted to them on principle. . . .
>
> I will hold responsible under military law for failing to carry out this order, all commanders and officers who either have neglected their duty of instructing the troops about this order or acted against this order where it is to be executed.
>
> SIGNED: Adolf Hitler

The men of Panzer Group Afrika never read this order. Rommel and Colonel Westphal burned it on the spot. This was a man who had spent 30 years in the German Army, who accepted the principle of unquestioning obedience, and who demanded that his own men follow his orders without question or comment, burning an order that he was obligated by (Nazi) military law to pass on. The incident shows how deep was Rommel's devotion to the proper code of military conduct. He would not abandon it, even if everyone else did. It is also clear that he was beginning to think about the political situation and was beginning to see Hitler for what he was. This process, however, was far from complete in 1941, and the correct conclusions had not yet been drawn. At the moment he was more concerned with the distressing inefficiency of his allied formations.

In 1941, the Italian forces were of doubtful value at best. Their equipment, stratified social classes, and poor leadership resulted in defeat after defeat. They had developed a marked inferiority complex and kept it throughout the war.

Perhaps the most outdated facet of their army, other than their ridiculous tanks, was their class system. The Italian officers' corps went into battle with a huge baggage train. Waiters from the best Roman hotels served as orderlies to higher-ranking officers; even near the front,

Italian generals were waited on hand and foot. There were even mobile officers' brothels for their use in the field. Rommel was especially horrified to learn that the Italians had different field rations for officers, NCOs, and enlisted men, in sharply descending order. While officers received a three-course cooked meal, even in active campaigning, the private had to be content with a can of *Alter Mann,* which was barely edible. The Italian soldiers were shocked to find German generals and German privates eating the same field rations.

The average Italian soldier in North Africa seemed to love Erwin Rommel as much as the average German soldier did. He, at least, seemed to care about them, and what did it hurt if he frequently flew off the handle with the Italian generals? Rommel liked the Italian soldier and had a very high regard for some of their fighter pilots. However, he considered their officers, particularly at the senior levels, worse than useless. For their part, Italian generals found Rommel rude, mean, and overly demanding. Certainly there was no love lost here. One Italian general, Count Ugo Cavellero, fooled Rommel for a time. The count succeeded Badoglio in December 1940 as commander-in-chief of the Army. Rommel liked him because he had beautiful manners and appeared to be competent. Count Galeazzo Ciano, the Italian foreign minister, had a more realistic view. He called Cavallero a "shameless liar, who . . . would bow to the public lavatories if this would advance him. . . ."[26]

Cavallero had a spotted career at best. He had distinguished himself in Italy's war against the Turks in Libya in 1912 and had won the Bronze Medal for Valor. He later served in World War I and as a member of the Versailles Inter-Allied Military Committee after the war. In 1928, however, he resigned all his public offices and became manager of the Ansaldo Shipbuilding Company of Genoa. This company built two of Italy's new 10,000-ton cruisers, *Trento* and *Trieste,* one of which was constructed under Cavellero's supervision. Later it was discovered that both cruisers had been built of ordinary steel rather than the shellproof steel ordered by the Navy. Cavallero would have gone to prison except for the intervention of Costanzo Ciano—the father of the foreign minister. The scandal, however, could not be completely covered up, and Cavallero did not make any further public appearances until he replaced Badoglio.[27]

The appointment of Cavallero took everyone in Italy by surprise. "For the next few days, circles of all classes buzzed with indignation," one American correspondent recalled.[28] Naturally, the Italian Army was

shocked by his selection, which caused a further decline in the troops'
morale.

Rommel, who was not usually deceived for long, soon came to
recognize Cavellero for what he was and came to despise him as much as
Ciano did.

Rommel's view of the Italian people was summed up in one statement:
"Certainly they are no good at war, but one must not judge everyone in
the world only by his qualities as a soldier; otherwise we should have no
civilization."[29] This is a remarkably humane view, considering that it
came from a German professional soldier and a man who was once the
chief bodyguard of Adolf Hitler.

Brigadier Desmond Young described Rommel's attitude toward the
enemy as "friendly, if suspicious, hostility."[30] Upon first encounter, he
considered the Australians the best fighters in the Allies' camp. He
revised this original estimate, however, because they were too rough and
inclined to get out of hand. Still, he regarded them as excellent warriors
and amusing men with good hearts. He seemed to like the men from
"down under" more than any of his other opponents.

General Rommel placed the South Africans in the same general class
but slightly below the Australians. The South Africans were good raw
material, he felt, but not trained well enough to be considered top choice.
He did, however, admire their skillful handling of armored cars, a field in
which they had no equal on either side throughout the Second World
War.

The New Zealanders, Rommel told his son, were the best fighters on
the Allied side.[31] His admiration for them grew with each campaign,
although he really did not understand why they joined the war on the
side of the British in the first place.

As for the Indians, Rommel resented the use of non-European, "non-
Aryan" forces in North Africa. They were well disciplined and "correct,"[32] but the Desert Fox never did think much of the British use of
these colonial troops in a European war.

As for the British themselves, almost always his main opponent until
1944, Rommel admired their courage and tenacity but did not admire
their rigidity of mind, tactical inflexibility, and inadequate training for
modern warfare. The Desert Fox appreciated the fact that the Allies
upheld the principles of humane warfare. Both sides occasionally violated this unwritten code, but such incidents were rare, and then often
accidental. The worst incident occurred when the Free French Brigade

fired on some German prisoners. The South Africans immediately put a halt to this fire, and Rommel either never heard of the incident or, more likely, considered the source and chose to ignore the incident. Certainly the bitterness of these exiles, whose homeland was suffering under the Nazi regime, was understandable. However, when a British order instructed their men not to give water to German prisoners until after they had been interrogated, Rommel became furious. He promptly retaliated by issuing the same order to his soldiers, and he demanded that the Allied commander-in-chief revoke the unlawful brainchild of his staff. The British commander-in-chief, who apparently was unaware of these instructions, did so immediately. British prisoners began to receive water again as soon as the Allied order was canceled.

Rommel's indignation at Allied infractions of the rules of warfare was exceeded only by his anger at the liberties his own allies occasionally took. Certainly Rommel cannot be accused of having a double standard. Desmond Young described an incident that illustrates this point: "Hospital ships were a sore point with Rommel," he wrote. "He became angry when he heard that the Royal Navy was pulling them into Malta for inspection and furious when he heard one of them was strafed by the R.A.F. He became upset when it was reported to him that an Italian general, who feared flying across the Mediterranean, had been taken, unwounded, from a hospital ship at Malta. One day in July [1942], just before El Alamein, three tankers had been sunk in two days. Cavallero, apparently quite proud of himself, informed Rommel that a new method of supplying him had been adopted. Petrol was being sent over on false-bottom hospital ships. Rommel jumped on him immediately. 'How can I protest against British interference with hospital ships when you do things like that?' he barked. Cavallero's feelings were hurt because of this exchange."[33]

While Rommel struggled vainly with his supply problems, the Allies took advantage of the lull to replace the 9th Australian Infantry Division at Tobruk with the British 70th Infantry Division, the 32nd Army Tank Brigade, and the Polish 1st Carpathian Infantry Brigade. The British War Office did not want to make the change at all, but Australian Prime Minister Fadden insisted on the return of Morshead's division. The Japanese were threatening their homeland in the fall of 1941, and the new Prime Minister wanted his troops home. The relief of the Australians came in three shifts. From August 19 to 29 the Royal Navy withdrew the Australian 18th Infantry and Indian 18th Cavalry brigades and landed the Polish Brigade. All operations took place at night, without losing a man. A month later the 16th Infantry Brigade of the 70th Division completed its trip from Syria to Tobruk and relieved the Australian 24th Brigade. At the same time the headquarters of the 32nd Army Tank Brigade and the 4th Royal Tank Regiment were ferried in, again without loss. The third lift, from October 12 to 25, was less successful. All but two Australian infantry battalions were extracted, and the remainder of the 70th Infantry Division was disembarked, but this time the Royal Navy's ships suffered several hits from ground and aircraft fire, and three were sunk: a storeship, a fuel carrier, and a minelayer. Admiral Sir Andrew Cunningham, the commander of the British Mediterranean Fleet, decided it was too risky to continue operations. Still, he had essentially accomplished his mission. The Allied resistance in Tobruk was, if anything, even stiffer than before.[34]

Although the lull put most of the men of Panzer Group Afrika out of danger in the summer of 1941, Rommel himself wanted to return to action as soon as possible. In September he decided to lead a raid into Egypt personally, in hopes of destroying some British supply installations. A kindred soul, Major General Johannes von Ravenstein, decided to accompany him on the foray. Rommel was in high spirits and, according to his aide, looked "like a U-Boat commander on his bridge."[35] However, they found no forward supply dumps. All they captured was a messenger truck with several important codes. Ravenstein was delighted, but Rommel was not. The commander of the 21st Panzer Division tried to cheer up his friend. "Herr General," he exclaimed, "the capture of these documents alone is enough to have justified the expedition." Rommel politely murmured his agreement, but his tone indicated that he did not really believe it.[36]

The RAF responded to the raid by bombing and strafing the raiders on their way back. Yet another one of Rommel's drivers received a critical wound. Rommel "hit the dirt." After the planes left he picked himself up and, to the horror of his men, began to limp. Lieutenant Schmidt rushed up to him. "Are you hurt, Herr General?" he asked.

"I don't feel anything," Rommel replied, patting himself. Further investigation revealed that a bomb splinter had ripped the left heel off his combat boot.[37]

On the way back the general's Mammoth became separated from the rest of the column; then one of its huge tires went flat, the delayed reaction to another bomb splinter, which had struck the tire and gone unnoticed in the excitement. They changed the huge tire, alone and unprotected, at night, with British pursuit forces in the area. It took hours, but Erwin Rommel's luck held again. He eluded his antagonists and reached his own lines at dawn.

This incident further added fuel to the growing legend of Rommel's invincibility. Perhaps the general was growing to believe it himself. He seemed convinced that he could not be killed. Undoubtedly he had a sixth sense for danger. Soon the Allies stood in as much awe of Rommel as did his own men. Like the panzer soldiers, they attributed superhuman powers to him. His men, most of whom were drafted or called up in the usual way, took on all the attitudes of elite, specially trained warriors. They were not any different from the men in other German divisions in 1941, but he made them feel as if they were the pick of the lot, and they loved him for it. Surely, they felt, Erwin Rommel was one of the greatest leaders in history, a pure genius who made the Afrika Korps unbeatable. Some of this emotion crossed the line and infected Allied ranks. It reached the point where the British commander-in-chief had to do something about it. He responded with the famous "Rommel Order." It read:

To all Senior Officers and Department Heads at G.H.Q. and with the Middle East Troops:

There is a real danger that our friend Rommel will become a "bogy man" for our troops in view of the fact that he is so much discussed. However energetic and capable he may be he is no superhuman. Even were he a superman it would be undesireable that our troops should endow him with supernatural attributes. I must beg you to make every effort to destroy the concept that Rommel is anything more than an ordinary German general. Firstly we must stop speaking of Rommel when referring to the enemy in Libya. We must speak of the Germans, the Axis troops or the enemy, but never, in this particular context, of Rommel. I must ask you to see that this order is carried out and that all our junior commanders be instructed that the matter is of great psychological significance.

SIGNED: C. I. Auchinleck

C-in-C Middle East Forces

P.S.: I do not envy Rommel.

Rommel himself found the legend a mixed blessing. In late 1942, when he desperately needed reinforcements but could not get any, he remarked, "At times it is a disadvantage to have a great military reputation. A man usually knows his limitations, whereas others always expect miracles and attribute any defeat to pure malicious intent."[38]

Rommel's popularity with his men, Hitler (during the period of his victories), and the general public helped cause increasing hatred for him to develop among several of the highest-ranking officers at Fuehrer Headquarters. Between him and Colonel General Halder, a mutual dislike had existed for some time. Rommel once called Halder a "bloody fool" to his face and asked him what he had ever done in wartime except sit on his backside in an office chair. For his part, the chief of the General Staff referred to Rommel as "this soldier gone stark mad."[39]

Field Marshal Wilhelm Keitel, the chief of the Armed Forces High Command (OKW), and Colonel General Alfred Jodl, chief of operations at OKW, both thoroughly disliked Rommel. These sentiments were returned in full. Rommel called the trio "chairborne soldiers" and despised them for their subservience to Hitler and the Nazi Party.[40] Halder, Keitel, and Jodl all tried to turn Hitler against Rommel. They also played a major part in keepig North Africa a secondary front, not to be significantly reinforced. North Africa was and would remain a sideshow for Hitler and the High Command, at least until it was too late to win the Desert War.

Rommel did have one friend at Fuehrer Headquarters. Major General Rudolf Schmundt, the chief adjutant of OKW, was handsome, smart, and highly ambitious. Schmundt rose from the rank of major in 1938 to general of infantry in 1944. Apparently he was quite fond of Rommel and was one of the few in Berlin to recognize the strategic possibilities of the North African Front. He even accompanied Rommel to Libya in February 1941. Whenever Rommel wanted something brought directly to Hitler's attention, he either sent Berndt to Germany or wrote directly to Schmundt. Hitler's Army adjutant was to meet a tragic death. On July 20, 1944, he was crippled and blinded by the bomb that was meant to kill Hitler. Two months later Schmundt succumbed to his injuries, only one month before his friend Rommel met his own tragic end.

7

Sidi Rezegh

The German situation in Africa in late 1941 was as follows: Rommel's successes had been brilliant, but he had extended his resources to the limit. The failure to capture Tobruk had left the Axis forces without a port close to the front. Benghazi, a badly damaged port, was 300 miles away, and Tripoli was 1,000 miles to the west. Important German and Italian units were tied up in the siege of Tobruk. An enemy offensive, coupled with a simultaneous attack from Tobruk, would place Rommel in an extremely critical position. The British, Rommel correctly guessed, would not shift their Middle Eastern reserves from Palestine to the Libyan-Egyptian front as long as the German armies in Russia threatened them with a possible invasion through the Caucasus Mountains. In November this threat receded as Hitler's legions advanced northward from Kiev, toward Moscow and their destiny. Rommel now expected the offensive to come in the last half of November. Characteristically, he planned to forestall it with an offensive of his own. However, another battle of an entirely different nature was already raging. This was the battle for supplies, and the German-Italian forces were losing it.

As the bulk of Hitler's Wehrmacht raced across Russia in the summer and fall of 1941, less and less could be spared for the North African Front. As they became obsessed with the fighting in the East, the High Command in Berlin came more and more to view the Desert War as a sideshow. Rommel could not muster the necessary strength to capture Tobruk, which was the key to freedom of maneuver for Panzer Group Afrika. The fortress tied down the four divisions of the Italian XXI Infantry Corps as well as three battalions of German soldiers. Without the port of Tobruk and the forces it tied down, Rommel was too weak to invade Egypt and capture the vital Suez Canal and the oilfields beyond. Even if he had had the required manpower, he lacked the fuel, ammunition, food, and other supplies essential for an offensive. The major reason for these deficiencies was the British air and naval base at Malta.

Until the beginning of the Balkan campaign in the spring of 1941, Malta had been relatively ineffective as an Allied base. The Luftwaffe's X Air Corps dominated the skies and held Allied pressure on Rommel's supply lines to a minimum. Then the X Air Corps was shifted to the East, to support Hitler's invasion of Yugoslavia and Greece. After Athens and Belgrade fell, the airmen were left in the Balkans, "against all sensible advice to the contrary," as General Warlimont of the High Command remarked.[1] This comment came from an orthodox member of the General Staff and certainly not a friend of Rommel's. Still, the vacuum created by the departure of the air corps was not filled for several months. As a result, the Royal Navy and Air Force were gradually able to reassert their control over the central Mediterranean.

In July the forces on the island became active again, and Rommel lost 17 percent of his assigned supplies to Allied attacks. In August, British warships, aircraft, and submarines operating out of Malta sank 35 percent of the supplies bound for Panzer Group Afrika. In September they increased this percentage to 38, and in October they destroyed a whopping 63 percent of the tonnage sent to North Africa. Only 18,500 tons arrived in Tripoli and Benghazi that month. A supply ship departing Genoa or Naples now had less than a 50–50 chance of reaching Libya.[2] It was small wonder that the Italian merchant marine was reluctant to leave port. The length of his supply line in Libya further added to Rommel's problems. He found that he had to expend 10 percent of his total fuel supply just to get the remaining 90 percent to the front. Thirty-five percent of his transport vehicles were undergoing or awaiting repair at all times: They were simply being worn out by the constant 1,000-mile one-way trips from the main supply base to the forward units.[3]

The troops' rations, which were already bad enough, became even worse. Rommel, who had no control over the Luftwaffe or the Italian Navy, was powerless to stop the deterioration of his group's position. He could only fume in his tent while the Allies, unhindered, built up vast stockpiles of materiel and filled their assembly areas with fresh units. Colonel Bayerlein summed it up later when he wrote: "By the end of September only a third of the troops and a seventh of the supplies which we needed had arrived. This was a terrible handicap in our race for time with the British."[4]

Things were no better in November than they had been the previous month as far as the supply race was concerned. On the night of November 8–9, a seven-ship merchant convoy, protected by two heavy Italian cruisers and six destroyers, was attacked and wiped out by two British light cruisers and two destroyers. Of the Italian escort vessels, one destroyer was sunk and another was damaged. Thirty-nine thousand more tons of supplies went to the bottom. This exceeded the Axis supply losses for the entire month of October and was approximately equal to the amount Rommel received in September and October. The British suffered no casualties in this naval engagement.[5]

Disasters of this type left little doubt in anyone's mind who controlled the central Mediterranean in late 1941. The fact that the Italian Navy outnumbered the Royal Navy in almost every category testifies to the inefficiency of the former and the skill of the latter. Table 5 gives a more exact breakdown of naval strength in terms of battleships, aircraft carriers, etc.

The naval disaster of November 8–9 prompted Hitler to take some action to restore the balance of power in the central Mediterranean, or face the risk of losing Panzer Group Afrika to starvation. He withdrew the 2nd Air Fleet from the Russian Front and sent it to Italy. On November 28 he named the fleet commander, Field Marshal Albert Kesselring, to the newly created post of commander-in-chief for the South. The energetic Kesselring, one of Germany's best officers, soon set out to redress the balance of power over the sea lanes. By the time his main force arrived, however, it was too late to help Rommel take Tobruk, because the British Winter Offensive was already well underway. Rommel faced it with less than 15 percent of the ammunition and fuel he needed.[6]

Rommel flew to Germany in late July. The purpose of the trip was to discuss his latest ideas with Hitler and the High Command. Rommel spent July 29 and 30 with his family at Wiener Neustadt. Lucie was horrified at his physical condition. The desert was especially tough on him, because Erwin Rommel was no longer a young man. His skin was yellow and his complexion unhealthy. She urged him to go to a doctor, but he refused. "I don't trust doctors," he half joked. "In 1915 they wanted to amputate my leg!" On the last day of July he ended his brief vacation and flew to Fuehrer Headquarters, the Wolf's Lair, in East Prussia.[7]

Table 5

Naval Strength in the Mediterranean, November 1941

Type of Vessel	Italian	German	British Med. Fleet Alexandria	British Force K Malta	British Force H Gibraltar
Battleships	5	0	3	0	1
Aircraft carriers	0	0	0	0	1
Heavy cruisers	3	0	0	0	0
Light cruisers	8	0	6–8	2–4	1
Destroyers	34	0	21	0	7
Submarines	46	6	11	12	6

Source: Warlimont, p. 186.

Rommel presented his strategic plans for the rest of 1941 to the Fuehrer and the top Nazi generals on August 1. He called for the capture of Tobruk and the seizure of Cairo and Alexandria, along with the Suez Canal. He would not stop here, however: the Afrika Korps would drive on to the Persian Gulf via Syria, thus dealing a crippling blow to the British Empire.

General Halder naturally denounced the scheme as impossible. It turned out to be exactly what General Sir Claude Auchinleck, the Allied commander-in-chief for the Middle East, feared most. The British were extremely weak in Syria, Iraq, and Persia. Cyprus also lay vulnerable to an airborne attack. Auchinleck was praying that the Nazis would not adopt the very strategic plans that Rommel was advocating. Auchinleck's prayers, of course, were answered: Rommel's ideas were rejected out of hand.[8] This conference does, however, demonstrate that Rommel had a much greater strategic grasp than he is commonly given credit for.

Not only did Rommel return from Europe empty-handed, he also almost got killed in the process. On the flight back, his airplane developed engine trouble and had to land in Athens for repairs. He spent the night of August 7 in the Greek capital, but he was kept up all night by an enemy air raid. The plane was still not functioning properly the next day when it landed in Bardia, Libya, near Rommel's forward headquarters. Later that day, while Rommel was conferring with Italian Marshals Cavallero and Bastico, he learned that the same plane had taken off again and crashed, killing everyone on board. "Just goes to show how quickly it can come to you," he wrote Lucie.[9]

Perhaps because of his wife's urging, or perhaps because of his close call with death in the airplane, Rommel went to see the Army doctors in August. They told him he had jaundice and prescribed a bland diet with much bed rest. Rommel went on the diet but ignored the rest of their advice. In September he contracted one of the "bugs" that commonly afflict soldiers in the field. "It's going to be the usual three-day race," he wrote Lucie. When word leaked to the troops that he was sick, they brought him gifts of fruit, eggs, live chickens, and other luxuries, which they purchased from the Arabs with their own money.[10] No matter what the High Commands in Rome and Berlin thought of him, there was no doubt about his men's devotion.

As if jaundice and the British weren't enough, Rommel was now involved in yet another of his periodic battles with the General Staff. Instead of being given the green light to advance on the Persian Gulf, he had a very hard time even obtaining permission to attack Tobruk again. Hitler, Jodl, Halder, von Brauchitsch, and Italian Marshal Bastico, Rommel's nominal superior, all opposed making the effort before January 1942. The top brass remained preoccupied with the Russian invasion, which was rapidly bogging down in the snow and mud of the Eastern Front. Hitler and Jodl told Rommel to prepare to repulse the British Winter Offensive, which Auchinleck was obviously preparing to launch in the near future.

The Luftwaffe also opposed the Tobruk venture. It seemed as if everybody was against it, except for Rommel. When the German Air Force sent him aerial photographs of the railroad the British were building west of Mersa Matruh, Egypt, Rommel flung them to the ground. "I will not look at them!" he shouted at General von Ravenstein. He categorically refused to accept the finality of Hitler's order and, with the commander of the 21st Panzer Division, flew to Rome to get it revoked.[11]

Rommel's first stop was the office of Lieutenant General Enno von Rintelen, the German military attaché in Rome. Here Rommel "blew his top." He called Rintelen a coward and a "friend of the Italians," which the Desert Fox seemed to consider synonymous. Obviously Rommel believed von Rintelen had played a part in the rejection of his strategic plans.[12]

Next Rommel phoned Colonel General Jodl in Berlin. "I hear that you wish me to give up the attack on Tobruk," Rommel said. "I am completely disgusted." Jodl brought up the subject of the coming Allied offensive. Rommel replied that he had the commander of the 21st Panzer Division with him. Major General von Ravenstein and his men would hold off the British while Rommel stormed Tobruk with the rest of the Afrika Korps. As usual, Jodl covered himself. "Can you guarantee that there is no danger?" the OKW operations officer asked. "I will give you my personal guarantee!" Rommel replied, emphatically. With this promise Jodl relented. Rommel scheduled the attack for November 23.[13]

Since it was already mid-November, Rommel decided to mix business with pleasure and remain in Rome for his birthday, November 15. Frau Rommel and Countess von Ravenstein joined their husbands in the Eternal City. Later, while their men attended to business, the two ladies went sight-seeing together. They rejoined the generals for lunch at the Hotel Eden a few hours later. The women were quite excited about the wonders of St. Peter's and the other sites they had seen. Rommel listened to them for some time without comment. Then he turned to his deputy and said, "You know, von Ravenstein, I have been thinking again about what we ought to do with those infantry battalions. . . ."[14]

Although he did not go sight-seeing, Rommel did take in a movie at the invitation of the Italian High Command. The film, entitled *On to Benghazi,* showed the victorious Italians, unaided by the Germans, charging forward while the disorganized British panicked and fled before them. "Very interesting and instructive," commented the sarcastic Swabian. "I often wondered what happened in that battle."[15]

If Rommel was preoccupied by the present situation in North Africa, he had good reason to be. The race for the initiative was reaching its climax. If the British struck first, the attack on Tobruk would have to be postponed indefinitely. If the Germans struck first, they might be able to take the fortress before the British Winter Offensive began. If they could do so, the four divisions and various other units employed in the seige could be used against Auchinleck's main thrust. Equally important, the threat to Rommel's rear would be eliminated. There was, however, a third and extremely dangerous possibility. If Auchinleck attacked while Rommel was decisively engaged in the assault on Tobruk, the Eighth Army could take him in the rear. This would mean a severe if not decisive defeat for the Afrika Korps. Conceivably the bulk of the assault force could be surrounded between the strong garrison and the Eighth Army. This possibility is why Hitler, Jodl, Keitel, Halder, Bastico, and all the rest wanted the Desert Fox to defeat the Eighth Army first, then turn on

Tobruk. Naturally, however, Rommel set his own course and opted for taking the risk, no matter who disagreed with him or how violently.

The Italian ground commanders in North Africa also feared a major British offensive. To quiet their apprehensions, Rommel ordered his officers to adopt a tone of confidence in all discussions with the Italians. Although he denied the possibility when in the presence of Mussolini's officers, Rommel's chief of Intelligence was also quite concerned over the threat of a major Allied attack in the very near future.[16]

The British Secret Service played a decisive part in forestalling the German attack on Tobruk. They delivered a map to General Auchinleck that showed all of Rommel's plans and the units involved. It had been drawn by the Desert Fox himself! How they obtained it is still a mystery, but it caused Auchinleck greatly to speed up his offensive preparations. With his superior logistical resources, Auchinleck was able to win the supply race against Panzer Group Afrika. He stood ready to attack several days before the Germans. For once in his life, Erwin Rommel would not get in the first blow.

Paul Carell, a noted German author, implies that the Italians betrayed this and other vital secrets to the Allies. He states that Italian Admiral Maugeri was a British agent and that he and other traitors were the major reason that 75 percent of the supplies dispatched from Italian ports during the war were sunk.[17]

The British Secret Service found the Italian councils easy to infiltrate for a number of reasons. Primary among these was the Royalist officers' corps, which hated Mussolini and the Fascists, whom they looked upon with disdain. They also disliked the Germans in general and Rommel in particular. Many senior Italian officers were jealous of him for his numerous victories over foes they could never come close to defeating. Other Italians were offended by Rommel's tactless manner and, as noted before, not without reason.

General Auchinleck, who was a much better commander than he is commonly given credit for, laid a trap for Rommel. Auchinleck wanted to delay the start of his offensive until the Desert Fox was decisively engaged outside of Tobruk; then he would strike and take Panzer Group Afrika in the rear. However, like Rommel, he was overruled by his chief. Churchill was overeager again. He set November 18 as the starting date and insisted that the Allied commander-in-chief stick to it, no matter what. This inflexible timetable severely hamstrung Auchinleck and his men, for a rare desert rainstorm took place on the night of November 17–18. The bad weather denied the Allies the air support they needed on the critical first day of the battle.[18]

As the time for battle grew nearer, Major General Walter Neumann-Silkow, the commander of the 15th Panzer Division, attended to the final details of his carefully laid plan to storm Tobruk. For this assignment he was given his own unit and the 90th Light Division under the command of Major General Max Summermann. They would be supported by a strong artillery force of 461 guns under Panzer Group Afrika's chief of artillery, Major General Karl Boettcher.[19]

The major problem in the assault force, as in the rest of the Afrika Korps, was disease. Outbreaks of dysentery, jaundice, and scurvy had reduced some units to skeleton organizations. The 15th Panzer was at 50 percent of its assigned strength, mainly due to illness. The German forces facing the Eighth Army and the Tobruk garrison were much weaker than they had been in June. This was a major factor in Rommel's decision to set the date for the Tobruk assault as late as he did.[20] He did not know it yet, but this decision postponed it permanently.

Following the defeat of Operation "Battleaxe," Auchinleck reorganized his command in preparation for another offensive. The commander-in-chief for the Middle East created two new armies: the Ninth in the Palestine-Transjordan area, and the Eighth in Egypt. General Sir Maitland Wilson was named commander of the Ninth Army, and General Sir Alan Cunningham, the brother of Admiral Sir Andrew Cunningham, was given the Eighth. Churchill wanted to name Wilson commander of the Eighth Army, but Auchinleck preferred Cunningham, so the Prime Minister let him have his way. The Western Desert Force was redesignated the XIII Corps and subordinated to the Eighth Army. The unlucky Lieutenant General Sir Noel Beresford-Peirse was given command of the Sudan and replaced at the XIII Corps by Lieutenant General A. R. Godwin-Austen the former commander of the 12th African Division, effective September 18.[21]

Two other British corps headquarters were activated in the Western Desert in the autumn of 1941. The XXX Corps' headquarters, staffed mainly by officers from the 2nd Armoured Division, was designated to control British armor. Its first commander was Lieutenant General V. V. Pope, a tank expert and former director of the Armoured Fighting Vehicles Department in the War Office. Unfortunately, Pope and two of his senior staff officers, Brigadiers Russell and Unwin, were killed in an airplane crash on October 5. Pope was succeeded by Major General C. Willoughby M. Norrie, the commander of the 1st Armoured Division, which was just beginning to arrive in Egypt.[22]

The British X Corps under Lieutenant General W. G. Holmes was also brought to Egypt to construct a last-ditch Allied defensive line at El Alamein; however, after new British reinforcements landed and the Allies prepared for their own offensive, the X Corps was stripped of its troops units and its headquarters was transferred to the Ninth Army in Syria.[23]

While Auchinleck and Cunningham reorganized and made ready, Churchill sent them forces, equipment, and supplies of every description. The threat of a Nazi invasion of Britain had disappeared in 1941 as the RAF checked the Luftwaffe and Hitler gambled everything on his invasion of Russia. With the Wehrmacht thus tied down, Churchill poured everything he could into Egypt, including a goodly quantity of supplies and equipment from the theoretically neutral United States. From July until the end of October, for example, the Eighth Army received 300 British cruiser (main battle) tanks, 300 American Stuart tanks, 170 "I" (infantry) tanks, 34,000 trucks, 600 field guns, 80 heavy anti-aircraft guns, and 900 mortars, plus other equipment. Cunningham was also reinforced by the South African 1st and 2nd Infantry divisions, the British 70th Infantry Division, the newly organized 1st and 32nd Army Tank brigades, the New Zealand 2nd Infantry Division, and other units. The 22nd Armoured Brigade of the 1st Armoured Division also arrived, and the rest of the division was en route when the offensive began. The RAF was also reinforced. Rommel would be at a disadvantage in all material categories when the British Winter Offensive began.[24]

While he organized and trained his reinforcements, Cunningham made sure Rommel's reconnaissance pilots and scouts remained ignorant of his dispositions and plans. The RAF had air superiority on the frontier (as Rommel had almost died confirming) and was strengthened to maintain it. Until August, the Egyptian side of the border was screened by the 22nd Guards Brigade and the 7th Support Group. Beginning in early September, however, Major General F. W. Messervy of the mobile Indian 4th Infantry Division took command of all Allied forces on the frontier. He was gradually reinforced by the Indian 5th, 7th, and 11th brigades. Since Rommel had only two ground reconnaissance battalions, acquiring useful tactical intelligence became very, very difficult.

Behind this screen, Cunningham made his plans for the relief of Tobruk. He gave all three armored brigades to the XXX Corps, which was to cross the frontier on the desert flank between Sidi Omar and Fort Maddalena and attack northwest toward Tobruk. This move would force Rommel to engage them in a decisive armored battle early in the campaign, or so the British thought. Meanwhile, the XIII Corps on the coastal flank would cover the Eighth Army's supply bases and pin down the frontier garrisons while Scobie would break out on General Norrie's command and link up with the XXX Corps in the vicinity of Sidi Rezegh after the Afrika Korps had been decisively engaged. The 4th Armoured Brigade, on the right flank of the XXX Corps, would protect the left flank of the XIII Corps from the German panzers. Table 6 shows the Eighth Army's order of battle.

The British plan was basically bad. The XIII and XXX corps—one heavy in infantry and the other heavy in armor—could not support each other, and their very compositions violated the principle of the combined-arms force. As usual, Allied tanks would be insufficiently supported by infantry, and the foot soldiers would be unprotected by tanks.

Rommel's initial dispositions were also weak because he had concentrated his main forces for the Tobruk assault, not for a major offensive from the opposite direction. The Italian Savona Division, backed up by strong German detachments with their 88's, held the frontier area, while the 21st Panzer Division guarded the area south of Gambut, ready to deal with any Allied move to interfere with the Tobruk attack. The 15th Panzer and 90th Light divisions were already in their jump-off areas, but Neumann-Silkow had orders to be ready to support von Ravenstein's men on 24 hours' notice. The 90th Light was of limited use at this time because most of its heavy equipment and transport had not been shipped from Naples. The XX Italian Motorized Corps (Ariete Armored and Trieste Motorized divisions) concentrated to the south, at Bir el Gubi and Bir Hacheim, respectively, but the XX Corps was not under Rommel's command. The gap from Bir el Gubi to Sidi Omar, between the 21st Panzer Division and the XX Motorized Corps, was screened by the 3rd and 33rd Reconnaissance battalions. General Navarrini's XXI Italian Infantry Corps, consisting of the Trento, Bologna, Brescia, and Pavia Infantry divisions, lay siege to Tobruk and was supported by elements of the 90th Light Division when the offensive began.[25]

In total armored strength, which would be the deciding factor in almost any desert battle, Rommel was badly outnumbered. According

Table 6

British Eighth Army Order of Battle, November 1941

Eighth Army—General Sir Alan Cunningham
XXX Corps—Lieutenant General C. W. M. Norrie
   7th Armoured Division—Major General W. H. E. Gott
      7th Armoured, 22nd Armoured, and 4th Armoured
      brigades; 7th Support Group
   South African 1st Infantry Division—Major General
   G. L. Brink
      South African 1st and 5th Infantry brigades
   22nd Guards Brigade—Brigadier J. C. O. Marriott

XIII Corps—Lieutenant General A. R. Godwin-Austen
   New Zealand 2nd Infantry Division—Major General
   B. C. Freyberg
      New Zealand 4th, 5th, and 6th Infantry brigades
   Indian 4th Infantry Division—Major General F. W.
   Messervy
      Indian 5th, 7th, and 11th Infantry brigades
   1st Army Tank Brigade—Brigadier H. R. B. Watkins

Tobruk Garrison—Major General R. M. Scobie
   70th Infantry Division—Major General Scobie
      British 14th, 16th, and 23rd Infantry brigades
   Polish 1st Carpathian Infantry Brigade—Major General
   S. Kopanski
   32nd Army Tank Brigade—Brigadier A. C. Willison

Army Reserve—
   South African 2nd Infantry Division—Major General
   I. P. de Villiers
      South African 3rd, 4th, and 6th Infantry brigades
   Indian 29th Infantry Brigade—Brigadier D. W. Reid

to Major General von Mellenthin, Panzer Group Afrika's Ic, the British had 748 tanks: 213 Matildas and Valentines, 220 Crusaders, 150 other heavy cruiser-model tanks, and 165 lightweight American Stuart tanks, which the British used as main-battle tanks in Operation "Crusader," as their offensive was code-named. Panzer Group Afrika, on the other hand, could commit only 249 German and 146 Italian tanks. These figures do not include the Italian L-3 or the British Mark VIB light tanks, which had only machine guns and were, in von Mellenthin's words, "quite useless."[26]

Lieutenant General (then Colonel) Fritz Bayerlein placed Rommel's tank strength at 414 (260 of which were of German manufacture) with none in reserve, except for 50 tanks in the repair shops. The British, he added, had 724 tanks on the front line, with some 200 in reserve.[27] Although the exact totals differ somewhat, the panzers must have been outnumbered by nearly 3 to 1.

The British *Official History* gives a slightly different picture, as Tables 7 and 8 indicate. According to Major General I. S. O. Playfair, the Eighth Army had 477 tanks in the main strike force, 261 in the Army tank brigades, 259 in reserve, and 236 en route to Egypt, or a total of 997, excluding those at sea. They opposed 244 tanks in the Afrika Korps and 146 limited-value Italian M13/40 medium tanks, as well as 162 useless Italian light tanks.[28]

The Italian M13/40, which weighed only 13½ tons, had a small 47mm main battle gun and was too lightly armored; also, its plates tended to crack when hit by almost anything. Its cross-country speed in the desert was only eight miles per hour, and it presented an extremely vulnerable target for the British;[29] nevertheless, it was probably Italy's best tank.

The Panzer Mark II (PzKw II) was scarcely better. The J model (PzKw IIj) weighed only 10½ tons and had very thin armor. It was, in

Table 7

Axis Tank Strength by Unit and Model, November 17, 1941

Unit	PzKw II	PzKw III	PzKw IV	M13/40	Totals
15 Panzer Div.	38	75	20		133
21st Panzer Div.	32	64	15		111
Ariete Armored Div.	—	—	—	146	146*
Totals	70	139	35	146	390*

*Excludes 52 Italian light tanks with Ariete and 110 light tanks distributed among the other Italian divisions.

Reserves: none.

Source: Playfair, III, p. 30.

fact, good only for reconnaissance. Seventy of the Afrika Korps' 244 tanks were, therefore, virtually useless in an armored battle.

Rommel's Panzer Mark IV's (PzKw IV's) were essentially infantry-support tanks, sporting a low-velocity 75mm gun that could shell enemy positions at ranges of up to 3,000 yards, even when on the move. It was faster than most British tanks and had equal armored protection. Also, like the PzKw III, its armor was face-hardened, while the British armor was not.

The workhorse of the Afrika Korps was the Panzer Mark III (PzKw III), which fired a 4½-pound armor-piercing shell from a 50mm gun. It had fairly thick armor (62mm) and averaged 12 miles an hour in cross-desert speed, which was equal to or better than all British tanks of the time, except the Stuarts, which were American-made.

Contrary to popular opinion, the Allied tanks were not greatly inferior to the panzers technologically. The British tanks fell into two

Table 8

British Tank Strength by Unit and Model, November 1941

Unit	Various early Cruisers	A-13 Cruisers	Crusaders	Stuarts	Total
HQ, XXX Corps				8	8
HQ, 7th Armoured Div.	6		2		8
4th Armoured Bde.				165	165
7th Armoured Bde.	26	62	53		141
22nd Armoured Bde.			155		155
Totals	32	62	210	173	477

1st Army Tank Brigade: 3 cruisers, 132 "I" tanks (approximately half Matildas, half Valentines).

32nd Army Tank Brigade: 32 assorted cruisers, 25 light tanks, 69 Matildas.

Reserves in Egypt: 92 cruisers (mostly the latest-model Crusaders), 90 Stuarts, 77 "I" tanks.

Reserves at sea (en route to Egypt): 124 Crusaders, 60 Stuarts, 52 "I" tanks.

Source: Playfair, III, pp. 27–44.

classes: the main battle or "cruiser" types and the infantry-support or "I" tanks, almost all of which were in the 1st or 32nd Army Tank brigades.

The heavy Matilda (26½ tons, or 6½ tons heavier than the PzKw IIIh) had 78mm of armor protection and had a 2-pounder main battle gun, like almost all British-made tanks in Egypt in late 1941. Its problem was speed: It averaged only six miles per hour across the desert, which was a rate even slower than that of the Italian M13/40.[30]

The Matilda was gradually replaced by the Valentine, which was originally a cruiser. It weighed 16 tons, had 65mm of armored protection, and averaged eight miles per hour in the desert.[31]

The main British cruiser was the Crusader, which weighed 19 tons, or five more than the older Cruiser A-13, which was being phased out. The Crusader fired a two-pounder, had 49mm of armored protection, and equaled the PzKw III's and IV's in speed. The Crusader's defect was its mechanical unreliability, as we shall see.

The newest British cruiser was the American M-3 Stuart or "Honey" tank, which was originally designed as a light or reconnaissance tank. It weighed only 12½ tons, had a 44mm armored thickness, and fired a 37mm main battle gun, which was slightly better than the 2-pounder.[32] It was the fastest tank on the desert in 1941 but was hampered by a short operating radius of only about 80 miles; nevertheless, the British tank crews loved it for its mechanical reliability, for it almost never broke down. The 4th Armoured Brigade was equipped entirely with this new tank.

The Allies also had another extremely valuable advantage in November 1941: limited air superiority. The Desert Air Force outnumbered the Luftwaffe 650 to 120 in aircraft. The Axis did have 200 Italian airplanes, but these were of no great value.

The RAF began using its advantages weeks ahead of the ground offensive by smashing Rommel's exposed supply lines. In September they bombed Naples on 12 consecutive nights and Tripoli on eight consecutive nights, often using 4,000-pound bombs. They also blasted Benghazi, Derna, and other supply points as well as the Mediterranean shipping lanes. In October, for example, five of the seven Axis ships sunk that month were done in by the RAF.[33] This Allied air superiority was of no use to the British on the all-important first day of the offensive, however, for the elements were against the RAF. The heavy rainstorms of November 18 grounded them.

The cloudburst, a rarity in the desert, was the worst in 60 years. Large elements of the 15th Panzer Division fell victim to a flash flood. Many men drowned—in the middle of the Sahara Desert. Tents and their occupants were swept away, while trucks and guns were overturned and buried in the sandy water. Mudslides and small avalanches caused protective minefields to blow up on their own. The 15th Panzer was severely damaged, crippled by nature on the very eve of the Allied offensive.[34]

Hundreds of miles away, the storm interfered with another drama. The British Secret Service had long been obsessed with a desire to rid themselves of their archopponent. Now they put into operation what they hoped would be their crowning achievement in the Desert War: They would eliminate Erwin Rommel on the very night the great Winter Offensive began. According to the Allied scenario, this would certainly cause the eventual defeat of the Afrika Korps and signal the beginning of the end of the Axis Empire in North Africa. They had discovered that Rommel's headquarters was located at Beda Littoria, a beautiful villa miles behind the lines, and they devised a daring plot to assassinate or kidnap him.

The man picked to lead the raid on Rommel's headquarters was Colonel Laycock, the commander of the Scottish commandoes. The assault group, which would actually seize the villa, was to be commanded by Lieutenant Colonel Geoffrey Keyes, the elder son of Admiral of the Fleet Sir Roger Keyes, a Member of Parliament. Geoffrey Keyes' men were the pick of the crop. After weeks of intensive training the best 50 commandoes in the British Empire were selected and transported by submarine to the Libyan coast. There, on the night of November 17–18, they surfaced in the middle of the storm. The sea was so rough that Colonel Laycock's group could not get off the submarine. On shore Geoffrey Keyes found he had only 28 men with him. He decided to continue the mission without any security element.[35]

The storm provided a perfect cover for Keyes' approach march to Beda Littoria. He decided that he, his second-in-command (Captain Campbell), and seven men would attack right through the main entrance, kill the guards with knives, and proceed upstairs to their rendezvous with General Rommel. If the decision to kill the Desert Fox had not been made previously, it was certainly made by this point. They could no longer expect to take him alive. The rest of Keyes' group would either provide covering fire from outside, or join a second raiding party, which would enter through the back doorway. They did not know that a German soldier had pushed a heavy water barrel against this entrance.

Despite all their efforts, this second unit never managed to break into the house and join the fighting. Keyes went into the building with eight men, all he would ever have to accomplish his mission.[36]

The headquarters staff considered Beda Littoria too far behind the lines to necessitate posting sentries. A lone military policeman was at the door. His duty was to accept late mail and to assign rooms to visitors who arrived late at night. Although unarmed, this anonymous warrior was quick, strong, and very brave. This combination proved fatal for Colonel Keyes. The first commando's knife only wounded the German MP. He blocked the corridor, grabbed the would-be killer, and cried out. A hand-to-hand struggle developed. The noise and screams woke up the noncommissioned officers who slept in the munitions office. One of them grasped the situation at a glance and started shooting at the British. A bullet struck Keyes in the thigh. Coolly the English colonel ignored the wound and tossed a hand grenade into the office. The ensuing blast put the NCO's out of action.[37]

Although he still had the element of surprise, Keyes had lost secrecy, and the stairs were yet to be reached. For Geoffrey Keyes, they were a lifetime away.

The struggle in the hall aroused a staff officer named Lieutenant Kaufholz, who had not yet gone to sleep. He grabbed his pistol and rushed to the head of the stairs just as Keyes threw his grenade. The light from the explosion revealed the figures of Keyes and Campbell in the dark hall. The German lieutenant did not hesitate: He fired a bullet right into the colonel's chest. The commando leader let out a short cry of pain and collapsed. Captain Campbell immediately opened up with his machine gun. The staircase splintered, and Kaufholz was hit in several vital spots. As he fell in his death throes, the young officer fired again, probably by reflex. This bullet, shot wild by a dying man, landed in the center of Campbell's leg, completely shattering his shinbone. This lucky shot left the British without a leader. The surviving commandoes fled, killing two more Germans as they retreated. The Allies suffered only one fatal casualty: Colonel Geoffrey Keyes lay dead on the villa floor, with a Luger bullet in his heart.[38]

Only three of the raiders ever made it back to friendly lines. The rest were betrayed by the Arabs, at a rate of 80 pounds of corn and 20 pounds of flour for each commando they turned in. The commandoes were treated as prisoners of war and were marched off to POW camps. Colonel Keyes, Lieutenant Kaufholz, and three other dead Germans were buried at Beda Littoria with full military honors.[39]

The irony of the raid was that the commandoes attacked the wrong target. True, Rommel had once used the villa as his headquarters, but he did not like to headquarter so far from the men he would have to lead in battle. He had moved twice since leaving Beda Littoria in August 1941. Even if this had been his temporary home, he would have been absent, since he was still on his way back from Rome. The villa at Beda Littoria had long since been occupied by members of the quartermaster's staff. All of these moves had gone unobserved by the British Secret Service.

During the night of November 17–18, the armor of the British XXX Corps marched to its jump-off points. While on the march, and long before they met the enemy, the 7th Armoured Brigade lost 22 of its 141 tanks due to breakdowns; the 22nd lost 19 of its 155 tanks for the same reason. The mechanical unreliability of the British cruisers was showing itself already. Only the 4th Armoured Brigade—with its M-3 Stuarts— did not report equipment trouble.[40] They surprised the Germans for a number of reasons when they crossed the frontier that night. British camouflage, dispersion, and radio discipline were excellent, while the bad weather and low cloud cover grounded the Luftwaffe. Early on the morning of November 18 they clashed with elements of the German reconnaissance battalions and the Italian Savona Division. In doing so they started a desert battle of unprecedented fury that lasted, with a few minor pauses, for three weeks. Of this fight, Brigadier Desmond Young later wrote:

> It was a real soldier's battle, a "proper dog-fight," like those great aerial mix-ups which we used to watch over the lines in 1918. It was fought at such speed, with such swiftly-changing fortune, under such a cloud of smoke from bursting shells and burning tanks, such columns of dust from careering transport, in such confusion of conflicting reports, that no one knew what was happening a mile away. Even to-day it is hard to follow. . . . [41]

This last remark is an understatement. Of all of Rommel's battles, this is the most complicated and most difficult to describe.

Rommel at first refused to believe that the British offensive had begun. He was a somewhat bullheaded man and was preoccupied with planning his own assault on Tobruk. On this occasion he let his stubborn streak affect his flexibility and dogmatically insisted that the British would not attack long after they had, in fact, crossed the wire. The commander of the 21st Panzer Division was more perceptive. On November 18, as British radio silence continued for the second consecutive day, Major General von Ravenstein grew quite nervous, for he correctly guessed that this represented the calm before the storm. Soon his fears were confirmed. Colonel von Wechmar reported that the 3rd Reconnaissance Battalion was being attacked by 200 enemy armored vehicles. The 33rd Reconnaissance Battalion was also engaged.[42] Ravenstein visited Cruewell, who, in turn, called on his chief. In the ensuing conference, Rommel became irritated. "We must not lose our nerve," he snapped at the commander of the Afrika Korps. Perhaps the fact that he had only just returned from Europe also affected his judgment.[43] He had left Rome early on November 16, but a thunderstorm forced him to spend the night in Belgrade. The next day his airplane developed engine trouble, and he had to lay over in Athens the night of November 17–18. It was sometime on November 18 before Rommel made it back to his headquarters.[44] No sooner than he got back Cruewell entered with his startling news. Rommel brushed it aside. He steadfastly refused to believe that his Tobruk assault had been spoiled.[45]

It had been, even if Rommel as yet refused to admit it. Ravenstein's men fought well but were no match for the bulk of the Eighth Army. Doggedly they were pushed back to the Bir el Gubi–Sidi Omar line (see Map 5). The hard-pressed commander called for immediate reinforcements. On the morning of November 19 General Cruewell reappeared at Rommel's door, this time determined to make him see sense. Cruewell reported that German forces had been driven across the Trigh el Abd* by strong British armored forces. The tough Rhinelander told his boss that he (Rommel) had been wrong the day before when he insisted that the British move represented only a reconnaissance in force. This indeed was a major offensive. Cruewell's arguments received a boost from an unexpected source: the enemy news media. The British Broadcasting Corporation in Cairo aired an interesting news item. "The 8th Army," the announcer said, "with about 75,000 men excellently armed and equipped, have started a general offensive in the Western Desert with the aim of destroying the German-Italian forces in Africa."[46] Reluctantly, Rommel faced facts. He agreed to order the 15th Panzer Division to assemble south of Gambut, where it could aid the embattled 21st. This move was tantamount to canceling the Tobruk assault altogether.

---

*A *trigh* is an unimproved road.

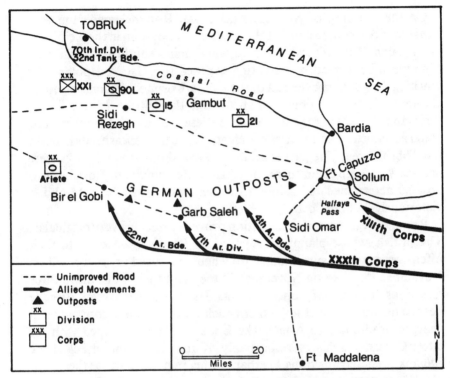

Map 5: Operation "Crusader": The British advance to contact, November 17-18, 1941. The German reaction to these attacks was slow, because Rommel simply refused to believe that the British were launching a major offensive before his planned assault on Tobruk, scheduled for November 23.

Rommel himself set out into the desert to assume personal command of the battle. "Crusader" has begun in earnest.

On the morning of November 19 Erwin Rommel made the very dangerous decision to commit the 21st Panzer Division in the vicinity of Gahr Saleh. This miserable village lay 40 miles southeast of Tobruk. Fighting here instead of retreating exposed the 21st to a potentially crushing defeat before the rest of the Afrika Korps could concentrate at Gambut. However, Rommel predicted that the British would not mass their tanks but scatter them all over the desert, as usual. He believed he could administer them a series of defeats before their spearheads reached the Tobruk area. The garrison must be kept bottled up. If risks were necessary to keep them there, then risks must be taken. Rommel was now as determined to maintain the siege as he had been to end it victoriously 24 hours before.

Rommel's estimate of the situation proved correct in every particular. The British, whose planning depended on Rommel's reaction to their offensive, were not sure what to do when he refused to react at all on November 18. Then on November 19 they sent their tanks off in three directions, instead of concentrating. The 22nd Armoured Brigade headed for Bir el Gubi, the southern anchor of Rommel's front, where it charged headlong into Ariete. The British tankers, equipped with the latest Crusader tanks, were probably overconfident and attacked the Italians' prepared positions, "perhaps rather impetuously," as their *Official History* later recorded. Certainly they failed to wait for their artillery to come up, and they were defeated in a sharp little battle that cost them 25 of their 136 remaining tanks. Ariete lost 34 inferior tanks and 12 guns destroyed and another 15 tanks damaged in the encounter.[47]

Meanwhile, Rommel dealt with the right flank of the XXX Corps. He still refused to believe the British were launching a major offensive, but he no doubt realized that they were up to something that had to be dealt with before Tobruk could be attacked. He therefore allowed Cruewell to move the 15th Panzer Division southwest of Gambut and send a battle group from the 21st Panzer Division toward Sidi Azeiz.

Cruewell's battle group was under Colonel Fritz Stephan, the commander of the 5th Panzer Regiment. With about 80 tanks, some artillery, and some anti-aircraft guns, Stephen reconnoitered toward Gabr Saleh. At 4:00 P.M. he ran right into Brigadier A. H. Gatehouse's 4th Armoured Brigade. Normally this unit had three line regiments—the 8th King's Royal Irish Hussars and the 3rd and 5th Royal Tank regiments—but the 3rd RTR was off supporting the armored cars of the King's Dragoon Guards, which was feinting near Sidi Azeiz. Consequently, the Battle of Gahr Saleh was about even in terms of numbers. The British got the worse of it in a running tank battle, losing 23 Stuarts against two PzKw III's and a PzKw II. When night fell, Stephen withdrew back to the 21st Panzer Division on the Trigh Capuzzo, south of Gambut.[48]

While all of this was in progress, the central British column (the 7th Armoured Brigade under Brigadier G. M. O. Davy) headed straight for Tobruk. At 1:00 P.M. it overran Sidi Rezegh airfield, only 13 miles from the fortresses' perimeter, and captured 19 airplanes. All that kept them from the rear of the XXI Italian Infantry Corps was a thin screen from the 90th Light Division, a screen that had only a handful of antitank guns. Davy, however, did not attack unsupported and without reconnaissance but instead decided to wait for reinforcements. He did not move the rest of the day. Meanwhile, on the night of November 19–20, Erwin Rommel decided to ignore the isolated 7th Armoured Brigade for the time being and gave Cruewell a free hand to "destroy the enemy battle groups . . . before they can offer any serious threat to Tobruk."[49] Cruewell apparently reasoned that if he could destroy the 4th Armoured Brigade in the deep right rear of the XXX Corps, Cunningham would have to retreat to maintain his supply lines. This would also have the effect of breaking the link between the Eighth Army's two wings and isolating the British armor in the desert.

Although Cruewell's plan was fundamentally good, he could not execute it. For one thing, he was nearly out of gasoline. To launch an attack at all he had to funnel his whole fuel reserve to the 15th Panzer Division. The 21st Panzer Division was virtually immobilized all morning on November 20. Even that afternoon its mobility was greatly restricted. Meanwhile, General Cunningham also issued his orders for November 20. Far from ignoring Davy, as Rommel had done, he sent the 7th Support Group to reinforce him at Sidi Rezegh airfield. The 1st South African Division was ordered to close in on Bir el Gubi (that is, the Ariete Armored Division) but to be ready to send one brigade to Sidi Rezegh during the afternoon. The 22nd Armoured Brigade, which the 1st South African relieved, was to remain near Bir el Gubi, where it could rush to the aid of the 1st South African, the 7th Armoured Brigade, or the 4th Armoured, as required. The 4th Armoured Brigade was to remain at Gabr Saleh, covering the left flank of the XIII Corps, which was pinning down the frontier garrisons and slowly working its way

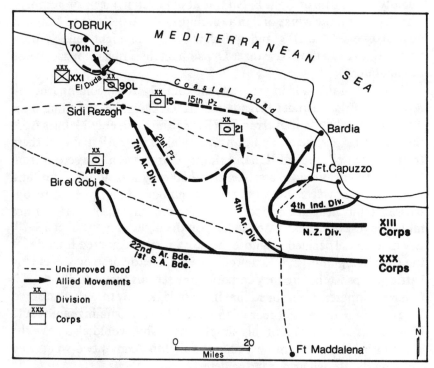

Map 6: Operation "Crusader": November 19-20, 1941. Although checked on the flanks, the central force of the British three-pronged attack penetrated Axis defenses and reached Sidi Rezegh, less than 10 miles from the Tobruk perimeter, thus bringing Rommel to the verge of defeat.

around the right flank of the Italian Savona Division.[50] Cruewell's initial efforts were in the Sidi Azeiz area, where he expected to find the 4th Armoured. Unfortunately for him, this unit was to the southwest at Gabr Saleh, so Cruewell wasted the morning chasing armored cars from the King's Dragoon Guards. (The 3rd Royal Tank Regiment of the 4th Armoured Brigade had been supporting the Dragoons the day before. It had returned to Gabr Saleh that night, a move that was apparently undetected by the Germans and that probably explains why Cruewell struck in the wrong place.) When he realized his mistake, the commander of the Afrika Korps turned southwest and attacked Gabr Saleh with 135 panzers (Rommel had reinforced him with the 21st Panzer Division), but by then British radio operators had intercepted messages revealing Cruewell's plans. Acting on this intelligence, Gott reinforced the 4th Armoured with the 22nd Armoured Brigade, which meant that the four German panzer battalions now faced six British tank battalions. The Afrika Korps was repulsed in indecisive fighting. The Allies lost 26 tanks, but the attackers lost about the same.[51] Map 6 shows the fighting on November 20.

While Cruewell chased Dragoons across the desert, Generals Gott, Norrie, and Davy met at Sidi Rezegh. Gott pointed out how easy it would be for the 70th Infantry Division to break out of Tobruk and link up with the 7th Armoured Brigade, attacking north from Sidi Rezegh. This notion was contrary to the original Allied plan not to break the siege until after the Afrika Korps was defeated, but General Norrie liked the idea. He ordered General Scobie to attack out of the fortress the next morning. Meanwhile, Norrie decided to reinforce Sidi Rezegh with the 5th South African Infantry Brigade, which began its move from Bir el Gubi that afternoon.[52]

That night Rommel, who was near Sidi Rezegh, came to the conclusion that the greatest danger now lay here. He concentrated elements of the 90th Light Division and Panzer Group Afrika's artillery under Major General Boettcher opposite Davy and ordered Ludwig Cruewell to attack Sidi Rezegh from the southwest the next morning with the entire Afrika Korps. In doing so he set the stage for a three-day fight that equaled any battle in World War II for intensity, complexity, and confusion.

8

Sidi Rezegh and
the Day of the Dead

The events of November 20 brought the German Army in Africa to the verge of defeat. The Allied armored spearhead made camp for the night north of the Sidi Rezegh airfield, within a dozen miles of the British siege lines in front of Tobruk. Within the fortress, the garrison made the final preparations for its own attack. They planned to attack through the Italian Bologna Infantry Division toward El Duda, a village three miles northwest of Sidi Rezegh. The attack started at dawn. Covered by diversions from the British 23rd and Polish 1st Infantry brigades, the 32nd Army Tank Brigade advanced on the Italian positions, closely supported by the 14th and 16th Infantry brigades of the 70th Infantry Division.[1] They gained ground more slowly than expected because the Bologna Division had been reinforced by elements of the 90th Light. Nevertheless, by afternoon they had penetrated 4,000 yards, overrun two battalions of Italian artillery, and taken 1,100 prisoners—half of them German.[2]

Erwin Rommel was determined that the British would not be allowed to exploit their gains. He launched a violent counterattack with his last reserves—the 3rd Reconnaissance Battalion and a few 88's. The Desert Fox managed to restore the siege line by his personal intervention but, with these units committed, his position was precarious indeed.[3]

Meanwhile, Gott and Davy also planned an attack from the south for the morning of the 21st. This assault, led by the 6th Royal Tank Regiment of the 7th Armoured Brigade and the 7th Support Group, had the objective of taking the ridge overlooking the Trigh Capuzzo and then pushing north for the linkup with Scobie. Three regiments of artillery were to support the attack, and the 7th Hussars and 2nd Royal Tank regiments were in reserve.[4] At 8:00 A.M., however, half an hour before the attack was to start, Davy received word that the Afrika Korps was approaching from the southeast. Since it was too late to alter his plans, Davy turned the main attack over to Brigadier "Jock" Campbell of the 7th Support Group and sallied out to meet the new threat with the 7th Hussars and 2nd RTR[5].

Without their reserves, the British attack north of Sidi Rezegh floundered. It was opposed by the entire 155th Infantry Regiment of the 90th Light Division—not just the Italians, as the Allies expected. Well dug in behind barbed wire and hasty minefields and supported by Boettcher's artillery and their own antitank guns, the German infantry held firm north of the Trigh Capuzzo. The 6th Royal Tank Regiment tried to force its way across the road and was almost annihilated. When it finally fell back, three fourths of its tanks were left burning north of the ruined airfield.[6]

Meanwhile, Brigadier Davy met Cruewell and the Afrika Korps southwest of Sidi Rezegh with only half of his command. By not calling off his attack toward Tobruk and by leaving the support group behind, Brigadier Davy denied himself his artillery and most of his antitank guns. General Cruewell, of course, did not make the same mistake. The two Allied regiments were cut to ribbons by concentrated gunfire. The 7th Hussars lost their commander and were reduced to 10 tanks.[7] The 2nd RTR suffered a similar fate. By 10:00 A.M. most of the British armor was burning. Cruewell burst through to the airfield itself, but the German effort to wipe out the other half of the 7th Armoured failed because of the determined stand of Brigadier Campbell, his 7th Support Group, and the remnants of the 6th Royal Tank Regiment. By now Gott realized the danger to his divided division and was on the way to Sidi Rezegh with the 4th and 22nd Armoured brigades. The 4th Armoured tried to catch the Afrika Korps in the rear by attacking from the southeast. However, a screen of antitank guns had been placed there for just such an emergency. The 4th Armoured was turned back. To the southwest the 22nd Armoured Brigade also tried to break through German lines to rescue Davy's battered force, but they ran straight into Neumann-Silkow's panzers and were soon halted.

As night fell on November 21, the Afrika Korps occupied a central position between the 7th Armoured Brigade and the 7th Support Group (both still under Davy) and the 4th and 22nd Armoured brigades under Gott. The situation was unbelievably confused. As General Playfair later wrote: ". . . both sides were sandwiched like the layers of a Neapolitan ice."[8] In all there were nine of these bent "layers" over a 20-mile area.

Roughly north to south, they were: (1) the British 70th Infantry Division and 32nd Army Tank Brigade, defending south of Tobruk and facing south; (2) the Italian Bologna Infantry Division, the German 90th Light Division, and the 3rd Reconnaissance Battalion, generally facing north; (3) the German 155th Infantry Regiment of the 90th Light, holding the ridge north of the Trigh Capuzzo, facing south against (4) elements of the 7th Support Group and the remnants of the 6th Royal Tank Regiment, hedgehogged north of the Sidi Rezegh airfield; (5) the rest of the 7th Armoured Brigade and the 7th Support Group, facing south against (6) most of the Afrika Korps, which lay north in the path of (7) the 4th and 22nd Armoured Brigades; meanwhile (8), the 361st Infantry Regiment of the 90th Light had taken up positions at Point 175, west of the airfield, and (9) the South African 5th Infantry Brigade was approaching approaching Sidi Rezegh from Bir el Gubi.

These "layers," of course, exclude the Ariete Armored and the bulk of the South African 1st Infantry divisions, still facing each other at Bir el Gubi; the British XIII Corps (the New Zealand 2nd and Indian 4th Infantry divisions and the 1st Army Tank Brigade) and the Italian Savona Infantry Division with its German detachments, fighting on the frontier. Also excluded are the Eighth Army's South African 2nd Infantry Division, 22nd Guards Brigade, and Indian 29th Infantry Brigade, all in reserve.

The movement of tens of thousands of vehicles—perhaps 35,000 in all—had ground the dirt around Tobruk into a fine sand that the wind easily transported. Dust flew everywhere, causing a screen of sand to cover the battlefield. The smoke from artillery fire and thousands of burning tanks, trucks, and armored cars further limited visibility and added to the confusion.

General Ludwig Cruewell, sandwiched between Davy's 7th Armoured Brigade and the 7th Support Group on the north and the 4th and 22nd Armoured brigades under Gott to the south, grew nervous under these circumstances. Greatly overestimating British strength and fearing he was about to be surrounded, he decided to regain freedom of maneuver by moving the Korps to Gambut under the cover of darkness. In this way he hoped to be able to catch the British in the flank the next morning. Major General Neumann-Silkow strongly disagreed with this plan but was overruled by his superior. At 10:40 P.M., when the march was well under way, Cruewell received orders from Rommel to send the 21st Panzer Division north to the Belhamed-Zaafram area, about two miles northeast of Sidi Rezegh. He also placed the 155th and 361st

Infantry regiments under Cruewell's command and ordered them to stand fast north of Sidi Rezegh, thus protecting the siege lines of the Italian XXI Infantry Corps. Cruewell sent the 21st Panzer to Belhamed as ordered but continued on to Gambut with the 15th Panzer. The effect of all of this was to split the Afrika Korps by a distance of 18 miles and allow the British 7th Armoured Division to reunite at Sidi Rezegh. This also gave the Allies a short breathing spell to regain their wits, a feat they accomplished with amazing rapidity.[9]

General Norrie interpreted the move of the Afrika Korps as a withdrawal and followed cautiously with the 4th and 22nd Armoured brigades. General Cunningham, also thinking the Korps was in retreat and that the German armor had been defeated, released the XIII Corps. He told Godwin-Austen to advance "as he pleased," and by the next morning the 2nd New Zealand Infantry Division was working its way behind the Savona Division and threatening Bardia and Sollum. One of the New Zealand brigades was already reconnoitering down the Trigh Capuzzo, preparing to advance on Tobruk.[10]

On November 22 the Battle of Sidi Rezegh entered its third day with no end in sight. The day's opening skirmish took place south of Gambut when a British tank column was shot up by some 88mm anti-aircraft guns from Neumann-Silkow's division. It is unclear whether this column represented an overly optimistic pursuit force, a reconnaissance in force, or just a lost body of tanks wandering around the battlefield. At Sidi Rezegh, the British massed 180 tanks and by noon the 7th Armoured Division was reformed. The South African 5th Infantry Brigade also came up (on the western flank of the 7th Armoured) and attacked Point 178 on the west end of the Sidi Rezegh ridge. The New Zealand 6th Brigade from the XIII Corps was moving west down the Trigh Capuzzo in an attempt to join the party. It could afford to do this because the XIII Corps had completed its first mission: the garrisons of Bardia, Halfaya Pass, and Sollum were now under siege, completely cut off from the rest of Panzer Group Afrika. In addition, Fort Capuzzo had been overrun. Soon the rest of the 2nd New Zealand Division would be available for transfer to the Sidi Rezegh sector. At last the Allies were beginning to concentrate.

Rommel, of course, was smart enough to know that this dangerous tendency must be broken up immediately. At about midday he turned up at von Ravenstein's headquarters near Belhamed. His orders were bold: The bulk of the 21st Panzer's infantry—mainly the 104th Panzer Grenadier Regiment—would attack Sidi Rezegh from the north, while the

5th Panzer Regiment, supported by the division's 88mm anti-aircraft guns, made a wide sweep north of Belhamed and attacked the airfield from the west.[11]

Rommel's daring stroke took the orthodox British totally by surprise. Initially the Panzer Group's heavy artillery opened up on them with an unexpected bombardment of terrible intensity. As soon as the bombardment lifted, the 104th Panzer Grenadier Regiment of the 21st Panzer Division attacked through the 1st Battalion, 155th Infantry Regiment and hit the airfield from the north, while the division's 5th Panzer Regiment swept in from the west, right across the ruined airstrip and into the gun positions of the 7th Support Group. Brigadier Campbell, who would meet his death within a few weeks, became a hero of the British Empire that day by again putting up an incredibly fierce resistance. He received aid from the 22nd Armoured Brigade, but for some reason the 4th Armoured stayed put while Rommel tore the other two units limb from limb. His panzers, artillery, 88's, and antitank guns destroyed about half of the 22nd Armoured Brigade's tanks before it withdrew.[12] The support group suffered similar losses. Gott now had only 144 tanks left: 10 with the 7th Armoured Brigade, 34 with the 22nd, and 100 with the 4th Armoured. Rommel had 173 panzers with the Afrika Korps. He had achieved a temporary quantitative superiority.[13]

Late that afternoon the 8th Panzer Regiment converged on Sidi Rezegh from the southeast. This move was not part of Rommel's original plan but something Colonel Hans Kramer, the commander of the 8th Panzer, did on his own initiative, answering a call for help from the 21st Panzer Division. The appearance of half of the Afrika Korps' panzers in their rear took the British by surprise once more. Just as darkness fell, the 8th Panzers ran right over the 8th Hussars Regiment, captured the Brigade Headquarters (including the commander), captured or destroyed 50 tanks, took over 200 prisoners, and dispersed the 4th Armoured, which was inoperable until the morning of November 24.[14]

Despite the staggering losses to the 4th Armoured and other units, the British soldiers refused to admit defeat. Far from that, they fought on with increasingly dogged determination. If the British had some bad traits, such as clinging to outmoded tactics and moving too slowly, they also had some truly fine ones, and the will to win despite the odds was perhaps their best. General Gott, for example, continued to try to batter his way toward Tobruk and improve his deteriorating position rather than retreat. West of Sidi Rezegh the 5th South African Infantry Brigade

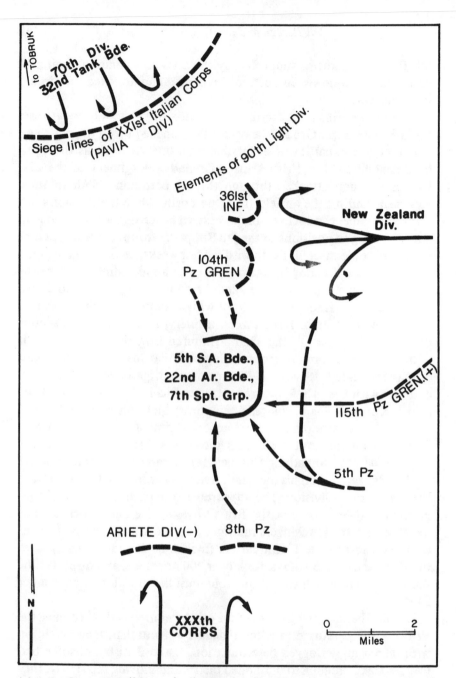

to TOBRUK

70th Div.
32nd Tank Bde.

Siege lines of XXIst Italian Corps
(PAVIA DIV.)

Elements of 90th Light Div.

361st
INF.

New Zealand
Div.

104th
Pz GREN

5th S.A. Bde.,
22nd Ar. Bde.,
7th Spt. Grp.

115th Pz GREN (+)

5th Pz

ARIETE DIV(−)   8th Pz

N

XXXth
CORPS

0   2
Miles

Map 7: Operation "Crusader": The third and fourth days of the Battle of
Sidi Rezegh, November 22-23, 1941. All German units are regiments
unless otherwise noted. Rommel's converging attack of November 22
prevented the Allies from lifting the Siege of Tobruk. The next day, in the
Totensonntag battle, General Cruewell annihilated the 5th South African
Brigade and eliminated the British relief force.

continued to try to take Point 178 on the Sidi Rezegh Ridge but was turned back by the 2nd Battalion, 155th Infantry Regiment.[15] That night it settled down two miles south of the ridge, where it was joined by Gott and the remnants of the 7th and 22nd Armoured brigades and the Support Group.

As darkness fell on November 22, the battlefield was lit up by burning Allied vehicles. The British armored concentration, which had looked so promising in the morning, was smashed. Now the survivors were caught between two fires: Rommel to the north and Cruewell to the south. Gott counted his losses that night and found that the fighting of November 22 had reduced the 7th Armoured Brigade from 28 tanks to 10. The 22nd Armoured Brigade had been reduced from 79 to 34 tanks, and the 4th Armoured had been so badly mauled and dispersed that it was impossible to determine how many of its tanks had survived the battle.[16] Some relief was near at hand, but not much. Elements of the New Zealand Division, fresh from their victory over the Italians at Fort Capuzzo, had moved to the northwest, into Cruewell's rear. The South African 1st Brigade was also nearby, at Bir el Gubi. The rest of the XXX Corps, however, was either pinned down or smashed, and the bulk of the XIII Corps was tied up in the Sollum–Bardia–Halfaya Pass area. The Indian 4th Division and the 1st Army Tank Brigade had taken Sidi Omar and most of Libyan Omar but had lost 37 tanks (mainly Matildas) to antitank guns and mines. They were still pushing the Germans and Italians back on the coast, but resistance was anything but weak.[17] No further help could be expected from the coastal flank in the immediate future.

Rommel's next move was predictable. He ordered a converging attack on the Sidi Rezegh pocket with all German and Italian armored units. Obviously he intended to wipe it out. This order sparked the Battle of Totensonntag, one of the hardest-fought actions of the Second World War.

The fourth day of the Battle of Sidi Rezegh was one of almost indescribable confusion. Heavy tanks and other armored vehicles had ground the sand into a very fine powder, which clogged engines and reduced visibility drastically. Smoke and haze further obscured things. Disorder increased throughout the day as communications failed and units and individual vehicles became separated from parent units and were left to wander about the battlefield on their own. It was still very much a multilayered battle. To the north, the Tobruk garrison formed layer one and the besieging Italians and German reserves represented layer two. Rommel and the 21st Panzer Division formed layer three, while layer four was comprised of the virtually encircled 7th Armoured Division and South African 5th Infantry Brigade. Layer five was Cruewell, the 15th Panzer Division, and elements of the 21st Panzer. Layer six consisted of the bulk of the New Zealand Division, approaching Cruewell's force from the east. The British rear area, which included their forward supply dumps and the 22nd Guards Brigade, may be classified as layer seven, while layers eight and nine were the units of the XIII Corps and German-Italian frontier garrisons, which were completely cut off from the rest of Panzer Group Afrika. Layer ten was the Eighth Army's reserve. Even this picture is an oversimplification, but a necessary one if one intends to make any sense out of the battle.

Totensonntag was the day Germany honored her World War I dead. It literally means day of the dead. It was an appropriate title for that day. At 5:30 A.M., General Cruewell set out from Afrika Korps Headquarters at Gasr el Arid, accompanied by his chief of staff, Colonel Fritz Bayerlein. Cruewell decided to lead the attack personally. From that moment on, Totensonntag was *his* day. Half an hour after his departure, New Zealanders burst into the village and captured the headquarters of the Afrika Korps, including the Ia. Although this loss caused no immediate damage, it did a great deal of harm later on, when defective staff work by inexperienced and/or unqualified officers hurt the Afrika Korps badly, particularly in the areas of transportation and resupply.

The Desert Fox was up very early on November 23 and won an important victory before dawn—this one in the political arena. He wired Mussolini directly, urgently requesting that all Axis forces in the battle zone be placed under a single commander. The Italian dictator responded at once: He placed Gambara's XX Italian Motorized Corps (Ariete Armored and Trieste Motorized divisions) under Rommel's personal direction.[18] Rommel himself remained under Bastico's nominal command, but even if that Italian marshal had attempted to influence the battle, Rommel would have ignored him. The Axis forces now had a unified command. Their commander, however, had no immediate chance to exercise his new authority, for he ran into bad luck on November 23.

Erwin Rommel was in the immediate vicinity of the Afrika Korps Headquarters, attempting to reach Cruewell, when the New Zealanders struck. He was chased and narrowly escaped to the 361st Infantry Regiment of the 90th Light Division, which guarded the eastern approach to Sidi Rezegh at Point 175. Soon this tough unit, which included many Germans who had served in the French Foreign Legion, was practically surrounded. When the New Zealanders tried to overwhelm this hedgehogged regiment, Rommel had no choice but to join the battle and leave the rest of Totensonntag to Ludwig Cruewell. This turned out to be an excellent decision, even if it were made under duress. On this day, the Germans finally won the First Battle of Sidi Rezegh.

The Afrika Korps commander's battle plan was not complex. He would link up with Ariete and then destroy the remaining Allied battle groups individually before they could regain their balance or the initiative.

At 7:30 A.M. the first of a series of armored clashes took place. A strong British armored group was smashed near Sidi Muftah. Meanwhile, Cruewell moved south with the 15th Panzer Division and the tanks of the 21st Panzer Division. His idea was for the Afrika Korps to swing south behind the Allied pocket, join with Ariete, attack north, and destroy the South African brigade. Besides attacking the Allies at an unexpected point, Cruewell's plan had the additional advantage of preventing the South African 1st Brigade from reinforcing the point from the south.

The maneuver worked out as planned. Cruewell swept south, smashed the remnants of the 7th Support Group, and continued on until the British pocket was behind him. Then the Afrika Korps turned east, joined with Ariete, and struck north. No one in the Allied camp expected an attack from this quarter, so the panzer soldiers burst into the South African rear before anyone realized what was happening. Neumann-Silkow's tanks shot up the brigade's transport columns in record time. The South Africans were now hopelessly trapped, but destroying these tough men proved to be a difficult task, even for the Afrika Korps. The first attempts were beaten off by the South African artillery and antitank guns. Cruewell was forced to bring up his own artillery and silence the Allied guns one by one. Slowly the South Africans were pushed back, until Cruewell felt it was time to launch another all-out attack. It was a battle of murderous intensity, with dust, flame, and smoke everywhere.

At one point Cruewell's Mammoth was surrounded by British tanks, probably from the 22nd Armoured Brigade, which had rushed to the support of the South Africans. The British, however, were unaware of the prize within their reach, because the German command vehicle was of British manufacture, captured at Mechili the year before. A British soldier got out of his vehicle and knocked on the hatch of Cruewell's

Mammoth. Imagine his surprise when he found himself staring face to face with the commander of the Afrika Korps! At almost that exact moment a German 20mm anti-aircraft gun opened up on the British soldier, who fled to the safety of his own tank. Cruewell's vehicle sped away in the confusion. Fortunately for him, the British tanks had already exhausted their ammunition. Neither side suffered any casualties in the incident.[19]

To the north, the Tobruk garrison did its best to help the men trapped in the Sidi Rezegh pocket. It attacked the Italian Pavia Division with 50 tanks. Probably they hoped this threat would force von Ravenstein to disengage the infantry of the 21st Panzer from the Totensonntag battle, where it formed the northern pincer. This would greatly reduce the odds against the South Africans, now caught between two fires. The Italians, however, again demonstrated their unpredictability by rising to the occasion and issuing the 70th Infantry Division and 32nd Army Tank Brigade an untimely check. The siege line was maintained without the commitment of a single soldier from the 21st Panzer Division.[20]

Despite the close call to Cruewell, the threat from the garrison to the north, and the desperate resistance within the pocket, the jaws of the pincers closed inexorably on the 7th Armoured Division and the South Africans. The main attack began at 3:00 P.M. Cruewell struck with 150 panzers, closely supported by the grenadiers of the 15th Panzer Division. The fighting was extremely bitter. The South African artillery particularly distinguished itself and knocked out many (if not most) of the 60 German tanks destroyed or damaged that day, but it could not stand against such odds indefinitely. The South African 5th Infantry Brigade was overwhelmed and destroyed; it lost 3,394 of its 5,700 men, most of them captured. The 22nd Armoured Brigade lost about a third of its remaining tanks before it escaped to the east.[21] The Allies were beaten at last, or so it seemed. Over 300 British tanks lay burned out or burning over the huge battlefield, and another 150 were heavily damaged. Gott and the 7th Armoured Division (or what was left of it) had had enough and escaped in the darkness and the smoke, the haze and the general confusion that dominated the 30-odd square miles south of Tobruk. Colonel Bayerlein described the entire area south of Sidi Rezegh as "a sea of dust, haze and smoke."[22] The Afrika Korps had also suffered tremendous casualties and its men were probably looking forward to a period of rest and reorganization. They were to be disappointed.

9

The Dash to the Wire

On the night of November 23, Erwin Rommel finally managed to make his way to his headquarters at El Adem, where Colonel von Mellenthin found him in a state of "excited exultation."[1] The Swabian general decided to launch a raid into the rear of the Eighth Army. He thought this would have the effect of stampeding the British into a headlong retreat. Colonel Mellenthin, Panzer Group Afrika's Intelligence officer, disagreed with his chief. He felt that Rommel had overestimated the decisiveness of Cruewell's Totensonntag victory. Major General Gause and Colonel Westphal agreed with his assessment, and they had some good arguments. True, the 5th South African Brigade had ceased to exist, but the Afrika Korps was down to 90 tanks.[2] The veteran officers pointed out that the New Zealand 2nd Division was left in an exposed position by the retreat of the remnants of the 7th Armoured and could be overrun fairly easily. Even Cruewell opposed the raid. "We have got to clean up the battlefield and salvage the immense booty before the enemy has time to come and fetch it himself," he told the Desert Fox.[3] Rommel, however, dismissed all their objections and could not be swayed.[4]

The next morning Rommel conferred again with Cruewell and Bayerlein. "The greater part of the force aimed at Tobruk has been destroyed," he told them. "Now we will turn east and go for the New Zealanders and Indians before they have been able to join up with the remains of their main force for a combined attack on Tobruk. At the same time we will take Habata and Maddalena, and cut off their supplies. Speed is vital. . . ."[5]

In making these plans, Rommel ignored the fact that the New Zealanders were not retreating; apparently he assumed they soon would. Erwin Rommel thought that the Eighth Army was defeated and that a major advance into their rear would spark a headlong retreat into Egypt. He would have been interested to know that General Auchinleck himself was at Cunningham's headquarters, demanding that the offensive be continued despite the losses. Godwin-Austen's XIII Corps was ordered to take charge of all operations against the Tobruk siege lines and to take Sidi Rezegh and El Duda "at all costs." The 70th Infantry and South African 2nd Infantry divisions and the Indian 5th Brigade were attached to the XIII Corps, which already had the New Zealand 2nd and Indian 4th divisions, as well as the 1st Army Tank Brigade. The XXX Corps was to be allowed to reorganize but was ordered to be prepared to protect the South African 1st or New Zealand 2nd divisions against panzer attacks if necessary. The 7th Armoured Brigade Headquarters, however, was withdrawn from the battle and sent to Egypt. Its tanks and most of its other equipment were given to the other two brigades.[6] Meanwhile, the pressure on the frontier garrisons was maintained. The New Zealand 5th Brigade took the Sollum barracks that afternoon while the rest of the New Zealand Division got ready to drive on Tobruk.

General Rommel, confident of victory, knew none of this, of course. He assembled a weak holding force of miscellaneous formations, placed them under Major General Boettcher, and stationed them south of Tobruk. The Boettcher Group consisted of one battalion from the 361st Infantry Regiment, the entire 155th Infantry Regiment, the 900th Engineer Battalion (all from Summermann's 90th Light Division), and elements of Panzer Group Afrika's artillery command. Rommel ordered Boettcher to deal with any new attempts to raise the siege. There was only one thing wrong with this order: Boettcher simply would not have the resources to carry it out when the XIII Corps struck. This fact, however, was not apparent to General Rommel. He was carried away. One of the dangers of Rommel's method of leadership from the front was that the commander tended to become overly impressed with local successes. He seemed to have forgotten that he had mauled only an armored division and a couple of brigades. The British still had an entire corps intact, as well as most of the 1st South African Division, two reserve brigades, the Tobruk garrison, and the 1st Army Tank Brigade. In retrospect, Rommel should have continued to defeat individual British units piecemeal, as he had throughout the first phase of the campaign. The Allies had already offered him yet another target: the New Zealand 2nd Division, which could easily have been destroyed, as subsequent events proved. However, hindsight is always superior to foresight.

In justice to Rommel, it must be pointed out that his plan almost worked: He nearly succeeded in routing the Eighth Army. Rommel bypassed an opportunity to wipe out a division in order to make a bid for the greater success. Had it worked, a victorious march across Egypt to the Suez Canal would have been a distinct probability. Rommel would not have been Rommel if he had not opted for the bolder move. This time it was the wrong choice.

At 10:30 A.M. on November 24, Rommel set off toward the Egyptian border at the head of the 5th Panzer Regiment, 21st Panzer Division. It was followed by the rest of the division and, two hours later, by the 15th Panzer Division. The tank strength in both divisions was now very low. The 5th Panzer Regiment had only 45 fit tanks (including 11 marginal-value PzKw II's), and the 8th Panzer Regiment had only 61 (18 of which were PzKw II's).[7] Nevertheless, disregarding his flanks, Rommel broke straight through the Indian 4th Division[8] and into the rear area of the XXX Corps. Several corps staff officers were captured, along with quantities of water, badly needed fuel, and other supplies. They did, however, fail to detect the main supply depot, which was defended by the fresh 22nd Guards Brigade. That afternoon the advanced columns of Rommel's army passed to the west of the 7th Armoured Division, which was covering the left flanks of the New Zealand and South African divisions. The 7th Armoured and South African 1st brigades and the 7th Support Group clashed with and delayed the 5th Panzer Regiment, but Rommel continued on and, at 4:00 P.M., reached the frontier wire near Gasr el Abid with elements of the 21st Panzer Division. They had covered 60 miles in six hours.[9] Behind him, scattered over 40 miles of desert, followed the entire Afrika Korps. Ariete was also supposed to follow, but it had been held up near Taiel el Esem by remnants of the 4th Armoured Brigade. Still, two panzer divisions were enough to throw the rear area of the XXX Corps into a panic bordering on rout. General Cunningham did not join the panic, but it was clear that he had lost control of the battle.

Cunningham himself was visiting the 7th Armoured Division at noon, but he had to leave hurriedly when the panzers approached the division's airstrip. The airfield was being shelled when the Eighth Army commander took off. That evening he discussed the situation with General Auchinleck, who was still at Eighth Army Headquarters. It was decided that the XIII Corps would continue advancing toward Tobruk. The Indian 4th Division was ordered to stand fast, while the Indian 5th

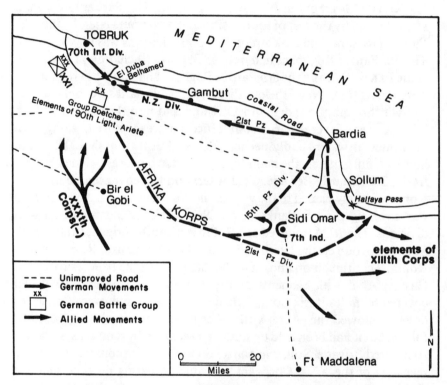

Map 8: "The Dash to the Wire," November 24-28, 1941. Following the Totensonntag victory, Rommel ordered a premature pursuit. Although gaining some minor successes, this move allowed the British to regain their balance and try again to break the Siege of Tobruk. Rommel was forced to turn back to meet this threat.

Brigade was sent to guard the Army's main railhead at Misheifa; the 22nd Guards Brigade, the 7th Armoured Brigade, and the 7th Support Group were detached to cover the rear of the XXX Corps.[10]

At 5:00 P.M. on November 24 Rommel met with Cruewell at Gasr el Abid. "The Desert Fox" set forth an ambitious plan to encircle and destroy all the British forces on the frontier. Ravenstein's 21st Panzer Division was to cross the border, drive north, and wheel west. The 15th Panzer Division was to attack north along the wire while the Ariete and Trieste divisions advanced eastward toward Fort Capuzzo. The 3rd and 33rd Reconnaissance battalions were sent toward Habath to raid the British main supply route. Rommel had already sent von Ravenstein off toward Halfaya Pass, but the 5th Panzer Regiment was too late to follow and spent the night at Gasr el Abid.[11]

Rommel's plan, for once, was utterly unrealistic and fell apart almost as soon as he issued the orders. The Trieste Motorized Division did not even get the orders due to an administrative foul-up and, apparently on the initiative of Lieutenant General Piazzoni, the divisional commander, moved from Bir Hacheim to the El Adem area—a good place to support the besiegers to Tobruk but 70 miles northwest of where it was supposed to be. Ariete, apparently still disorganized from Totensonntag, was still only a few miles east of Bir el Gubi.[12] The Afrika Korps itself was strung out over 60 miles of desert and in great confusion. Logistical support was strained to the breaking point, and disorganization was rampant. The loss of experienced staff officers suffered when the New Zealanders overran Cruewell's main headquarters was already paying dividends for the Allies. It would pay still more in the days ahead.

"The plot of movements on the frontier on 25th and 26th November resembled the scurrying of ants," the British *Official History* later recorded. "Neither side had much idea of what was happening...."[13] The day started badly for Rommel and got worse as it went along. The failure of Ariete to reach the frontier forced him to change his plan early that morning. He sent the 21st Panzer Division minus the 5th Panzer Regiment to relieve Major Bach at Halfaya Pass, while the 15th Panzer Division struck between Sidi Omar and Sidi Azeiz. The 5th Panzer Regiment was to deal with the Indian 7th Brigade at Sidi Omar, while the 3rd and 33rd Reconnaissance battalions launched their raid into the British rear. Ariete was again ordered to the frontier.[14]

Ariete again failed to reach the wire on November 25; it ran into the South African 1st Brigade west of Gabr Saleh and was pinned down all day. The reconnaissance battalions never even got off. They were strafed and bombed by the RAF, which began to dominate the air battle over Libya to an even greater degree than before. The 15th Panzer Division was spread out between Sidi Omar and Sidi Azeiz and was not able to concentrate. Due to supply and organizational problems it did not accomplish anything. Only the 21st Panzer Division—which reached Halfaya Pass with only about a company of tanks—accomplished its mission. The worst disaster of the day, however, occurred at Sidi Omar, in the sector of the 5th Panzer Regiment.[15] The Indian 7th Brigade was dug in here, along with the 1st and 25th Royal Field Artillery regiments. The 5th Panzer charged in full tilt and was promptly shot to pieces, losing 18 of its 43 remaining tanks. The distinguished regimental commander, Lieutenant Colonel Fritz Stephan, was critically wounded when the RAF bombed the attackers. Rommel personally saw to it that the valuable Stephen received immediate medical attention. He took the badly wounded leader to a captured British hospital. Stephen, who was conscious but in shock, had a sucking chest wound and his right lung was all but severed from his heart. Rommel waited in the hospital and watched the operation until the Allies began to shell the area. Obviously they were trying to destroy Rommel's vehicles, which were parked outside. The British anesthetist asked him and his entourage to leave, which they did. Colonel Fritz Stephan died a few hours later, despite the efforts of the Allied doctors to save him. He was replaced by Major Mildebrath.[16]

Following the repulse in which Colonel Stephan was mortally wounded, Rommel instructed von Ravenstein to proceed north, strike down the Allied forces besieging Sollum, and then penetrate into Egypt. Rommel escorted the 21st Panzer part of the way and then turned back, heading for where the 15th Panzer was supposed to be. En route his vehicle broke down. He was alone, in no-man's-land, without an escort, for he had once again outrun his *Kampfstaffel.* He did not know exactly where his other units were. Luckily he was picked up by General Cruewell, who was also roaming about the desert in his Mammoth. The danger was far from over, however, for Cruewell was also traveling without escort.[17] Their total strength was ten officers and five enlisted men—the brains of Hitler's Panzer Group Afrika. They were unable to find a hole in the large wire fence that separated Egypt from Libya, so they camped for the night. They would have been shocked to learn that they were within a few miles of Fort Maddalena—the Eighth Army's advance headquarters![18] The next day they found their way again and set out to rejoin Ravenstein and the 21st Panzer Division. After that Rommel planned to visit the coastal garrison at Bardia.

On the way back to the Afrika Korps, Rommel stumbled across a New Zealand field hospital. The panzer commander quickly realized he was at their mercy, so he played a skillful game of bluff. He dismounted; then he walked through the place as if he owned it. Fortunately for him the battlefield was in such a state of flux and confusion that nobody knew where the front was, and the New Zealanders assumed they had been captured. Rommel briefly visited with the doctors, asked if anybody needed anything, promised to send back medical supplies, and drove off. Ten minutes later, a British pursuit column arrived.[19]

Rommel's adventures on the way to Bardia were still not over. Several times he was chased by Allied vehicles. Once he even crossed an airfield still being run by the RAF. As if by a miracle, he escaped each time.

While Rommel was dashing about the desert, events elsewhere slipped beyond his control. On the evening of November 25, General Sir Claude Auchinleck made what for him must have been a painful decision. He had lost confidence in General Sir Alan Cunningham—his own appointee, chosen over Winston Churchill's own candidate—so he sacked him and replaced him with Major General Sir Neil Ritchie. Ritchie was Auchinleck's own deputy chief of staff and a man with little command experience; nevertheless, he knew how to take orders, and the orders Auchinleck gave him were uncompromising: The Eighth Army was to fight to the last bullet. It would win this battle or never return.[20] With these orders, General Ritchie had no choice but to rally all his forces southeast of Tobruk. He did not retreat, as Rommel expected. The absence of the Afrika Korps allowed the battered units of the XXX Corps to rest, reorganize, and repair their damaged tanks and other equipment. British mechanics worked feverishly to get their armor into working condition, and they succeeded to a large degree. Soon the New Zealanders were attacking Group Boettcher at Belhamed, but the German line held on the morning of November 25. That afternoon, however, the New Zealand 4th Brigade took the airfield at Gambut, threatening Tobruk and even further reducing the capabilities of the Luftwaffe by pushing it farther west—away from Rommel's zone of operations on the frontier.[21] The situation was critical for the Germans, for they had little prospect of holding off Ritchie's forces for long. The British were once again on the verge of relieving the fortress.

Colonel Westphal watched the enemy gather with increasing dismay.

As fresh forces from the 22nd Guards Brigade and elements of the New Zealand Division mauled Battle Group Boettcher, Westphal came to the realization that a major defeat was inevitable if reinforcements were not brought up immediately. Feverishly he tried to contact Rommel, but without success. As the chief operations officer of Panzer Group Afrika, Siegfried Westphal faced perhaps the greatest decision of his life. Should he, a mere colonel, put his career on the line and override the direct orders of his commander-in-chief? After a consultation with von Mellenthin, the Intelligence officer, Westphal showed his moral courage and did just that.

General von Ravenstein was probably a little puzzled at 2:00 P.M. on November 25. His men stood 19 miles inside Egypt and only 50 miles from the British supply depot at Bir Thalata.[22] Two hours before, orders from Rommel had arrived, instructing him to prepare to attack into Egypt. Now he received a totally opposite message from Westphal at Group Headquarters. "All orders given to you hitherto are cancelled," it read. "Twenty-first Panzer Division is to break through the Indian line in the direction of Bardia."[23] Ravenstein may have been puzzled, but he did what he was told and headed for the coastal towns with his division (minus the 5th Panzer Regiment, which was still with Cruewell in the desert). On the way back Ravenstein overran the New Zealand 5th Brigade at Fort Capuzzo. By dawn on November 26 he neared Bardia with his tired infantry and a handful of tanks.

Ravenstein found Rommel temporarily headquartered in the coastal town of Bardia. The Swabian was sitting up in his chair, sound asleep, obviously exhausted by the strain of the campaign that seemed as if it would never end. "General," von Ravenstein reported, "I am happy to tell you that I am here with my division."

This surprise announcement hit Rommel like a bolt from the blue. He was awake instantly. "What are you doing here?" he exploded. "Did I not give you an order to be ready to attack from Halfaya in the direction of Egypt?"

Perhaps von Ravenstein had doubted the authenticity of the Westphal order all along, because he promptly produced his copy of the order from his pocket and handed it to Rommel without saying a word. "A fake!" Rommel screamed. "This is an order from the British! They must have our code!"[24] It was too late to do anything about it now. Rommel took advantage of the situation to allow the 21st Panzer to refuel at Bardia. He himself joined the 15th Panzer and later returned to Panzer Group Afrika Headquarters, which he reached on the evening of

November 27. Here an unexpected confrontation with Westphal awaited him. At first he was completely furious at his Ia for ordering the return of the 21st Panzer. Instead of saying anything, Rommel simply turned on his heel and went directly to bed. Perhaps he realized that he might say something in the heat of anger that he might regret later. The next morning he emerged, completely rested and in control of his temper. Much to the relief of his staff he forgave Westphal and even admitted that his course of action had been correct.[25]

And what was happening to the rest of the Afrika Korps on November 26, while von Ravenstein was heading toward Bardia and Rommel was dodging desert patrols and the RAF? General Cruewell, who had never wavered in his opposition to the Egyptian raid, wanted to return to Tobruk at once. This is what he told the Desert Fox that morning (just before he left for Bardia), but Rommel wanted to crush the enemy south of Sollum first, and quickly. He ordered Cruewell to defeat these forces, then go to Bardia, refuel, and draw ammunition.[26]

Cruewell's efforts of November 26 were also crowned with failure. En route to Bardia with the 15th Panzer Division he clashed with the New Zealand 5th Brigade—further convincing him that they must return to Tobruk. Nevertheless, he decided that he had a chance to destroy the New Zealand 5th, so he set about trying to organize an attack on Sidi Azeiz with the 15th Panzer. The attack never came off, however: The division simply did not have the fuel to deploy, fight a battle, and then reach Sollum.[27] Instead, it continued on toward the coast.

Cruewell also tried to organize another attack against Sidi Omar with the 5th Panzer Regiment and the 3rd Reconnaissance Battalion, but again failed—again due to a shortage of fuel.[28]

Late that night Rommel finally drew the proper conclusions and realized that the situation near Tobruk was critical. He ordered all German units to converge on the fortress at once. The order came none too soon for Group Boettcher, the 90th Light Division, and the Italian XXI Infantry Corps.

Early on the morning of November 27 the yet unnamed battle entered its third phase. Unlike the first two phases (the First Battle of Sidi Rezegh and the Egyptian raid), Rommel no longer called the tune. Half of the original members of the Afrika Korps lay dead or wounded, or in POW cages. The British had been reinforced, many of their damaged tanks repaired, and the RAF had achieved and would continue to maintain complete air superiority. However, the wounded lion had not lost all his teeth. On this morning Major General von Ravenstein returned to the Tobruk area with his division, while Rommel dealt with the New Zealand 5th Brigade at Sidi Azeiz. He took personal charge of the refueled 15th Panzer Division and annihilated the Allied force. The brigade commander and his staff, along with 800 men and their six remaining artillery pieces, were captured. Following this victory, Rommel reassembled the panzer division and led it back toward Tobruk, where a real danger again existed.[29]

Rommel's raid, later called "the dash to the wire," was thus ended. It had been a disastrous failure. The Afrika Korps had exhausted itself, while the XXX British Corps had been allowed to recover. The XIII Corps had now joined the main battle, which threatened to become one of attrition. Perhaps most ironical of all was the effect the raid had on the frontier garrisons. Not only did Rommel fail to relieve them, but also his panzer troops had seriously depleted their supply stockpiles. Now they were once again isolated.

When Rommel resumed the Battle of Sidi Rezegh (actually, the Second Battle of Sidi Rezegh) on November 27, it was under vastly different circumstances than those under which he began it a week earlier. The Afrika Korps had only 40 PzKw III's and IV's left, along with 20 of the nearly useless Panzer Mark II's. The 32nd Army Tank Brigade in Tobruk outnumbered him in tanks almost two to one, all by itself.[30]

To explain what had happened in the Tobruk sector during the Egyptian raid, the author must backtrack a bit. On the morning of November 24, while the Afrika Korps was moving southeast from Sidi Rezegh, the New Zealand 2nd Infantry Division (minus the 5th Brigade) and the 1st Army Tank Brigade (minus one regiment) with 86 "I" tanks started to advance on Tobruk again. The next day the New Zealand 6th Brigade continued along the escarpment as far as the Sidi Rezegh airfield. General Godwin-Austen ordered them to take the tactically critical Belhamed–El Duda–Sidi Rezegh village triangle, which controlled the approaches to the fortress. After this, if all went well, the garrison would break out and join them. Major General Freyberg, the New Zealand divisional commander and an excellent tactician, ordered a night attack in which the 4th Brigade was to seize Belhamed and the 6th Brigade was to take Sidi Rezegh and El Duda. The assault began at 9:00 P.M. against stiff opposition; by dawn on November 26 most of Belhamed was in Allied hands. The New Zealand 6th had taken the Sidi

Rezegh village but could not go beyond. El Duda remained in German hands.[31]

The effect of their excursions must have told on the New Zealanders on November 26, because they could gain no ground in heavy fighting. That afternoon, however, the Axis troops faced a new threat, as Major General Scobie broke out of Tobruk from the north. At 3:00 P.M. the 32nd Army Tank Brigade took el Duda, three miles north of Sidi Rezegh. It seemed that Tobruk was about to be relieved, but this was not the case, for the Afrika Korps had returned at last. Southeast of the escarpment the 15th Panzer struck toward Gasr el Arid. General Gott ordered the 22nd Armoured Brigade to "head it off" while the 4th Armoured struck it in the flank. The 15th Panzer reacted quickly—"a good example of efficient battle drill," the British *Official History* noted—and the battle became general. Both sides suffered heavy casualties, but it was the British who were pushed back; nevertheless, the victory was far from decisive, and Rommel could ill afford the losses, especially in tanks. Still, the victory at Gasr el Arid separated the Allied infantry from most of its tanks, gave the Afrika Korps the advantage of the central position, and isolated the New Zealand 2nd Infantry Division.[32]

That evening Rommel arrived at Gambut. Cruewell and Bayerlein drove to the airfield that night to brief Rommel on the deteriorating situation in front of Tobruk. They did not find him right away. Finally they saw a captured British Army truck and decided to look in the back. "Inside," Bayerlein later remembered, "were Rommel and his chief of staff [Major General Alfred Gause], both unshaven, worn out from lack of sleep and caked with dust. In the truck were a heap of straw as a bed, a can of stale drinking water and a few cans of food. Close by were two radio trucks and a few dispatch riders. Rommel now gave his instructions for the coming operation."[33]

Later that night, at El Adem, Colonel Westphal made his report to Rommel. The Tobruk front, he said, was on the verge of collapse. The Italians wanted to retreat. Rommel decided to wipe out the New Zealand Division instead.[34]

No heavy fighting occurred on November 28, although the 15th Panzer Division drove on Sidi Rezegh that afternoon. It overran the New Zealand rear area, captured its field hospitals, and took 1,000 prisoners, most of them wounded. The Germans did not attack Freyberg's division, however, because their southern flank was exposed. Ariete was supposed to cover it but failed to do so because it was still pinned down by the 7th Support Group. The 7th, which was down to one motorized battalion, held the Italian armored division in check mainly with its 33 remaining 25-pounder antitank guns.[35]

That evening Rommel met Cruewell and objected to his plan for the next day's assault. Cruewell had hoped to drive the New Zealanders into the fortress. Rommel wanted them surrounded and destroyed, not driven to safety in Tobruk.[36] It was decided that the 21st Panzer, supported by the 90th Light's artillery, would try to take Belhamed from the east while the 15th Panzer overran El Duda from the southwest. Ariete was ordered to hold the ring to the south.

Because Rommel rejected Cruewell's plan of the day before, the Afrika Korps was not in position at daybreak on November 29. The Korps was further delayed by strong British armored attacks from the south, but finally the 15th Panzer and Ariete divisions beat back the British in bitter fighting and turned on the 70th Infantry Division and the 32nd Army Tank Brigade. In the evening a fierce battle raged at the pivotal point of El Duda. At last the 115th Panzer Grenadier Regiment took half of the village but was thrown out again during the night by the 4th Royal Tank Regiment. Meanwhile, Ariete took Point 175 from the New Zealanders, whose isolation was growing and whose position was deteriorating by the hour. Freyberg ordered Brigadier Pienaar to retake the position with his South African 1st Infantry Brigade that night, but Pienaar refused. He did not want to suffer the same fate as his sister brigade (the South African 5th), and he particularly did not want to start such an operation as darkness was falling and radio communications tended to fail.[37]

Rommel not only lost a few more precious tanks that day, he also lost one of his best men. In the confusion of the battle, Major General Johannes von Ravenstein drove right into the middle of a New Zealand battalion. He was promptly taken prisoner. This daring and capable commander would not be freed until 1948.[38] He was replaced by Major General Boettcher. Colonel Mickl took over Group Boettcher, still holding its positions south of Sidi Rezegh.

Dawn broke clear and cold on November 30. Both sides were near the end of their tether, but the Afrika Korps was in extremely bad shape. Its exhausted soldiers had little food and little or no water. The RAF dominated the skies, and several supply columns did not make it through. Each Panzer division was down to a handful of tanks, and they were short of fuel and ammunition. The New Zealanders were at last virtually encircled, true enough, but strong Allied forces to the south and in Tobruk gave them hope of early relief. Worse still, the Italian forces besieging Tobruk would never hold up against a determined attack, and the British inside the perimeter had long before proven that determination was their strongest point. Many other commanders would have considered the situation hopeless and ordered a retreat under such circumstances. Erwin Rommel ordered another attack. He directed Ariete to advance west from Point 175 against the New Zealanders east of Sidi Rezegh; the 15th Panzer, supported by Group Michl, was to attack Belhamed from the south while the 90th Light struck the village from the north. Of this move, Major General von Mellenthin later wrote: ". . . Rommel's decision to continue the battle until he had wiped out the New Zealanders is striking proof of his will power and determination."[39]

On the morning of November 30 Major General Neumann-Silkow's 15th Panzer Division left the El Duda area and attacked the southern sector of the New Zealand pocket near Sidi Rezegh. At the same time, elements of the 90th Light Division struck from the north. They made progress, and by nightfall Sidi Rezegh was back in German hands. Six hundred New Zealanders and 12 guns were captured by the two German divisions.[40] Meanwhile, Lieutenant General Norrie personally led the South African 1st Brigade in attacks toward Point 175. He was covered by the 4th Armoured Brigade, which had absorbed all the tanks of the 22nd Armoured, thus reducing the 7th Armoured Division to a single brigade. They gained a mile against Ariete (which lost 19 light and medium tanks) and the remnants of the 21st Panzer Division but were unable to prevent Rommel from again falling on the already mauled New Zealand 2nd Division with the bulk of his panzers. On December 1 the Desert Fox overran the tough New Zealand 4th Brigade near Belhamed. The fighting was heavy, but the New Zealand Division was cut in two.[41] Major General Freyberg, the hardened divisional commander, recognized the signs. Since the Axis southern flank was holding firm, he correctly assessed his own position as untenable and decided to break out on his own initiative while he still had the forces to break out with. The decision was not made any too soon. That night he assembled the remnants of his division at Zaafran (five miles east of Belhamed), broke the encirclement, and escaped to the southwest, losing another 1,000 men and 26 guns in the process. The 1st Army Tank Brigade, which had supported it so well, accompanied the New Zealanders out of the trap. It was down to its last 10 "I" tanks. The Siege of Tobruk was restored, and the New Zealand 2nd Division was thoroughly mauled and temporarily eliminated as an effective combat unit. It would be months before it could be restored to its former strength. During the morning of December 2 it began the trip across the Egyptian frontier, while the remnants of the 7th Armoured Division and the 1st South African Brigade retreated southward, into the desert south of Bir el Gubi. It seemed at that moment that Rommel had won the battle, but the cost had been very high indeed.[42]

10

The Retreat to Cyrenaica and the Death of the Frontier Garrisons

The Allied retreat of December 1-2 signaled a lull in the fighting that had been raging unabated for two weeks. Rommel radioed Hitler and reported the destruction of 814 enemy tanks and scout cars, along with 127 enemy aircraft. He also informed the Fuehrer that 9,000 prisoners had been taken.[1] Rommel's own losses were 142 tanks and 25 armored cars either damaged, destroyed, or missing. Over 4,000 Germans had been killed, wounded, or captured so far, including a divisional commander and sixteen other commanding officers.[2] The Afrika Korps was a shell of its former self, down to a strength of about 80 operational panzers. In addition, thousands of other Axis soldiers were still surrounded and under seige at Bardia, Sollum, and Halfaya Pass. Marshal Bastico and Rommel had signaled Rome on November 30. In the dispatch they virtually declared operational bankruptcy and urgently demanded troops, ammunition, and equipment of all kinds. In recent weeks they had received only about 40,000 tons (one source said 29,843 tons) of the 120,000 tons of supplies sent to North Africa.[3] The British stranglehold on the Mediterranean supply routes was crippling the Axis Army.

Contrary to Rommel's hopes, the campaign was not yet over. General Ritchie was unimaginative, but he could obey orders, and his orders from Auchinleck were still uncompromising. Resolutely, in the manner that reminds one of a bulldog, Ritchie reformed his damaged forces to strike again.

The two sides now resembled punch-drunk boxers, both battered beyond recognition but neither willing to concede victory to the other. The first three days of December represented only a break between rounds. However, one of the fighters was even now marshaling his strength for what proved to be the knockout blow.

About December 1, Ritchie sent most of his Eighth Army's reserves, the South African 2nd Infantry Division and the Free French 1st Brigade, to the frontier to relieve the Indian 4th Division and the New Zealand 5th brigade at Bardia, Sollum, and Halfaya Pass. This move freed five fresh brigades for use around Tobruk.[4]

Auchinleck was also again making his presence felt in a decisive way. The commander-in-chief for the Middle East was now at Eighth Army Headquarters and remained there for the rest of the campaign, but he did not interfere in tactical operations. His sole concern was getting reinforcements to Ritchie as quickly as possible. As soon as the 1st Armoured Division arrived in Egypt, Auchinleck ordered the 12th Lancers (an armored car regiment) and the divisional artillery forward.[5] The Royal Dragoons armored car regiment was ordered from Syria to the front, as was the Indian 38th Infantry Brigade from Egypt and the 150th Infantry Brigade from Palestine, as well as other, smaller units.[6] Perhaps more important for the Allied cause, battered units already at the front received replacements, new equipment, repaired equipment, supplies, and much-needed rest.

Ritchie reorganized his command during the lull by placing the Tobruk garrison (the 70th Infantry Division, the Polish 1st Brigade, and the 1st Army Tank Brigade) and the South African 2nd Infantry Division under XIII Corps command. The New Zealand 5th Infantry Brigade, which had not been involved in the Belhamed–Sidi Rezegh fighting, was attached to the South African 2nd Division. Norrie's XXX Corps was given the 7th Armoured and Indian 4th divisions as well as the 22nd Guards and the South African 1st brigades. Most of the newly arriving troops were also earmarked for the XXX Corps.[7]

After over two weeks of more or less continuous battle, defeat rapidly closed in on the Afrika Korps. On December 1, over Cruewell's objections, General Rommel decided to send a couple of mobile task forces (each with a reduced infantry battalion, an antitank company, and some artillery) to relieve, or at least take some of the pressure off of, the frontier garrisons. The next day one column started down the Coastal Road, the other down the Trigh Capuzzo. The northern force never came back: On December 3 it was ambushed by the New Zealand 5th Brigade and destroyed 10 miles from Bardia. At about the same time, the southern column clashed with the Indian 4th Division, was brought under heavy attack by the RAF, and was forced to withdraw.[8] Rommel didn't know it yet, but this turned out to be the last attempt to rescue the garrisons. Meanwhile, however, Rommel had more pressing problems, because the British were advancing on Tobruk again.

For Rommel, the latest phase of the British Winter Offensive began when reconnaissance units reported that a new force of British armor, reorganized from previously beaten units and supplemented by new formations, was concentrating at Bir el Gubi, about five miles south of the Axis outpost line. Their obvious plan was to thrust into Rommel's rear southwest of Tobruk and force him to fight them there. This move would also force the Desert Fox to lift the Siege of Tobruk, because he no longer had the resources to defend against the Eighth Army's armor and maintain his hold on the fortress at the same time. Abandoning the siege would, in turn, release the powerful garrison, which could join in the battle against Rommel's main force. Ritchie's move, though predictable and lacking in surprise, was very dangerous nevertheless. As if to underline the urgency of the situation, the Tobruk garrison grew aggressive again. On December 4 relatively fresh elements of the 70th Infantry Division and the 32nd Army Tank Brigade defeated the nearly exhausted 21st Panzer Division at El Duda and took the important Duda–Belhamed hill line, creating a dangerous salient in the weakened siege line. Meanwhile, the heretofore lightly engaged Indian 4th Division appeared south of El Adem. West of Tobruk the South African armored cars played havoc in Rommel's communication and supply zone, and the Royal Air Force strafed Panzer Group Afrika's vital supply columns. Things were getting too close, even for Erwin Rommel. During the night of December 4–5, he withdrew his mobile forces from between the garrison and the 4th Indian Division. In doing so he used the last escape route still open: the El Duda–Sidi Rezegh corridor, which had shrunk to a depth of two miles during the day's fighting. It is doubtful whether Rommel could have extracted these forces if he had waited another few hours to give the order to retreat. Their departure, along with that of the Italian Bologna Infantry Division, ended the Siege of Tobruk. It had been lifted after 242 days.[9]

Rommel, always the last to give up, refused to concede that the siege could not be reimposed. He regrouped rapidly and launched a spoiling attack on Bir el Gubi. He hoped to break up Ritchie's new concentration, turn around, and chase the garrison back into its cage. However, Rommel also sensed that this might well be the last roll of the dice. He must win at Bir el Gubi, or the campaign was lost. Urgently he summoned the Italians to join him, but they were no longer battleworthy.

December 5 was a wasted day for Panzer Group Afrika. Erwin Rommel ordered all his mobile forces to concentrate north of Bir el Gubi but, although the Afrika Korps assembled for the counterattack, Ariete never arrived and the Trieste Motorized Division never even left its assembly areas. The 8th Panzer Regiment did attack and overrun part of the Indian 11th Brigade but, with little support, went no farther.[10]

The Battle of Bir el Gubi raged on throughout December 6 and 7. Cruewell led the Afrika Korps, but General Gambara would not come up with the Italian XX Motorized Corps. "Where is Gambara?" Cruewell radioed again and again. "Where is Gambara?" was the battle cry under which Bir el Gubi was fought. "Where is Gambara?" was the epitaph for the entire campaign, because the Afrika Korps no longer had the strength to go it alone. Cruewell could not take Bir el Gubi or disperse the Allied armor. The worn-out 15th Panzer Division was the only really intact unit Rommel had left, and it was repulsed with heavy casualties by the fresh 22nd Guards Brigade.[11] Major General Walter Neumann-Silkow, the popular divisional commander, was killed by a shell burst on December 7. The Afrika Korps had lost both of its divisional commanders within 10 days. That same Sunday, thousands of miles away, even greater events took place. In Russia, Zhukov's winter offensive entered its second day. It was to cost Germany the lives of thousands of her best soldiers and push Army Group Center—then in the suburbs of Moscow—back a hundred miles in what was to be Nazi Germany's first really serious defeat on the ground. This defeat saved the Soviet Union and foiled Hitler's bid for a rapid conquest of the Communist state. The dreaded two-front war was and would remain a reality. Also that day, Japanese aircraft attacked the American naval base at Pearl Harbor, pulling the United States into the war against Germany as well. Adolf Hitler's legions would now have to face the combined might of most of the industrialized world. Although they did not realize it, the odds against the Nazis had become so great that they could no longer realistically hope to win.

The significance of these events was more appreciated by his African commander-in-chief than by Hitler himself. Rommel, however, had little time to ponder such momentous turns of fortune, for the issues of the moment were far more pressing. He had been forced to draw a painful conclusion: He had suffered his first major defeat. He now ordered the retreat to begin.

Marshal of Italy Ettore Bastico was a very upset man on December 7, not because of anything happening in Russia or America but because he had gotten word that Erwin Rommel was planning a major withdrawal without even asking permission. He ordered the German to report to him immediately, but Rommel sent word back that he was too busy to get away, so Bastico decided to pay a visit to Rommel instead. It was a stormy meeting. Bastico refused to authorize a retreat, and Rommel replied that he would do what he saw fit. He then blamed the Italians for his defeat in this campaign. The two men were soon screaming at each other. Bastico later recalled that Rommel "very heatedly, and acting like an overbearing and uncouth boor, yelled that he had struggled for victory for three weeks and had now decided to withdraw his divisions to Tripoli. . . ." Rommel curtly declared; "We haven't won the battle, so now there is nothing to do but retreat!"[12] The growling continued, but Erwin Rommel was still the commander of Panzer Group Afrika. On the night of December 7–8 it began moving west.

Rommel's delaying tactics on December 8 were so successful that General Gott actually believed that Panzer Group Afrika had been reinforced. By December 9 the retreat was well under way. Rommel sent the nonmotorized elements of the 90th Light (that is, most of the division) off to Agedabia, 100 miles south of Benghazi, to keep the Coastal Road open at that critical point. He still hoped to halt his retreat at the Gazala line, a fortified position previously constructed by the Italians, but he was taking no chances.

There were two bits of good news on December 9: First, the X Italian Corps under Lieutenant General Gioda was placed under Rommel's command. This unit's divisions were virtually immobile, so they could not be used now, during a fluid retreat, but they might come in handy later. The other piece of news was an unmixed blessing: At Rommel's insistence General Gambara was replaced as commander of the XX Motorized Corps by Major General Piazzoni, the commander of the Trieste Motorized Division.[13] Gambara became Bastico's chief of staff, but at least now Rommel wouldn't have to depend on him for help in the field.[14]

To have held at Gazala would have at least saved most of Cyrenaica, but it was not to be. The First Battle of Gazala was fought from December 13 to 17. Rommel's battle plan was simple: The Italian XXI Infantry Corps (Brescia, Trento, and Pavia divisions, running north to south) would hold the Coastal Road sector while the Italian XX Motorized Corps (Trieste and Ariete) held the center. The Afrika Korps (21st and 15th Panzer divisions, running north to south, respectively) covered the desert flank, and the 8th Panzer Regiment formed the reserve.[15]

Godwin-Austen's XIII Corps pursued the Panzer Group and launched a major attack on December 15. The New Zealand 5th and Polish 1st brigades pushed back the XXI Corps and took Gazala itself, as well as a number of prisoners. The Indian 4th Division launched the main blow at Rommel's center but were turned back by a counterattack from the 8th Panzer Regiment. About 1,000 Indians were taken prisoner, but the 8th Panzer lost nine tanks. The Afrika Korps was now down to 33 operational tanks: 14 in the 15th Panzer Division and 19 in the 21st.[16] Losses in the infantry were as high or higher. The 15th Motorized Infantry Battalion, for example, had only five officers, 14 NCO's, 58 men, three support guns, 10 Volkswagens, five heavy trucks, and six motorcycles left on December 17. Before "Crusader" began they had had 480 officers and men. As the retreat continued they formed part of the rear guard and suffered even more casualties.[17]

Casualties among the senior officers were also high. On December 9 Major General Max Summermann, the commander of the 90th Light Division, was killed in an air attack.[18] He was soon replaced by Major General Richard Veith, a veteran of the Eastern Front.[19] Rommel had lost all three of his German divisional commanders in one campaign: two dead and one captured.

The retreat was very hard on the rank and file, who had been in almost continuous combat for three weeks. An advance is much easier than a retreat. The sun beat down brutally overhead, and the desert nights were cold. Familiar names were passed as they continued west, including Gazala, Derna, Mechili, and Msus.

Unlike that of the Italians, German morale did not sag. Rommel, ever present in victory, was even more in evidence now. He realized that, in North Africa, holding terrain meant nothing. What was a few hundred square miles of desert worth anyway? Germany could certainly live without them. What mattered was keeping Panzer Group Afrika intact.

The British, who did not yet grasp the insignificance of occupying thousands of acres of barren rock, thought that this was the beginning of the end for Rommel. One English newspaper reported: "The remains of the German Afrika Korps and the Italian Army are retreating along the Coastal road of the Bay of Sirte to Tripoli. The main objective, the destruction of enemy forces in the Western Desert, has been achieved. The German armor has been defeated. Only a handful of German tanks have survived and they are fleeing in panic to Tripoli."[20]

Marshal Bastico, the Italian commander-in-chief for North Africa, did almost panic because he feared the political consequences of retreat. He wanted Gazala held indefinitely; then he wanted the retreat halted at Derna and Mechili.[21] Along with Luftwaffe Field Marshal Kesselring, he met with Rommel on the last day of the Battle of Gazala. "I'm retiring because I must do so," Rommel snapped at them, "or else I shall lose not only a battle but my whole army."[22]

The next day Marshal Cavallero, the head of the Italian Army and a favorite of Mussolini, arrived from Rome to register his objections. "An obvious defeat would be dangerous for Mussolini's prestige," he lectured Rommel.

"And what about total defeat with the loss of the whole army and North Africa?" Rommel replied tartly.

Cavallero nevertheless demanded the order to retreat be canceled. Rommel refused to be intimidated. The argument grew stormy, but the retreat continued.[23]

The retreat was not the disaster some commanders expected. The new commander of the 90th Light Division was puzzled over the success of the withdrawal. "Nobody can see any escape," he told his staff on December 20. "The British outnumber us enormously. The puzzle is, why are they following us so slowly? Time and again they have enabled us to dodge encirclement. There is only one explanation: their awe of General Rommel, and his capacity to surprise—that's why they're following so hesitantly."[24]

On December 20, just the day after the British vanguard reached Derna,[25] the 15th Panzer Division took up positions south of Benghazi. Rommel was greatly relieved. He could not be cut off now. He was also reinforced by 40 new tanks, fresh from Europe and complete with crews. They had arrived in Tripoli on December 17.[26]

Six days later, elements of the 7th Armoured Division tried to cut the Coastal Road between Benghazi and Agedabia. The British armor made the mistake of splitting up into various columns, separated over a wide area. As a result they were defeated in detail by the concentrated attacks of the panzers.[27]

The next day the retreat resumed, and Rommel evacuated Benghazi.

Three days later, on December 27, the Afrika Korps again turned on its tormentors. It could do so at last, since Panzer Group Afrika now had a total of 70 tanks. In a three-day battle at least 65 British tanks were knocked out, and the 7th Support Group and 22nd Armoured Brigade were again mauled.[28] Ritchie was forced to follow at an even slower pace.

Rommel managed to embarrass himself at Agedabia that week. The Italians had only a dozen 88mm anti-aircraft guns left, so Rommel ordered them to dig in the real 88's far apart and construct dummies for the sake of British reconnaissance units. A few days later he inspected the area again and found the 88's in full view, attracting heavy shelling. He immediately flew into a rage and went off to find the Italian commander responsible. He came back red-faced. "They *are* dummies," he said. "The Italians have knocked them together from telegraph poles. It's the camouflage paint that fooled me." He then complimented the Italian he had set out to reprimand.[29]

Rommel continued his retreat to the Mersa el Brega line, which the last unit reached on January 12. Ritchie halted at Agedabia. Rommel would now have time to reorganize refit, re-equip, and strike again. For the Axis garrisons trapped on the Egyptian-Libyan frontier, however, time was running out.

They were the best of the German infantry: proud, tough, resourceful, and self-reliant. They were trapped, 450 miles behind enemy lines, without hope of relief. Nevertheless, they fought like tigers, denying the British a clear supply route from Alexandria and tying down forces Ritchie would rather have used against Rommel. The Eighth Army could never concentrate as long as they held out, and they intended to hold out as long as possible.

Bardia was the first to fall. Here Major General Artur Schmidt was cornered with 2,200 Germans (mostly from the administrative services) and 4,200 Italians from the Savona Infantry Division. Schmidt was besieged by elements of Major General I. P. de Villiers' South African 2nd Division, along with the rebuilt 1st Army Tank Brigade, artillery from the New Zealand Division and the Polish Brigade, other nondivisional units, and strong detachments from the Royal Navy and Air Force. The Italians were of little use in the battle. Around New Year's Day the last water hole was lost. Finally, on January 2, 1942, General Schmidt surrendered the garrison with Rommel's approval. Over 1,100 British POW's were released when the town fell.[30]

Sollum was defended with equal skill by the 300th Oasis Reserve

Battalion under Captain Ennecerus. The siege began on November 21. By January 10, his two companies were reduced to 70 men. Their daily rations were 20 grams of bread, a handful of rice, and a spoonful of currants per man per day. On January 12 the British launched their final assault. The German soldiers resisted fanatically, and the first attack was beaten back with heavy losses. Massive concentrations of British artillery and mortars continued to shell the town relentlessly, while the Allied infantry prepared another attack. The last buildings of the ruined town were destroyed in the fierce bombardment. The British foot soldiers, sensing that the end was near, struck again. Soon the last round of ammunition was fired. Ennecerus ordered his men to destroy their weapons and surrender. The agony of Sollum was over. The siege had lasted 56 days.[31]

While Sollum reeled in its death throes, the Halfaya garrison also neared the end of its resistance. The position was held by Major General Fedele De Giorgis, with some 4,200 veterans of the Savona Division, and by 2,100 Germans under Major Reverend Wilhelm "Papa" Bach, a chaplain from Mannheim and a battalion commander in the 104th Panzer Grenadier Regiment.[32] All day, every day, the men lay in their trenches and foxholes, awaiting attacks that seldom came. The Allies had learned the folly of launching direct, frontal assaults against the vital pass. They decided to starve Bach and his men into submission.

The defenders ate one meal a day, at about midnight. They got two cups of watery soup and one canful of beef. The cooks also served a jug of coffee, made with salt water, for every three men.[33]

Rommel tried to organize food and water parachute drops from Crete. One of these attempts actually took place and dropped the supplies to the troops. The next night, however, the Luftwaffe transport squadron found the RAF waiting: Every German plane was shot down. This was the last attempt to resupply the garrison by air.[34]

On January 17, 1942, Major Bach and Major General de Giorgis surrendered. All German weapons were destroyed. After the South Africans gave the survivors a much-needed meal, they were formed up. As they got ready to march off, an incident almost unparalleled in the Desert War occurred: They were fired on by elements of the Free French Brigade. After recovering from their initial shock, the South Africans stopped the shooting. The French had committed one of the most disgraceful acts of the war in North Africa.[35]

The loss of the frontier garrisons cost the Axis 14,000 men, of whom

4,000 were German. These losses ran the Panzer Group's casualty list to 38,300, or 32 percent of Rommel's original total. Most of these losses were Italian infantrymen, captured in the retreat or trapped on the frontier, where the Savona Division ceased to exist. A total of 14,600 Germans were killed, wounded, or missing. The Allies lost 17 percent of their force, or 17,700 men killed, wounded, or missing.[36]

According to Brigadier Young, two thirds of the Axis Army had been destroyed, and barely half of its personnel had escaped death, capture, or disablement. Of Rommel's 412 tanks, 386 were lying "burnt out, blackened wrecks around the battlefield."[37]

The defeats around Tobruk and Sidi Rezegh brought Rommel back to his starting point. The British thought that they had permanently cleared eastern Libya of the German Army and that the Third Reich's tide in Africa had reached its peak and was receding. They were wrong on both counts.

Epilogue

Contrary to British hopes and beliefs, the German defeat in "Crusader" represented only a momentary phase in the war in North Africa, and a very brief one at that. The real significance of the battle and the preceding campaigns was that the weapon had been forged. The Afrika Korps had survived its birth and growing pains and was well on the way to becoming perhaps the most feared and respected military formation in World War II. Likewise, Erwin Rommel had completed his professional development. The tactics, strategies, and leadership principles he developed and used in World War I, in France, and in Cyrenaica would remain unchanged in the 2½ years left to him. His innovative thought processes, which the world had labeled genius, also remained unaltered. The legend of the Desert Fox had been born and would continue to grow. He would soon be recognized as one of the great captains of all time.

After "Crusader," Rommel recaptured Benghazi in January 1942 in a brilliant counteroffensive since known as the Second Cyrenaican Campaign. Later that year, despite odds of 3 to 1 or more, he overran the British Eighth Army's vaunted Gazala Line, took Tobruk, and drove to the gates of Alexandria. Finally decisively defeated in the two-week Battle of El Alamein, he conducted a brilliant retreat to Tripoli before turning on his pursuers in Tunisia. He successively commanded Panzer Army Afrika, the German-Italian 1st Panzer Army, and Army Group Afrika before his health broke down and he was evacuated to Europe two months before the final collapse of the Axis front in North Africa. Once home, Hitler gave him command of Army Group B and eventually charged him with repulsing the Allied invasion of France in 1944. Rommel begged Hitler to withdraw the Afrika Korps from Tunisia while there was still time, but the dictator would not listen. The Korps was forced to surrender in May 1943. Today its name is synonymous with courage and gallantry in the face of overwhelming odds.

Like his men, Erwin Rommel remained true to his code. He survived the Afrika Korps only a little more than a year. Finally recognizing

Hitler for what he was, Rommel became involved in the plot to rid Germany of her, by now, clearly unbalanced dictator. When the plot failed, Rommel was given the choice of committing suicide or facing the People's Court. The Nazis promised to spare his family if he chose the first course, so the Desert Fox took poison on October 14, 1944. He is buried at Herrlingen, West Germany, not far from the village of his birth.

Notes

Chapter 1

1. Paul Carell, *The Foxes of the Desert* (New York: E. P. Dutton and Company, 1960) pp. 109–10 (hereafter cited as "Carell").
2. Reynolds and Eleanor Packard, *Balcony Empire* (New York: Oxford University Press, 1942), p. 25 (hereafter cited as "Packard").
3. W. G. F. Jackson, *The Battle of North Africa, 1940–43* (New York: Mason/Charter, 1975), pp. 15, 39 (hereafter cited as "Jackson").
4. Jackson, p. 19; Pietro Badoglio, *Italy in the Second World War* (Westport, Conn.: Greenwood Press, 1976), p. 32.
5. B. H. Liddell Hart, *The German Generals Talk* (New York: Quill, 1979), p. 155 (hereafter cited as "Hart, 1979").
6. Ibid., pp. 156–58. Lieutenant General Ritter von Thoma later commanded the 17th Panzer Division in Russia and the Afrika Korps in Egypt in 1942. During his career, von Thoma was wounded 17 times. See Samuel W. Mitcham, Jr., *Rommel's Desert War: The Life and Death of the Afrika Korps* (Briarcliff Manor, N.Y.: Stein and Day, 1982).
7. See I. S. O. Playfair et al., *The Mediterranean and Middle East,* Vol. I–IV (London: Her Majesty's Stationery Office, 1954–66), Vol. I, pp. 237–38 (hereafter cited as "Playfair").
8. Packard, p. 267.
9. John Strawson, *The Battle for North Africa* (New York: Bonanza Books, 1969), p. 10 (hereafter cited as "Strawson").
10. Erwin Rommel, *The Rommel Papers,* ed. B. H. Liddell Hart (New York: Harcourt, Brace & Company, 1953), p. 93 (hereafter cited as "Rommel"); Richard Collier et al., *The War in the Desert* (Alexandria, Va.: Time-Life Books, 1979), p. 27 (hereafter cited as "Collier"); Packard, pp. 294–95.
11. Robert Goralski, *World War II Almanac, 1931–1945* (New York: G. P. Putnam's Sons, 1981), p. 141; Rommel, p. 93.
12. Jackson, pp. 44–45.

13. Collier, p. 28.
14. Packard, pp. 297–98.
15. Collier, p. 29; Packard, pp. 297–98.
16. Rommel, p. 94.
17. Packard, pp. 298–99.
18. Collier, p. 32.
19. Rommel, p. 94.
20. United States Army, "Order of Battle of the Italian Army, June, 1943" (Washington, D.C.: U.S. Army Military Intelligence Division, 1943), p. 63 (hereafter cited as "Italian OB"); Jackson, p. 39.
21. Rommel, pp. 94–95.
22. Ibid., p. 97.
23. Ibid.
24. Desmond Young, *Rommel: The Desert Fox* (New York: Harper & Row, 1950), p. 82 (hereafter cited as "Young").

Chapter 2

1. Young, p. 28. Erwin, Sr. was appointed director of the *Realgymnasium* at Aalen in 1898. He moved his family there when the future field marshal was six years old.
2. David Irving, *The Trail of the Fox* (New York: E. P. Dutton & Company, 1977), p. 10 (hereafter cited as "Irving").
3. Young, p. 28.
4. Irving, pp. 9–10.
5. Young, p. 29.
6. Irving, pp. 9–10.
7. Young, p. 30.
8. Irving, p. 10.
9. Charles Douglas-Home, *Rommel* (London: Excalibur, n.d.), p. 20 (originally published by Saturday Review Press, New York, 1973); Young, p. 14.
10. Young, p. 30.
11. Irving, p. 11.
12. Ibid., pp. 10–11; Young, p. 30. Lucie's family was of Italian origins. She was introduced to her future husband by one of Rommel's fellow officer-cadets.
13. Irving, p. 449.
14. Erwin Rommel, *Attacks* (Vienna, Va.: Athena Press, 1979), pp. 1–2

(originally published in Germany as *Infantry Greift an,* 1936, and hereafter cited as "Rommel, 1936").

15. Irving, pp. 13–14.
16. Young, p. 31.
17. Ibid., p. 32.
18. Ibid., p. 41.
19. Rommel, 1936, pp. 8–15.
20. Ibid., pp. 58–59.
21. Ibid., pp. 59–60.
22. Young, p. 33. Rommel was the first lieutenant in his regiment to receive this award (Rommel, 1936, p. 73). He lost less than a dozen men in this exploit (Young, p. 33).
23. Rommel, 1936, p. 88.
24. Irving, p. 14.
25. Rommel, 1936, p. 91.
26. Irving, pp. 14–15.
27. Ronald Lewin, *Rommel as Military Commander* (New York: Ballantine Books, 1970), p. 4 (originally published by D. Van Nostrand Company, New York, 1968); also see Young, p. 35.
28. Young, pp. 36–37.
29. Ibid., p. 37.
30. Ibid., p. 49.
31. Ibid.
32. Irving, p. 22, and Young, pp. 46–47. Rommel turned down an offer to join the Stuttgart Police at this time.
33. Young, p. 50.
34. Irving, p. 23.
35. Ibid., p. 24.
36. Ibid., pp. 23–24.
37. Young, pp. 34–35.
38. Ibid., p. 35.
39. Ibid., p. 34.
40. Hans Speidel, *Invasion, 1944* (New York: Paperback Library, 1950), p. 145 (originally published as *Invasion 1944, Ein Beitrag zu Rommels und des Reiches Schicksal*) (Tubingen and Stuttgart: Rainer Wunderlich Verlag Hermann Leins, 1949).
41. Ibid., p. 146.
42. Irving, p. 31. Mrs. Schirach married her husband for social and political reasons, while he was after her money, according to Alfred Speer, Hitler's minister of munitions. She broke with him in 1948

after he had been sent to prison as a war criminal. See Alfred Speer, *Spandau: The Secret Diaries* (New York: Pocket Books, 1977, by arrangement with Macmillan Publishing Company, New York), pp. 159–60.

43. Young, pp. 56–57.
44. Irving, p. 29.
45. Ibid., p. 30.
46. Ibid., p. 27.
47. Ibid., p. 29.
48. Young, pp. 58–60; David Irving, *The War Path: Hitler's Germany, 1933–1939* (New York: The Viking Press, 1978), p. 190 (hereafter cited as "Irving, 1978").
49. Irving, p. 32.
50. Young, p. 61.
51. Ibid., p. 63.
52. Irving, p. 37.
53. Heinz Werner Schmidt, *With Rommel in the Desert* (London: G. Harrap & Company; New York: Ballantine Books, 1972), p. 89 (hereafter cited as "Schmidt"; page numbers are from the Ballantine edition).
54. Rommel, p. 4.
55. Heinz Guderian, *Panzer Leader* (New York: Ballantine Books, 1967), p. 18 (originally published in the United States by E. P. Dutton & Company, New York, 1957).
56. Irving, pp. 40–42.
57. Ibid., p. 41.
58. Ibid., p. 43.
59. David Irving, *Hitler's War* (New York: The Viking Press, 1977), pp. 57–81 (hereafter cited as "Irving, 1977"); Erich von Manstein, *Lost Victories* (Novato, Calif.: Presidio, 1982), pp. 94–127 (originally published as *Verlorene Siege,* Athenaum-Verlag, Bonn, 1955); William L. Shirer, *The Rise and Fall of the Third Reich* (New York: Simon & Schuster, 1960), p. 718.
60. Rommel, p. 7.
61. Ibid., pp. 8–9.
62. Ibid., p. 9.
63. Ibid., p. 10.
64. Ibid., pp. 10–11.
65. Ibid., p. 11.
66. Ibid.
67. Ibid., p. 12.

68. Ibid., pp. 12–13.
69. Ibid., p. 13.
70. Ibid., p. 16.
71. Ibid., p. 17.
72. Paul Carell, *Scorched Earth* (New York: Ballantine Books, 1971, by arrangement with Little, Brown and Company, Boston), p. 507; Rommel, p. 17.
73. Rommel, p. 17.
74. Ibid., pp. 18–19.
75. Ibid., pp. 20–21.
76. Ibid., pp. 22–24.
77. Ibid., p. 26.
78. Ibid., pp. 24–25.
79. Ibid., p. 27.
80. Ibid., p. 29.
81. Ibid., pp. 29–30.
82. Ibid., p. 30.
83. Young, p. 70; Rommel, p. 32. According to Young, the 42nd Anti-tank Battalion of the 7th Panzer Division was overrun in this action.
84. Rommel, p. 33.
85. Ibid.; Irving., p. 42.
86. Irving, p. 54.
87. Young, p. 74. Major General Victor M. Fortune, commander of the British 51st Highlander (Infantry) Division, was among the prisoners, as was the commander of the French IX Corps and three French divisional commanders.
88. Rommel, pp. 82–84; Young, p. 75.
89. Rommel, pp. 82–84; Young, pp. 76–77.
90. Irving, p. 56.
91. Young, p. 77.
92. Ibid., pp. 76–77.

Chapter 3

1. Irving, p. 59.
2. Many of Rommel's photos taken at this time may be seen at the U.S. National Archives, Microfilm T-84, Roll 276, "The Rommel Collection" (Washington, D.C.: unpublished documents, n.d.).
3. Irving, p. 58.

4. Ibid., pp. 58–59.
5. Ibid., p. 60.
6. Marshal Rodolfo Graziani had been commander of the Italian forces in North Africa, governor of Libya, and chief of staff of the Italian Army, all at the same time. After his fall from grace following the Libyan debacle, he lost all three posts. Marshal Italo Gariboldi became governor of Libya, Bastico became his operations officer, and Roatta was named chief of staff of the Italian Army. Bastico eventually became the Italian commander-in-chief for North Africa.
7. Rommel, pp. 99–100.
8. Ibid., pp. 100–1.
9. Ibid., p. 100.
10. Italian OB, p. 36.
11. Ibid., pp. 55–60.
12. Irving, p. 68.
13. Rommel, p. 102.
14. Irving, p. 207.
15. Rommel, p. 103.
16. Ibid.
17. Stumme had commanded the 7th Panzer Division before Rommel took over in February 1940. Later Stumme commanded the XXXX Panzer Corps in Russia and was acting commander of Panzer Army Afrika before dying of a heart attack on October 23, 1942, during the Battle of El Alamein (see Mitcham, *Rommel's Desert War,* pp. 141–51).
18. Irving, pp. 51 and 62–63. Funck later served in Russia and in Rommel's Army Group B as commander of the XXXXVII Panzer Corps. See Samuel W. Mitcham, Jr., *Rommel's Last Battle* (Briarcliff Manor, N.Y.: Stein and Day, 1983).
19. Schmidt, p. 23.
20. Ibid.
21. Ibid., p. 25.
22. Rommel, p. 104.
23. Strawson, p. 42.
24. Rommel, p. 103.
25. Collier, pp. 31–32.
26. Irving, pp. 70–71.
27. Rommel, p. 104.
28. Ibid., pp. 106–7.
29. Playfair II, pp. 1–7.

30. Ibid., p. 8.
31. Ibid., p. 2.
32. Collier, p. 63.
33. Rommel, pp. 107–9; Carell, p. 9.
34. Playfair II, p. 19; Rommel, pp. 109–10.
35. Playfair II, p. 19.
36. Rommel, p. 110.
37. Erwan Bergot, *The Afrika Korps* (New York: Charter, 1975), p. 61 (hereafter cited as "Bergot").
38. Playfair II, p. 21.
39. Bergot, p. 61.
40. Rommel, p. 111.
41. Carell, p. 11; Playfair II, p. 22.
42. Playfair II, pp. 23–24.
43. Rommel, pp. 109 and 112–13.
44. Rommel, p. 112; also see Playfair II, p. 23.
45. Collier, p. 65.
46. Rommel, p. 113.
47. Bergot, pp. 60–61.
48. Playfair II, p. 27.
49. Irving, p. 78.
50. Rommel, p. 114.
51. Ibid., p. 115.
52. Rommel, p. 117; Bergot, p. 249.
53. Elements of the Indian 18th Cavalry Regiment broke out and the 2nd Support Group escaped with the Australian infantry, eventually retreating all the way to Egypt. Parts of the Australian 3rd Anti Tank Regiment, however, were also trapped inside Mechili (Playfair III, p. 30).
54. Rommel, p. 116.
55. Ibid.
56. Jackson, pp. 105–6.
57. Schmidt, p. 35.
58. Ibid.
59. Collier, p. 65.
60. Ibid.
61. Several sources give various versions of the details of the captures of Neame and O'Connor; for example, see Carell, pp. 12–13; Bergot, pp. 70–71; Playfair II, p. 29; and Rommel, p. 118.
62. Playfair II, p. 29.

Chapter 4

1. Playfair II, p. 34.
2. Rommel, p. 34.
3. Andrew Kershaw and Ian Close (eds.), *The Desert War* (New York: Marshal Cavendish Promotions, 1975), p. 14 (hereafter cited as "Kershaw and Close").
4. Strawson, pp. 56–57.
5. Playfair II, pp. 34–35; Strawson, pp. 56–57.
6. Rommel, p. 121.
7. Irving, p. 82.
8. Ibid.
9. Ibid.
10. Rommel, p. 123; also see Playfair II, pp. 35–36.
11. Bergot, p. 78.
12. Rommel, pp. 128–29.
13. Ibid., p. 123; Playfair II, p. 37.
14. Rommel, p. 124.
15. Ibid., pp. 125–26; Playfair II, p. 37.
16. Bergot, pp. 89–91.
17. Schmidt, p. 45.
18. Ibid.
19. Bergot, p. 79.
20. Rommel, p. 127.
21. Ibid., pp. 126–27.
22. See Irving, pp. 90–92. Johannes von Ravenstein commanded a panzer regiment in the Balkans and apparently briefly commanded the 8th Panzer Regiment in Africa before being promoted to divisional command.
23. Irving, pp. 90–92.
24. See Irving; Irving, 1977; and Mitcham, *Rommel's Last Battle.*
25. Carell, p. 18.
26. Playfair II, p. 31.
27. Schmidt, p. 45.
28. Playfair II, p. 41.
29. Ibid., p. 153.
30. Ibid.
31. Schmidt, p. 53.
32. Irving: pp. 51 and 62–63; Rommel, pp. 129–30.
33. Rommel, pp. 131–32; Kershaw and Close, p. 15.

34. Schmidt, p. 51.
35. Ibid., p. 49.
36. Irving, p. 74.
37. Rommel, p. 134; Playfair II, p. 156.

Chapter 5

1. Playfair II, pp. 33–36.
2. Strawson, p. 59.
3. Ibid., p. 61.
4. Irving, p. 91.
5. Playfair II, p. 157. Halder also wrote: "If history succeeds in un-ravelling the threads of what went on in Africa, it will have achieved a miracle, for Rommel managed to get things into such an unholy muddle that I doubt whether any one will ever be able to make head or tail of it." (Young, p. 83).
6. Young, pp. 100-1.
7. Ibid., p. 90.
8. Ibid, p. 91.
9. Carell, p. 21.
10. Ibid.
11. Frederick Wilhelm von Mellenthin, *Panzer Battles: A Study in the Employment of Armor in the Second World War* (Norman: University of Oklahoma Press, 1956), p. 54 (hereafter cited as "von Mellenthin").
12. Playfair II, p. 160.
13. Ibid., p. 160.
14. Ibid., p. 162.
15. Ibid., p. 163.
16. Irving, p. 96.
17. Carell, p. 25.
18. Playfair II, p. 163.
19. Irving, p. 101.
20. Rommel, p. 140.
21. See Playfair II, p. 166, for additional details on aircraft strengths.
22. Playfair II, p. 164.
23. Ibid., p. 167; Carell, p. 37.
24. Ibid., pp. 36–39.
25. Carell, pp. 42–43.
26. Ibid., pp. 40–42.

27. Ibid., pp. 41–42.
28. Rommel, pp. 144–45.
29. Ibid., p. 144.
30. Carell, p. 45.
31. Ibid.
32. Schmidt, p. 42.
33. Irving, p. 117.
34. Theodor Hartmann, *Wehrmacht Divisional Signs, 1938–1945* (London: Almark Publications, 1970), p. 59.

Chapter 6

1. Young, p. 135.
2. Ibid., pp. 132–33.
3. Ibid., p. 133.
4. Schmidt, p. 91.
5. Gause later became chief of staff of Army Group B in 1943–44, and of the Fifth Panzer Army in France in 1944. Westphal became chief of staff of Army Group C and OB South in Italy in 1944–45, where he rose to the rank of lieutenant general. After serving a period on the Eastern Front, Bayerlein commanded the Panzer Lehr Division on the Western Front, 1944–45, and briefly commanded a corps in the Ruhr Pocket in 1945. F. W. von Mellenthin did a tour of duty on the Russian Front with the XXXXVIII Panzer Corps (1942–43) before being transferred back to the West. He served as chief of staff of Army Group G in France and Germany, 1944–45.
6. Young, pp. 90–91.
7. von Mellenthin, pp. xi–xiii.
8. See ibid., pp. 183–436.
9. Young, p. 92.
10. Ibid., pp. 92–93.
11. Schmidt, p. 10.
12. Ibid., pp. 106–7.
13. Ibid., p. 107.
14. Young, p. 11.
15. Ibid., pp. 100–1.
16. Schmidt, pp. 78–80.
17. Ibid.
18. von Mellenthin, p. 63.

19. Young, p. 135.
20. Ibid., p. 136.
21. von Mellenthin, p. 63.
22. Ibid.
23. Schmidt, pp. 81–82.
24. von Mellenthin, p. 54.
25. Carell, pp. 178–79.
26. Young, p. 144.
27. Packard, p. 277.
28. Ibid.
29. Young, p. 147.
30. Ibid.
31. Ibid., p. 148.
32. Ibid., p. 147. Also see Young, pp. 152–53, for part of General Westphal's testimony at Nuremberg relating to Rommel's attitude toward the rules of warfare.
33. Ibid., p. 159.
34. Playfair III, pp. 23–25. Major General R. M. Scobie replaced Morshead as fortress commander.
35. Schmidt, p. 96.
36. Ibid., p. 97.
37. Ibid.
38. Young, p. 84.
39. Ibid., pp. 84–85.
40. Ibid., p. 85.

Chapter 7

1. Walter Warlimont, "The Decision in the Mediterranean," in H. A. Jacobsen and J. Rohwer, eds., *Decisive Battles of World War II: The German View* (New York: G. P. Putnam's Sons, 1965), p. 186 (hereafter cited as "Warlimont").
2. See Carell, p. 114; Strawson, p. 72; and Rommel, p. 155.
3. M. van Creveld, "Rommel's Supply Problem, 1941–42," *RUSI Journal* (London: Royal United Service Institute for Defence Studies, September 1974), pp. 67–73 (hereafter cited as "Creveld").
4. Strawson, p. 75.
5. von Mellenthin, p. 68.
6. Carell, p. 114; Strawson, p. 72; Rommel, p. 155; and Warlimont, p. 186.

7. Irving, p. 12.
8. Carell, pp. 46–47.
9. Irving, p. 113.
10. Ibid., pp. 116–17.
11. Young, pp. 101–2.
12. Irving, p. 120.
13. Young, p. 102.
14. Ibid.
15. Ibid.
16. von Mellenthin, p. 70.
17. Carell, p. 62.
18. Ibid., p. 66.
19. Irving, p. 122.
20. Schmidt, p. 105.
21. Playfair III, p. 1.
22. Ibid., pp. 1–2.
23. Ibid., p. 2.
24. Ibid., pp. 1–31.
25. von Mellenthin, p. 72.
26. Ibid., p. 63.
27. Rommel, p. 158.
28. Playfair III, pp. 27–31.
29. Ibid., pp. 27, 440–41. All armored thickness figures refer to frontal, or maximum, thickness.
30. Ibid.
31. Ibid.
32. Ibid., pp. 27–30, 440–41.
33. Ibid., pp. 16–17.
34. Carell, pp. 60–66.
35. Ibid., pp. 49–50.
36. Ibid., pp. 49–51.
37. Ibid.
38. Ibid., pp. 54–55.
39. Ibid.
40. Playfair III, p. 38.
41. Young, p. 81.
42. Irving, p. 125.
43. von Mellenthin, pp. 73–74.
44. Irving, p. 125.
45. von Mellenthin, pp. 73–74.

46. Irving, p. 131.
47. Playfair III, p. 40.
48. Ibid.; von Mellenthin, pp. 73–74. In addition to the units mentioned, the 4th Armoured Brigade had the 2nd Artillery Regiment, the 102nd Northumberland Hussars Antitank Regiment, and the 2nd Scots Guards Battalion (Playfair III, p. 40).
49. von Mellenthin, p. 76.
50. Playfair III, p. 41, Map 4.
51. von Mellenthin, p. 76; Playfair III, pp. 41–42.
52. Playfair III, pp. 41–43. Brigadier B. F. Armstrong was commander of the South African 5th Brigade at this time.

Chapter 8

1. The 14th and 16th Infantry brigades were commanded by Brigadiers B. H. Chappel and C. E. N. Lomax, respectively.
2. Playfair III, pp. 43–45; Rommel, p. 160.
3. Rommel, p. 160.
4. The 3rd and 4th Royal Artillery and the 60th Royal Field Artillery regiments were in support (Playfair III, pp. 44–45).
5. Playfair III, pp. 44–45.
6. Ibid., p. 45.
7. Jackson, p. 164.
8. Playfair III, p. 46.
9. Rommel, p. 160; Playfair III, p. 46.
10. Playfair III, p. 46.
11. Jackson, p. 164.
12. von Mellenthin, p. 86; Playfair III, p. 47 and Map 8.
13. Jackson, p. 164.
14. Rommel, p. 160; Carell, pp. 72–75; Playfair III, p. 47.
15. Playfair III, p. 47 and Map 8.
16. Ibid., p. 47.
17. Ibid.
18. Ibid., p. 49.
19. Carell, pp. 78–79.
20. Ibid., pp. 77–78; Rommel, p. 162.
21. von Mellenthin, p. 88.
22. Rommel, p. 162.

Chapter 9

1. von Mellenthin, pp. 88–89.
2. Jackson, p. 169.
3. Irving, p. 136.
4. von Mellenthin, pp. 88–89.
5. Rommel, p. 163.
6. Playfair III, pp. 50–52, 62
7. Ibid., p. 54.
8. Rommel, p. 163.
9. Playfair III, p. 54.
10. Ibid., pp. 54–56.
11. Ibid., p. 55.
12. Ibid.
13. Ibid., p. 56.
14. Ibid., pp. 56–57.
15. Ibid., pp. 57–58.
16. Irving, pp. 127–28.
17. Carell, pp. 83–84.
18. Irving, pp. 137–39.
19. Carell, p. 85.
20. Ibid., p. 81.
21. Playfair III, pp. 57–58.
22. Schmidt, p. 120.
23. Young, p. 111.
24. Ibid., pp. 111–12.
25. Rommel, p. 167; Carell, p. 84.
26. Playfair III, p. 58.
27. Ibid.
28. Ibid.
29. Rommel, p. 168.
30. Irving, p. 141. These figures exclude Italian tanks.
31. Playfair III, p. 61. The 1st Army Tank Brigade included the 8th Royal Tank Regiment with 49 Valentine tanks and the 44th RTR with 37 Matildas.
32. Playfair III, p. 62.
33. Irving, p. 142.
34. von Mellenthin, p. 94.
35. Playfair III, p. 64.
36. von Mellenthin, p. 94.

37. Rommel, pp. 168–69; Playfair III, pp. 65–66.
38. Carell, 86–87; Ravenstein's driver was wounded by the New Zea-landers in this incident.
39. von Mellenthin, p. 96.
40. Ibid., pp. 96–97.
41. Playfair III, pp. 67–68.
42. von Mellenthin, pp. 96–97; Rommel, pp. 169–70; and Playfair III, pp. 67–69.

Chapter 10

1. Carell, p. 90.
2. Jackson, p. 178; Rommel, p. 170.
3. Playfair III, pp. 69–70.
4. Ibid., p. 69.
5. The 2nd Armoured Brigade, which also arrived, would require desert training before it met the Afrika Korps, so it was held back.
6. Playfair III, pp. 69–74.
7. Ibid., pp. 73–74.
8. Ibid., pp. 74–75.
9. von Mellenthin, pp. 97–98; Bergot, p. 116; and Carell, pp. 90–91.
10. Playfair III, pp. 75–76.
11. Ibid., p. 77; Carell, p. 91.
12. Irving, p. 146; von Mellenthin, pp. 98–99.
13. Playfair III, p. 78.
14. Ibid., p. 80.
15. Ibid., pp. 81–82.
16. Ibid.
17. Carell, p. 93.
18. Ibid., p. 129; Playfair III, p. 80.
19. Carell, p. 129.
20. Ibid., pp. 116–17.
21. Playfair III, p. 84.
22. Carell, p. 117.
23. Ibid., pp. 114–15.
24. Irving, p. 150.
25. The 7th Indian Brigade was the vanguard at this time (Playfair III, p. 85).
26. von Mellenthin, p. 99.

27. Rommel, p. 177.
28. Ibid. The British *Official History* put their losses at 37 on December 28 and at 23 on December 30. Their losses of December 29 apparently were unrecorded (Playfair III, pp. 91–92).
29. Irving, p. 151.
30. Carell, p. 98; Playfair III, pp. 94–96. Brigadier H. R. B. Watkins commanded the 1st Army Tank Brigade at this time.
31. Carell, p. 98.
32. Playfair II, pp. 94–95; Carell, pp. 98–101. Bach commanded the 1st Battalion, 104th Panzer Grenadier Regiment, 21st Panzer Division.
33. Carell, p. 99.
34. Ibid.
35. Ibid., pp. 100–1.
36. Jackson, p. 181.
37. Young, p. 118.

Bibliography

Agar-Hamilton, J. A. I., and L. C. F. Turner. *The Sidi Rezegh Battles, 1941.* Oxford: Oxford University Press, 1957.

Badoglio, Pietro. *Italy in the Second World War.* Westport, Conn.: Greenwood Press, 1976.

Carell, Paul. *The Foxes of the Desert.* New York: Bantam Books, 1972 (originally published by E. P. Dutton, New York, 1960).

_____. *Hitler Moves East, 1941-1943.* New York: Bantam Books, 1966 (originally published by Little, Brown and Company, Boston, 1965).

_____. *Scorched Earth: The Russian-German War.* New York: Ballantine Books, 1971 (originally published by Little, Brown and Company, Boston 1966).

Chant, Christopher, Richard Humble, William Fowler, and Jenny Shaw. *Hitler's Generals and Their Battles.* New York: Chartwell Books, 1976.

Collier, Richard, et al. *The War in the Desert.* Alexandria, Va.: Time-Life Books, 1979.

Douglas-Home, Charles. *Rommel.* London: Excalibur, n.d. (originally published by Saturday Review Press, New York, 1973).

Esposito, Vincent J., ed. *A Concise History of World War II.* New York: Frederick A. Praeger, 1964 (originally published by The Americana Corporation, 1964).

Fuller, J. F. C. *A Military History of the Western World* (3 vols.). Minerva Press, 1956.

Goebbels, Joseph. *The Goebbels Diaries.* Louis P. Lochner, ed. Garden City, N.Y.: Doubleday & Company, 1948.

Goralski, Robert. *World War II Almanac, 1931-1945.* New York: G. P. Putnam's Sons, 1981.

Guderian, Heinz. *Panzer Leader.* New York: Ballantine Books, 1967 (originally published by E. P. Dutton & Company, New York, 1957).

Hart, B. H. Liddell. *The German Generals Talk.* New York: Quill, 1979.

————. *History of the Second World War* (2 vols.). New York: G. P. Putnam's Sons, 1972.

————. *The Tanks: The History of the Royal Tank Regiment and Its Predecessors* (2 vols.). London: Cassell & Company, 1959.

Hartmann, Theodor. *Wehrmacht Divisional Signs, 1938–1945*. London: Almark Publication, 1970.

Irving, David. *Hitler's War*. New York: The Viking Press, 1977.

————. *The Trail of the Fox*. New York: E. P. Dutton & Company, Thomas Congdon Books, 1977.

————. *The War Path: Hitler's Germany, 1933–1939*. New York: The Viking Press, 1979.

Jablonski, David. *The Desert Warriors*. New York: Lancer Books, 1972.

Jackson, W. G. F. *The Battle for North Africa*. New York: Mason/Charter, 1975.

Jacobsen, Hans-Adolf, *Kriegstagebuch des Oberkommandos der Wehrmacht,* Band I (1 August 1940–31 Dezember 1941). Frankfurt am Main: Bernard & Graefe Verlag fuer Wehrwesen, 1965.

———— and J. Rohwer, ed. *Decisive Battles of World War II: The German View*. New York: G. P. Putnam's Sons, 1965.

Keitel, Wilhelm. *In the Service of the Reich*. Briarcliff Manor, N.Y.: Stein and Day, 1979.

Kennedy, Robert M. *The German Campaign in Poland (1939)*. Washington, D.C.: U.S. Department of the Army Pamphlet No. 20–255, April 1956.

Kershaw, Andrew, and Ian Close, eds. *The Desert War*. New York: Marshal Cavendish Promotions, 1975.

Lewin, Ronald. *Rommel as a Military Commander*. New York: Ballantine Books, 1970 (originally published by D. Van Nostrand Co., Princeton, N.J., 1968).

Manstein, Erich von, *Lost Victories*. Novato, Calif.: Presidio, 1982 (originally published as *Verlorene Siege,* Athenaum-Verlag, Bonn, 1955).

Mellenthin, Frederick Wilhelm von, *Panzer Battles: A Study in the Employment of Armor in the Second World War*. New York: Ballantine Books, 1976 (originally published by the University of Oklahoma Press, 1956).

Mitcham, Samuel W., Jr. *Rommel's Desert War: The Life and Death of the Afrika Korps*. Briarcliff Manor, N.Y.: Stein and Day, 1982.

————. *Rommel's Last Battle*. Briarcliff Manor, N.Y.: Stein and Day, 1983.

Moorehead, Alan. *The March to Tunis: The North African War, 1940-1943*. New York: Dell Publishing Company, 1968 (originally published by Harper & Brothers, New York, 1943).

Packard, Reynolds and Eleanor. *Balcony Empire*. New York: Oxford University Press, 1942.

Playfair, I.S. O. et al. *The Mediterranean and Middle East* (4 vols.). London: Her Majesty's Stationery Office, 1966.

Rommel, Erwin. *Attacks*. Vienna, Va.: Athena Press, 1979 (originally published in Germany as *Infantry Greift An* [*Infantry in the Attack*], 1936).

———. *The Rommel Papers*. B. H. Liddell Hart, ed. New York: Harcourt, Brace & Company, 1953.

Schmidt, Heinz Werner. *With Rommel in the Desert*. New York: Ballantine Books, 1968 (originally published by G. Harrap & Co., 1951).

Shirer, William L. *The Rise and Fall of the Third Reich*. New York: Simon & Schuster, 1960.

Speer, Alfred. *Spandau: The Secret Diaries*. New York: Pocket Books, 1977 (originally published by Macmillan, New York, 1976).

Speidel, Hans. *Invasion, 1944*. New York: Paperback Library, 1950 (originally published as *Invasion 1944, Ein Beitrag zu Rommels und des Reiches Schicksal*. Tubingen and Stuttgart: Rainer Wunderlich Verlag Hermann Leins, 1949).

Strawson, John. *The Battle for North Africa*. New York: Bonanza Books, 1969.

Toland, John. *Adolf Hitler*. New York: Ballantine Books, 1977 (originally published by Random House, New York, 1976).

United States Army Military Intelligence Service. "Order of Battle of the German Army." Washington, D.C.: Military Intelligence Service, October 1942 and April 1943 (on microfilm at U.S. National Archives, Washington, D.C.; hardcover copies may be found at the Library, Army War College, Carlisle Barracks, Pa.).

———. "Order of Battle of the Italian Army." Washington, D.C.: Military Intelligence Service, June 1943 (on microfilm at U.S. National Archives, Washington, D.C.).

United States National Archives. "The Rommel Collection." Washington, D.C.: U.S. National Archives *Microfilm T-84*, Roll 276, n.d.

Warlimont, Walter. "The Decision in the Mediterranean," in Hans-Adolf Jacobsen and H. Rohwer, eds., *Decisive Battles of World War II: The German View*. New York: G. P. Putnam's Sons, 1965.

Young, Desmond. *Rommel: The Desert Fox*. New York: Harper &
Row, 1965.

Appendix I

Comparisons of U.S. and German Ranks

U.S. Rank	German Rank
General of the Army	Field Marshal (*Generalfeldmarschall*)
General	Colonel General (*Generaloberst*)
Lieutenant General	General of Panzer Troops, General of Infantry, General of Artillery, etc. (*General*)
Major General	Lieutenant General (Generalleutnant)
Brigadier General	Major General (*Generalmajor*)
Colonel	Colonel (*Oberst*)
Lieutenant Colonel	Lieutenant Colonel (*Oberstleutnant*)
Major	Major (*Major*)
Captain	Captain (*Hauptmann*)
First Lieutenant	First Lieutenant (*Oberleutnant*)
Second Lieutenant	Second Lieutenant (*Leutnant*)

Appendix II

German Units, Ranks, and Strengths

Unit	Rank of Commander*	Strength†
Army Group	Field Marshal	2 or more armies
Army	Colonel General	2 or more corps
Corps	General	2 or more divisions
Division	Lieutenant General/ Major Heneral	10,000–18,000 men 200–350 tanks (if panzer)
Brigade‡	Major General/ Colonel	2 or more regiments
Regiment	Colonel	2–7 battalions
Battalion	Lieutenant Colonel/ Major/Captain	2 or more companies (approximately 500 men per infantry battalion; usually 50–80 tanks per panzer battalion)
Company§	Captain/Lieutenant	3–5 platoons
Platoon	Lieutenant/ Sergeant Major	Infantry: 30–40 men Panzer: 4 or 5 tanks
Section	Warrant Officer/ Sergeant Major	2 squads (more or less)
Squad	Sergeant	Infantry: 7–10 men Armor: 1 tank

---

*Frequently, units were commanded by lower-ranking men as the war went on.
†As the war progressed, the number of men and tanks in most units declined accordingly. SS units usually had more men and tanks than Army units.
‡Rarely used in the German Army.
§Called batteries in the artillery (4 or 5 guns per battery).

Appendix III

German Staff Abbreviations

Ia—Staff Officer, Operations
   (equivalent to G-3 or S-3 in the U.S. Army)
Ib—Staff Officer, Supplies
   (equivalent to G-4 or S-4 in the U.S. Army)
Ic—Staff Officer, Intelligence
   (equivalent to G-2 or S-2 in the U.S. Army)
IIa—Staff Officer, Personnel
   (equivalent to G-1 or S-1 in the U.S. Army)

The U.S. staff position G-5 or S-5 (Civil Affairs) had no equivalent in the German Army during World War II.

Subject Index

General Index*

*Whenever possible, the rank an individual held in 1941 is given.